A LAWYER IN INDIAN COUNTRY

A Lawyer in Indian Country

A MEMOIR

Alvin J. Ziontz

FOREWORD BY *Charles Wilkinson*

UNIVERSITY OF WASHINGTON PRESS *Seattle & London*

© 2009 by the University of Washington Press
Printed in the United States of America
Designed by Thomas Eykemans
14 13 12 11 10 09   5 4 3 2 1

UNIVERSITY OF WASHINGTON PRESS
PO Box 50096, Seattle, WA 98145, USA
www.washington.edu/uwpress

LIBRARY OF CONGRESS CATALOGING-IN-PUBLICATION DATA
Ziontz, Alvin J.
A lawyer in Indian country : a memoir / Alvin J. Ziontz ;
foreword by Charles Wilkinson.
p. cm.
Includes bibliographical references.
ISBN 978-0-295-98935-8 (hardback : alk. paper)
1. Ziontz, Alvin J. 2. Lawyers—United States—Biography. 3. Indians of North
America—Civil rights. 4. Indians of North America—Legal status, laws, etc. I. Title.
KF373.Z56A3 2009
340.092—dc22
[B]
2009010167

The paper used in this publication is acid-free and 90 percent recycled from at least
50 percent post-consumer waste. It meets the minimum requirements of American
National Standard for Information Sciences—Permanence of Paper for Printed
Library Materials, ANSI Z39.48–1984.

FRONTISPIECE: The author in 1982 in front of *Yellow Magpie, Arapaho,* a print by
Leonard Baskin. By permission of the Estate of Leonard Baskin. © Estate of Leonard
Baskin. Photo: *Mercer Island Reporter*

This book is dedicated with deepest affection to Lennie, my wife,
who gave of herself during a lifetime of love and enabled me
to have a career, a family, and a home.

Contents

Foreword by Charles Wilkinson   *ix*
Preface   *xv*
Acknowledgments   *xvii*

1   The Road to Neah Bay   *3*

2   The Road to Neah Bay Begins in Chicago   *8*

3   The University of Chicago, the Army, and Seattle   *14*

4   Becoming a Lawyer   *24*

5   Seven Years of Lawyering in West Seattle   *35*

6   Creating a Law Firm   *44*

7   Indian Fishing Rights: Joining the Struggle   *49*

8   The Makahs   *59*

9   Recovering Lost Property: Ozette, Tatoosh, and Waadah   *68*

10   The Lummi Tribe   *79*

11   Indian Fishing Rights: Eighty Years of Suppression,
Twenty Years of Confrontation   *82*

12   The Big Bang: *U.S. v. Washington* Begins   *92*

13 *U.S. v. Washington*: The Trial *100*

14 *U.S. v. Washington*: Closing Arguments
and Judge Boldt's Decision *116*

15 The U.S. Supreme Court Has the Last Word:
Consequences of the Boldt Decision *127*

16 The Confederated Tribes of the Colville Reservation *134*

17 The Northern Cheyennes Fight Strip-Mining *146*

18 The Northern Cheyennes and the *Hollowbreast* Case *159*

19 The *Oliphant* Case: A Setback for Tribal Government *166*

20 Writing about the Indian Civil Rights Act *172*

21 Leaving Law for Academia *180*

22 A Firm of Tribal Attorneys *191*

23 Representing Fishermen of the Alaska Peninsula *198*

24 The Mille Lacs Band of Chippewas *203*

25 The Wanda Boswell Case *216*

26 The Northern Arapaho Tribe *226*

27 Photographing the Northern Cheyennes *236*

28 The Makah Whale Hunt *253*

29 A Life in Being *265*

Notes *271*
Selected Bibliography *281*
Index *285*

Foreword by Charles Wilkinson

WHEN AL ZIONTZ MADE HIS FIRST DRIVE ACROSS THE OLYMPIC Peninsula to the Makah Indian Reservation in 1963 to meet with the tribal council, he had no grounding in Indian law or tribal life. He had represented members of a Makah family on miscellaneous civil matters and, out of intellectual curiosity, had done some reading on Indian law. But he had never taken a course in the field. No one had—Indian law was not taught in any law school. Most of the few lawyers representing tribes took only "claims cases," where attorneys could recover contingent fees when tribes were awarded money damages for loss of their lands. Indian law was as far from the mainstream of American law as the distant Makah reservation, the northwesternmost point of the continental United States, was from American society.

Indian tribes, due to the great many treaties and other laws passed since the earliest days of the republic, have pressing needs for specialized legal representation. Their reservation lands have always been coveted by timber, mining, grazing, and other development interests. Legal work is important even when lands are not threatened by confiscation: the Bureau of Indian Affairs holds the reservations of these land-based peoples in trust, and leases and other transactions need oversight. The states have regularly attempted to exert jurisdiction over governmental functions that should be handled by tribal courts and legislatures. Special federal laws apply to Indian education, health, housing, bank accounts, crimes, and numerous other areas.

The need for legal representation was especially acute in the early 1960s, when Al Ziontz began work for the Makah. Washington and other states were aggressively cracking down on Indian salmon fishing—treaty rights, backed by the solemn promises of the United States, described by the U.S. Supreme Court as "not much less necessary to the existence of the Indians than the atmosphere they breathed." As for Congress, its official policy (since discredited) was "termination," that is, selling off the reservations one by one, thereby breaking up Indian societies and bringing an end to "the Indian problem" once and for all. Poverty-stricken tribes could rarely afford lawyers in private practice, and federal legal services programs for dispossessed peoples did not yet exist.

Although tribes lacked the resources to put it to work, Indian law held many promising doctrines. In *Cherokee Nation v. Georgia*, Chief Justice John Marshall emphasized the distinctive place of Indian tribes in American law, policy, and history ("the relation of the Indians to the United States is marked by peculiar and cardinal distinctions which exist nowhere else"), and Marshall held that the federal government had a unique and high trustee's duty to tribes.

Marshall also wrote the 1832 decision in *Worcester v. Georgia*, one of the great opinions in the nation's constitutional law. Indian tribes are one of the three sources of sovereignty, along with the United States and the states, in our constitutional system. In holding that Georgia could not enforce its laws within the Cherokee reservation, where Cherokee sovereignty was protected by the United States–Cherokee treaties, Marshall explained: "The Indian nations had always been considered as distinct, independent political communities...The very term 'nation,' so generally applied to them, means 'a people distinct from others'...The Cherokee, then, is a distinct community, occupying its own territory,... in which the laws of Georgia can have no force."

Tribal sovereignty, as announced by our greatest jurist, with its honoring of the treaties and its promise of self-determination, took many batterings from Congress and the courts as the nation moved west. The tribes saw a steady erosion of land and a stifling of sovereign authority by the Bureau of Indian Affairs. Nonetheless, Chief Justice Marshall's opinions in the Cherokee cases remained the law, even if it went mostly unenforced. A saving grace came in 1942 when the U.S. Interior

Department published *Felix S. Cohen's Handbook of Federal Indian Law.* Cohen, one of the country's leading legal scholars, rightly extolled tribal sovereignty as "perhaps the most basic principle of all Indian law, supported by a host of decisions." Cohen's rigorous and courageous scholarship revived Marshall's vision of tribal powers.

Tribal leaders knew about Marshall, Cohen, and tribal sovereignty—the latter, like the salmon, ran in their veins. Indians were determined people, but even as late as the early 1960s they lacked an understanding of how to deal with the legislators, judges, and administrators of the literally foreign U.S. government. Then, more Indian people began graduating from college. Veterans returned home after honorable service in World War II and the Korean War. Tribal leaders began to stand up to the Bureau of Indian Affairs. In 1964, Congress enacted the War on Poverty legislation, which authorized tribes—not the BIA—to administer valuable social and economic programs. Not incidentally, the poverty funds also funded offices, telephones, and plane tickets to the seat of power, Washington, D.C. By the mid-1960s, Indian country started to assert itself. With law so pervasive, the tribes had a critical need for lawyers if the burgeoning movement was to become a reality.

It is, of course, here that Al Ziontz moved into the heartland of his career. Idealistic and public-spirited, he was one of the very first private practitioners to come forward and represent tribes, which had compelling causes but little ability to pay other than minimal attorneys' fees. By the late 1960s, Ziontz was joined by a handful of private lawyers and Legal Services attorneys.

In Ziontz's case, as he explains in this memoir, he represented Northwest Washington tribes and in time worked for tribes as far away as the Great Plains. He closed the circle with his work for the Makahs on the tribe's controversial return to traditional whaling. Witnessing such a hunt, animal-rights activists will see desecration, while tribal advocates will see a profound cultural revival. Readers of this memoir, though, will have no trouble appreciating—and feeling—Ziontz's satisfaction in his role, thirty-five years after that first drive across the Olympic Peninsula, in once again bringing a measure of justice to the Makahs. With the Makahs and other tribes, his affection for Indian people and his passion for their causes are palpable.

The most prominent event in Ziontz's long and productive career (as it was in the careers of virtually everyone involved) was the Indian fishing rights litigation that culminated in federal District Court Judge George Boldt's decision in *U.S. v. Washington*, handed down in 1974 and affirmed by the U.S. Supreme Court five years later. The conflict over Indian off-reservation fishing had stewed for generations and then boiled over after World War II as many new non-Indian commercial fishing boats began taking fish from Puget Sound and the ocean. The action became truly frenetic over a period of about fifteen years beginning in the mid-1960s: determined tribal members continuing to fish under their own tribal laws and refusing to obey state restrictions; the violent scenes as police arrested Indian fishers as "poachers" violating state law; the tribes' success in persuading federal officials to file *U.S. v. Washington*, with the government suing as trustee on behalf of the tribes; the tribes' bold assertion of a 50 percent share of the fishery under the treaties; the colorful trial; Judge Boldt's historic ruling on February 12, 1974 (which he knew to be Lincoln's Birthday) upholding the tribal 50 percent share and the tribes' right as sovereign to manage their members' salmon fishing; the defiance by non-Indian fishers of Boldt's decree, including the hanging of the judge in effigy; the state of Washington's refusal to implement Boldt's order until a definitive ruling by the U.S. Supreme Court; the affirmation of Judge Boldt's decision by the Supreme Court; and the decline in non-Indian commercial fishing as the tribal share was implemented. In especially poignant passages, Ziontz puts forth his view, punctuated by long passages from the trial transcript, of how the powerful, authentic testimony of tribal elders—Indian people who had been plagued by the state's denial of their cherished treaty rights their whole lives—may well have won the case for the tribes.

Ziontz offers us a truly invaluable account—at once an insider's view and solid, accurate history as well—of these epic events. He probably can be twitted, though, for understating his own role. Ziontz was by then a senior attorney, well-regarded in the Seattle legal community, while his co-counsel were much younger Legal Services lawyers. In addition to his lawyering skills, he brought heft to the case.

U.S. v. Washington stands as a monument for how our legal system, for all of its warts, can in some bright moments bring justice to dispossessed peoples. In addition to being one of the most important court decisions ever handed down in the Pacific Northwest, the case had national dimensions. It remains the strongest affirmation of Indian treaty rights since John Marshall's time. It was a thunder clap warning to the states against unwarranted assaults on tribal sovereignty; in time, the state of Washington responded, and today the tribes are respected partners with the state and the federal government as co-managers in the sacred cause of restoring the once-teeming runs of Pacific salmon. As much as any single event, the Boldt decision marked the end of the "vanishing Indian" notion and the beginning of a far-ranging tribal sovereignty in which Indian leaders have brought many benefits to Indian people and an engaged, progressive participation in public policy beyond the reservations. Ultimately, this saga is a stirring reminder of how, when things break right, people of ability, staying power, and idealism can change the world.

Preface

I UNDERTOOK THIS BOOK AT THE URGING OF COLLEAGUES AND friends who have heard me talk about my career as a tribal attorney. It is a story of my life in the law and my part in the making of Indian history. As I wrote, I had in mind young men and women who might be inspired by my personal history to become tribal attorneys themselves—one of the book's central themes is that being a tribal attorney is a noble calling and fulfills an attorney's quest for justice. Another audience consists of those who are interested in Indian life and history and who want to know how the Indian nation has used the American legal system to survive and recapture lost property and rights. But the most important group of readers I hope to reach are the Indian people who have shared their experience with me and who have shown me their common sense, wisdom, and courage. Most of what is in this book is their history, and I am happy to offer my retelling of it to them. I hope they find it to their liking.

I began to write this memoir in 2006, at the age of seventy-eight. In it I recall events stretching back over fifty years and, because human memory is often faulty, I may have erred in reconstructing some of these events. For this, I take full responsibility. The dialogues are recreated as faithfully as I can remember them; some I recall completely, and others I have had to reconstruct from imperfect memory.

Although this book's main focus is on my work with Indian tribes, it also describes the making of a lawyer. My family and childhood imparted values to me that have strongly shaped my career. I try to describe my personal background to provide some insight into the extraordinary trajectory of my life. The story of my career begins with the alienation I experienced in law school, followed by the baptism of fire as a neophyte coping with sole responsibility for a law practice, jury trials, and appeals without the benefit of any help or guidance. I also describe the stresses and strains involved in creating and running a public-service law firm, believing that the firm's internal dynamics will be of interest to lawyers and law students as well as the general public. I survived all of these challenges, of course, and ultimately developed into a mature advocate, able to assume responsibility for important and difficult legal cases.

This is a memoir, not a history book. For the most part, the facts I recount are those that I personally experienced. Where I have used secondary sources, I have cited them in the endnotes. For example, I found that after thirty-five years I was not able to recall the specific testimonies of witnesses in *U.S. v. Washington*, so I relied on court transcripts. I have also had the benefit of a research assistant who sought out references for some of the stories I tell.

I look back at writing this book with satisfaction. Many of the events I report have never been told elsewhere. Some of what I tell is personal, revealing emotions of grief, anger, elation. I also speak frankly and voice my opinions about those who oppose Indian rights. I make no apologies for the scorn I hold for anti-Indian racism. I conclude with my assessment of the position of the American Indian in the American political system today and my hope for the future. I have tried to help the reader understand the reality of tribal and reservation life from the unique perspective of a tribal attorney. It has been my privilege to serve the Indian people who sought my help.

ALVIN J. ZIONTZ

Bellevue, Washington

Acknowledgments

I WANT TO EXPRESS MY GRATITUDE TO ALL THE PEOPLE WHO MADE this book possible. Old friends among the Indian people have taught me important lessons. Sadly, many are now gone, including Quentin Markishtum, Charlie Peterson, and Bruce Wilkie. But Ed Claplanhoo is still with us, and I thank him for the many kindnesses he and his wife, Thelma, have shown me. I also greatly appreciate the hospitality and friendship of Ed Dahle and his wife, Donna. Ed has unfortunately passed away, but Donna carries on. Special mention is due Joe and Charlene Alden, who made me welcome in their home on the Northern Cheyenne Indian Reservation; and thanks to their children as well, who put up with my intrusion into their lives. I also extend thanks to the wonderful people on the Northern Cheyenne reservation who opened their lives to me and to my camera. The warm-hearted Colvilles, Arapahos, Lummis, and Mille Lacs have my gratitude for teaching me the truths about Indian life. But it is the Makahs who have taken me into their hearts and shown me the meaning of the word *tribe*. They hold a special place in my life and in this book.

I thank Beth Fuget and Marianne Keddington-Lang of the University of Washington Press for their patience and helpfulness in shepherding this book from manuscript to publication, and particularly Julie Van Pelt, whose editing brought the book into sharp focus. Anonymous readers made critical comments that helped me convert my original, flawed manuscript into a much improved work. A great debt is owed to my law partners—Steve Chestnut, Marc Slonim, and Rich Berley—for reading the manuscript and offering helpful suggestions.

In the largest sense, there are two people who enabled me to enjoy the wonderful career I have had: Lawrence M. Friedman, my classmate at the University of Chicago Law School, who extended kindness and generosity that helped lead me through the thicket of law courses and enabled me to pursue a career in law, and my devoted wife, Lennie, who sustained me and gave me her unconditional love during the most daunting periods of my life. It was she who often urged me to write about my experiences, seconded by a lawyer in my firm, Brian Gruber. Without these promptings, this memoir would probably never have been written.

A LAWYER IN INDIAN COUNTRY

ONE

The Road to Neah Bay

NOVEMBER IS A DARK, RAINY MONTH ON THE PACIFIC COAST OF Washington State. The light was already fading and rain was falling intermittently this late-fall night as I drove west to Neah Bay. It was 1963 and I was on my way to a meeting with the tribal council of the Makah Tribe, thinking about the possibility of becoming the tribe's attorney. It was a call from the tribe's young executive director, a Makah named Bruce Wilkie, that brought me to travel the road to Neah Bay that night. He had asked if I might be interested in being the tribe's attorney. It was an exciting prospect and of course I immediately said yes. I would be interviewed by the tribe's governing body, the tribal council. Now my mind was turning over what I might say—this could be an important new client, but I had never met with a tribal council and I was feeling apprehensive. The meeting was set for eight in the evening and I wasn't even sure I could find the council office.

Neah Bay is the home of the Makah Indian people. It was then a village of about six hundred Makahs (now more), at the farthest north-west tip of the continental United States. From Seattle you cross Puget Sound by ferry and drive west to Port Angeles. Out of Port Angeles you turn onto Highway 112, which soon becomes a treacherous two-lane road, twisting along the coast of the Olympic Peninsula. In many places it skirts the cliffs rising out of the Strait of Juan de Fuca and runs alongside dense forests. That night in the steady drizzle, following the hairpin curves took all my concentration, leaving little time to worry about what I was going to say to the council.

I was thirty-five years old and had been a practicing lawyer in Seattle for nine years. Bruce Wilkie and I had met six years before when he was a high-school student. I had prosecuted several cases successfully for members of his family when he came to see me concerning a used car he had bought. The car had serious mechanical defects and the dealer refused to make repairs or refund Bruce's money, claiming Bruce had bought it "as is." It was a simple matter to write the dealer advising him that Bruce was a minor when he bought the car. Since no parent had signed the purchase contract, I demanded that the dealer rescind the contract and return Bruce's money. The money was returned. Afterward, Bruce and I talked about Indians and their treatment in America, a subject about which Bruce was passionate.

Bruce's appearance was striking. He had a large, bulky body and his face, though very round with full cheeks, was handsome. His presence was imposing and he spoke with a gravity and thoughtfulness unusual for a seventeen-year-old. We spoke about the Makah Tribe and his desire to return to the reservation to work for the tribe. As we talked, his resentment over the injustices Indians had suffered dominated the conversation. I told him what I had learned about tribal sovereignty from reading Indian cases and what I understood about the nature of sovereignty. He was deeply interested in my comments and we seemed to establish a comfortable rapport.

During the next six years I had no contact with Bruce at all, so his call took me by surprise. But I remembered him immediately. Since we last talked, Bruce had graduated from college and then traveled, even going to France and giving a talk at the Sorbonne. After knocking around for a while, he finally did go back to the reservation at Neah Bay. The tribal council was looking for someone to run the day-to-day business of the tribe—to be their executive director—and he was hired.

"I'll tell you why I'm calling," he said. "You know I've always felt the Makahs were getting a raw deal. Their treaty rights mean nothing to the state. A lot of us younger Indians around the country feel it's time to kick ass. Our council is no different than other tribal councils. They're all afraid to stand up to the white man, to the state. Instead, they turn to the Bureau of Indian Affairs and expect them to defend their rights. Well, that's useless."

Then he told me the council was unhappy with their tribal attorney and they wanted to replace him. Two firms were under consideration, one in Port Angeles and another in Seattle, but, Bruce said, "I remembered the work you did with my family, and I've heard about your work with the American Civil Liberties Union and I'd like to nominate you. Would you be interested?"

My three-man firm had barely been in existence a year and we were struggling to pay the bills. Every new client was important. But an Indian tribe was not a run of the mill client; it was a category of client that few lawyers encountered. Of course I was interested.

After what seemed an endless series of sharp curves, the road finally ran straight and I entered the Makah Indian Reservation. Night had fallen and it was still raining. I strained to make out the buildings as I drove through the village. The street ran along the oceanfront, but most of the buildings were on the landward side. I was looking hard for any building with a sign on it. At last I spotted it—a small white cottage with a sign that read, "Makah Tribal Office."

I walked up a short flight of steps and entered the building. Inside was a single room, dominated by a large table with a plate-glass top covering a map of the reservation. Seated around the table were five men and Bruce. They stood up and Bruce introduced me to each, one by one. First was a short, bald-headed man who shook my hand with a friendly smile. "This is Quentin Markishtum, our chairman," said Bruce. "They call me Squint," Quentin said good-humoredly. Then, Charlie Peterson, middle-aged with a serious face and piercing dark eyes, and David Parker. "Call me Ty," he said with a grin. A tall man with a deep resonant voice came next, Hillary Irving. "They call me Zab," he smiled. And finally a youngish looking man with a pleasant manner, Joe Lawrence Jr., whom I later learned was called Bobe. Seated at a small desk in the rear was a young woman with a pad of paper, seemingly poised to take notes.

Bruce began. "Al, the council wanted to meet you, so just go ahead and tell them anything you want." I gathered my thoughts.

"Well," I said, "I've never done any legal work for a tribe and I am not an expert in Indian law. But I did do some work for the Wilkies, Bruce's family, several years ago, and that's when I studied the law pertaining to Indians. I discovered something important—under the law Indian tribes are sovereign. I know something about sovereignty because I studied it in college and again after law school. It seems to me that this principle of Indian law can be a powerful tool. I know only a little about Indian affairs, but from what I've read it doesn't look like state governments have shown much respect for tribal sovereignty. If I were representing the Makah Tribe, the principle of tribal sovereignty would be the way I would go about defending your rights."

Then I told the council something about myself;

"I came to the Pacific Northwest in 1954, after I was discharged from the army. My legal career started in a small law office in West Seattle, and that's where I met the Wilkies and Bruce. During the past nine years I have built up my knowledge by representing people in all kinds of cases. I have gone to court, presented cases in jury trials, and argued cases in the Washington Supreme Court and the U.S. Ninth Circuit Court of Appeals. I have always felt strongly about injustice and so I joined the American Civil Liberties Union. I believe in the protection of rights, human rights and constitutional rights. I would be proud to represent the Makah Tribe."

The council members listened respectfully. Then, one by one, each spoke of the Makahs' need to be able to fish, as they believed they had a right to do under their treaty with the United States. Again and again I heard their expressions of tension with the state of Washington.

This was news to me. I had lived in Washington for ten years and thought of it as an enlightened and tolerant place. I learned then and later that this was only a partial truth. There was indeed racial prejudice in the state, and state government held to a philosophy that Indians must eventually be brought under state laws. Like most Washingtonians of the time, I knew next to nothing about the local tribes. If I ever read anything about them in the newspapers, it was usually a small article in the sports section headed "Indian Poachers Arrested," describing some Indians seized for fishing in violation of state law. Sometimes the article mentioned in passing that the Indians claimed a right to fish "under some old treaty." Usually the Indians were convicted and given jail sentences. To the average reader, the Indian fishermen appeared guilty of endangering conservation, and the claim to fishing rights "under some old treaty" seemed specious. It would take ten more years of struggle on the rivers and in the courts before that "old treaty" was given the respect it deserved.

My meeting with the council was over in about an hour. The councilmen had been polite and friendly, but I had no idea what they would decide. I drove back to Seattle excited by my experience—it had been nothing like I'd expected. Meeting the council had been stimulating, but I thought it unlikely that they would retain my firm. We were tiny and had no background in Indian law. So I was surprised when three days later Bruce called and told me that they had voted to hire us.

This one meeting with the Makahs changed my life. For the next thirty years, I was immersed in the problems of American Indian tribes. My three-man law firm grew to fourteen, and we were retained by other tribes in Washington as well as in Montana, Wyoming, South Dakota, Minnesota, Nevada, California, and Alaska. I was to travel the road to Neah Bay hundreds of times, and my life and the life of the Makahs would become closely intertwined.

TWO

The Road to Neah Bay
Begins in Chicago

I WAS BORN AND RAISED IN CHICAGO. MY MOTHER AND FATHER came to America from Russia before the First World War, among the flood of Jews leaving that country to look for a better life and freedom from persecution. Ultimately, both settled in Chicago. My mother, Rose Bolasny (later changed to Block), left behind her entire family—parents, three sisters, and two brothers. She apprenticed as a seamstress when she was a teenager, and once in America she employed her skills making fashionable women's dresses. After marriage, she settled into life as a homemaker.

Mom observed all the customs and traditions of Orthodox Judaism, but Harry Ziontz, my dad, totally rejected them. To him they represented an archaic, benighted way of life that he associated with the primitive conditions of the Russian shtetl, or little village. He had the equivalent of a fourth-grade education, but he had taught himself to read and he read the English and Yiddish newspapers.

Every day he went to the tavern he owned in a Chicago working-class neighborhood. He embraced America and modernity: cars, radio, skyscrapers, sports. And he idolized Franklin D. Roosevelt. He admired Roosevelt's wit and loved to listen to the president's speeches on the radio. He would shake his head in admiration: "He can hold a speech."

Until I was five, we lived in a predominantly Jewish neighborhood and my Jewishness was unselfconscious. My parents spoke Yiddish at home and I, of course, understood them. It was the language of our relatives and family friends. The Jewish holidays were part of our lives. But then we moved so my father could be near his tavern, and the new neighborhood was entirely Gentile. When I started elementary school, I suddenly became aware of my "otherness," and I soon experienced the world as hostile. After incidents of name calling and harassment, I became apprehensive. Every strange boy approaching me seemed a threat.

Derogatory names for Jews were in common usage in America during the 1930s, and as I grew older I heard them from otherwise nice people. You never knew when one of these epithets would pop up casually in conversation: "I Jewed him down." "He's as cheap as a Jew." "Look at those kikes." And if such comments were uttered in my presence, I faced the dilemma of either announcing my membership in the despised class or swallowing my self-respect and remaining silent.

The question of my Jewishness inevitably arose whenever I had to tell someone my name was Ziontz. "What nationality is that?" came the typical response. I knew what that meant. Sometimes I would say "Russian," sometimes "Jewish." This constant awareness of my separateness, of being a member of a disparaged minority in America, I believe, was responsible for the powerful empathy I later felt toward Indian people. But as a child I experienced my Jewishness as a liability, and it remained that way until well into adulthood.

Growing up, the most important figure in my life was my father. He was just over five feet tall and people called him "Little Harry." But he was well muscled and self-confident. He was like no other father, I thought—affectionate, even soft-hearted, and he was a self-made man. Coming to America at the age of twelve and going to work as a hawker plying the trains between Detroit and Chicago, selling sandwiches and candy, and later, loading sacks of vegetables on peddlers' wagons, gave him enormous self-reliance. Still later, he took a horse and wagon into the countryside of Michigan, buying scrap metal from farmers. Meeting America face-to-face gave him an easy manner with everyone he met. Eventually he moved to Chicago, and after a stint as a bootlegger he gravitated to the tavern business when Prohibition ended.

His tavern was his whole life and formed a backdrop to my childhood. He was there every day from ten or eleven in the morning till closing; one in the morning on weekdays and two on Saturdays. I loved talking with him. He seemed to know about everything, and he was curious about even more. He had a way of challenging questionable statements, rubbing his chin and delivering a drawn-out, "Well, I don't know." He called me Sonny, changing to Alvin only when I got older. I walked over to the tavern to spend time with him two or three times a week. Sometimes I carried his dinner over in a shopping bag. His face always brightened when I came in.

A long bar ran along one side of the tavern, with a plywood partition separating the front of the tavern from the rear, where there were booths. Usually there was a single bartender working, but sometimes Dad worked alone behind the bar. Early on, I started going behind the bar with him, and sometimes he let me draw a beer from the tap for a customer. To the customers, I was "Harry's kid" and they accepted my presence. They were working men, employed in nearby factories or in the Chicago and North Western railroad yards. They sat at the bar, sipping beer or downing a shot and talking about life and work, or offering anecdotes for amusement or confirmation of accepted truths.

These men seemed to hold my dad in their affection. No matter what he called his tavern—and it went by several names over the years—to the customers it was always "Harry's." Dad also had a way of diffusing tension. "Tom, you've had enough," he would say. Occasionally, the man would become angry, but my father always seemed able to tactfully persuade him to leave. There were some incidents of violence. Usually I heard about these at home, listening in on conversations between my parents. But once I was in the tavern when two big, brawny guys got into a violent argument. One minute there was just the sound of raised voices; the next, the two men were swinging at each other. With amazing swiftness, my dad ran out from behind the bar and intervened. The sight of my father, barely five feet two inches tall, struggling and grappling with these big men, sent a flash of fear through me. Yet he was bold and strong enough to halt the melee. I think the respect he commanded induced the men to stop their fighting.

The tavern also taught me important lessons about racial tolerance and kindness. For Dad, the issue of bigotry toward black people was one of compassion. "Give the man a break," was the way he usually phrased it. We didn't often see black people. They lived almost exclusively on the South Side of Chicago and it was rare for a black man to come into the tavern. But occasionally one or two did. One of them, a man named Henry, got caught up in a tragic chain of circumstances. He had gone over to the dice table where two white men were playing and asked if he could get in the game. They ordered him away using an ugly epithet. Henry got belligerent and an argument started. My dad, sensing trouble, quickly intervened and asked Henry to leave to avoid a fracas. "Okay, Harry," the man said, "I'm going," and he left. But he walked to the nearby factory where he worked, went to his locker, got a pistol, and returned to confront the two men. Words were exchanged, and Henry shot one of them. Henry ran out of the tavern, but the police soon found him. His victim died and Henry was sentenced to a long term in the state penitentiary.

The killing meant serious trouble for my father. His license could be revoked over an incident like this. But he was also troubled for another reason. Henry, he felt, had been mistreated by those men in his tavern, and he felt deep sympathy toward him for what had happened. My father drove to the state prison in Joliet to visit Henry, who was happy to see him. He told Dad that he had sore feet and could sure use a comfortable pair of shoes. Two weeks later, my father returned to Joliet, bringing Henry new shoes.

My boyhood was dominated by books. I had discovered the riches of the local library and became a voracious reader. It was reading that led me to do well in school and to become a confident public speaker, a skill that would later enable me to make a mark as a lawyer. But there was another side to school. I was drawn to the "bad" boys in my class, the ones who were indifferent to school and who engaged in adventures of the street. With them I tasted the delights of forbidden activities and staged a quiet rebellion against the staid existence of a "nice Jewish boy." This came to an end when I was thirteen and my parents, concerned about the bad influence of my friends, sent me off to a distant high school that had a large Jewish enrollment.

In high school I began working a part-time job. Because of the manpower shortage during the Second World War, at the age of fourteen I got a job as a stock boy and later as a salesman at a women's shoe store. Three years of selling shoes, kneeling at the feet of women and girls of all ages, were enough for me, and I looked for a change, for work that would be physical. Through a friend's uncle who owned a small construction company, I hired on as a laborer. Although the job was strenuous, I liked working outdoors with my hands and my body.

For three years, every summer I returned to construction work, earning money for college. I found dignity in being a workman, wearing overalls and work boots and getting dirty and tired. I developed an ability to talk plainly and directly, without airs. Perhaps because of this, I was later comfortable talking to Indian people, many without higher education, and able to establish an easy rapport despite their awareness that I was a lawyer.

College for me meant a local junior college—there was no money for university. I was lucky that Wright Junior College had an extraordinary program and fine instructors, and I experienced an intellectual awakening there. I absorbed the social sciences, physical sciences, biological sciences, and humanities. I was particularly intrigued by international relations, where I first learned the concept of national sovereignty and its importance.

As I neared the end of the two-year program, I became increasingly uneasy about not having a clear vocational goal. What would I do? Where would I go? I thought I might become a college instructor, modeling myself on the teachers I admired. But my father, largely silent on the topic up to this point, spoke up. When I told him I was thinking of becoming a teacher, he made a face.

"A teacher! No! You should be a lawyer."

"Dad, I'm not cut out to be a lawyer. Besides, I don't think much of lawyers."

I had never actually met a lawyer, but I had formed opinions of them, largely shaped by the movies. Lawyers were bombastic, argumentative, and largely the instruments of the business world. But my father idolized them. To him, lawyers represented the highest virtues: using your mind, speaking eloquently, and making a handsome living. I knew how he felt, but I rejected the idea. I was intensely idealistic and thought lawyers stood for values that I opposed. While I wasn't at all sure what I wanted, being a lawyer didn't fit my self-image. My father would not give up, however.

A few days after our initial conversation, he said, "Alvin, you're a smart boy, you're a good talker and you would make a very good lawyer."

I tried to persuade him that he was overlooking something. "Dad,

I'm not the kind of person who likes to argue, I'm not that interested in studying legal documents and I'm really not suited to be a lawyer." He persisted and finally I said, "Look, Dad, there's a scientific way to find out if a person is really suited to becoming a lawyer—they have tests. I could take those tests and if they show I'm not cut out to be a lawyer would you be satisfied?"

"Okay," he said, "but if they show you are cut out to be a lawyer?"

The unspoken answer hung in the air, and finally I relented. "If they show that, then I'll go to law school and become a lawyer."

Three weeks later, I sat in the office of a psychologist at the Illinois Institute of Technology and listened while she told me the meaning of my test scores. "You scored in the ninety-sixth percentile and you would do very well in law."

"What about teaching?" I asked.

"No," she replied. "Your scores point toward law, business, or journalism."

I sat in disbelief. I was confident I had answered the test questions in ways that would suggest teaching. Suddenly, everything was different. But at least the uncertainty was over. I knew what I was going to do with my life. I was going to be a lawyer.

THREE

The University of Chicago, the Army, and Seattle

IN THE FALL OF 1948 I ENTERED THE LAW SCHOOL OF THE UNIversity of Chicago. As I approached the law school for the first time, it looked intimidating. It was housed in a massive English Gothic stone structure dating from the early 1900s, and it stood apart from other buildings on campus. The university was on Chicago's South Side, a section of the city foreign to me. I was going to live at home and travel an hour on the El, the elevated train, to get there.

My first class was torts. I took my seat near the rear of the classroom, an amphitheater with the lecturer below and a small desk in front of a blackboard. I looked around at my classmates as the room filled. They were almost entirely male. I spotted only three women; there was only one black man and one Asian. For the most part the group was much older than me. Then the professor came in, and law school was about to begin.

It was not an auspicious beginning. Professor Gregory immediately began asking questions about a case. Though I had bought the casebook, I had only glanced through it, expecting there would be reading assignments given in the class—my junior college experience. Instead, to my dismay students began raising their hands. They had read the cases! How did they know? This was a hell of a way to begin! I sat through the remainder of the class listening to other students' confident commentaries and vowing to catch up. After class, I asked one of them how they knew what to read and learned there was a reading assignment sheet posted in the office. I hadn't even thought of going there. It foreshadowed the trouble that lay ahead for me.

I came to the law school with only two years of junior college behind me, in contrast to most of my classmates who had three or four years of undergraduate schooling and some who were World War II veterans. Still, I was confident of my abilities. But while my college reading had trained me to understand the language of the social sciences, the language I was reading in these law books seemed to come from a different universe. In fact, it was a different universe. The books were casebooks, compendiums of court decisions, some of them dating back to the eighteenth century, written by judges. While the recitals of the facts were easy enough to grasp, when the decision turned to legal analysis, I found the application of rules and the reasoning process murky and elusive. Much of what I read was turgid, dreary, and often deceptive, nothing like the straightforward language of political science or history. The opinions seemed to move toward one outcome, only to announce a different one.

I struggled to master "the law." I underlined, made notes, read and reread the cases, but the classroom discussion left me confused. I found the Socratic style of teaching only raised questions, but (of course) didn't answer them. My classmates seemed to be agile thinkers who grasped the elusive legal principles and spoke up with confidence, while to me the subject matter was narrow and technical and unconnected to world problems. The focus was on conflicts between individuals or on disputes over property. Who wins? Who gets the property? Who gets the money? I almost never volunteered a response, particularly in the classroom of Professor Edward Levi, the intellectual avatar of the school. Levi was intimidating, cutting down unworthy remarks with superior wit and sarcasm. He later became dean of the law school and served as attorney general of the United States. The intellectual excitement I had felt in junior college was gone, and I found it difficult to sustain interest in the arcane world of the law. My confidence oozed away and I sank deeper into feelings of inadequacy. I began to doubt that law school was right for me.

We had no midterm exams or quizzes, only a year-end comprehensive examination. My tendency to procrastinate was dangerous in such a system. I studied sporadically and as the time for exams neared, I vacillated between panic and depression. I had never experienced such a feeling of academic inadequacy. When the grades were posted, I was not surprised to find that my final mark was the equivalent of a low C, placing me in the lowest 10 percent of my class.

That year stamped me with a badge of inferiority that haunted me for most of my career. I felt that I had no aptitude for law, though the truth was more complicated. I did have a fairly good mind and I had an exceptional ability to see broad principles. I could write clearly and speak even better. But I was so discouraged by my experience that I limped through the remainder of my law school years alienated, troubled, and dispirited. My sour attitude also affected my feelings toward the people in my class. They seemed to be bursting with their own sense of importance—glib, confident, and noisy.

I spent my second year in deep anxiety. I studied only desultorily and lived in a state of unreality, blocking out the consequences of my behavior. The comprehensive exam was a year off, and in the meantime I discovered the life of Hyde Park, the campus neighborhood. I took a part-time job driving a school bus and moved into a house on Woodlawn Avenue, an elegant tree-lined street running past old brick homes, built for the wealthy, many converted into student rooming houses or fraternities for graduate students.

As I grew increasingly alienated from my studies and my classmates, I was drawn into the bohemian life of the neighborhood, where I was exposed to a society unlike any I had ever known. The students outside the law school spoke of literature, politics, and the arts. They disdained middle-class, or "bourgeois," values and style. The girls affected unconventional manners and were unlike any of the girls I had known in high school. Their language seemed shockingly free in their casual use of vulgarity. I discovered folk music and experimental film. Instead of studying the abstruse language of law cases, I plunged deeply into literature.

My horizons were broadening, intellectually and socially, and I was getting an education—but not a legal education. One night some acquaintances asked me to go to a rent party. I didn't know what that was. They told me they were going to an apartment in the heart of the South Side, Chicago's black ghetto, to help raise rent money for the family that lived there. I had never been in the black ghetto. There would be music and beer, and all I had to do was bring five or ten dollars. I went.

We walked upstairs to a second-floor apartment in a dilapidated building. The party was for Jimmy Yancey, a jazz pianist who, my friends told me, was famous in the world of jazz. Admission was collected at the door and on entering I saw twenty or thirty people crowded into the small apartment, sitting everywhere or standing around. The furnishings were old and shabby. We were the only white people there. Music was playing on a phonograph and a woman was dancing alone in the center of the living room. Her appreciative audience was laughing and shouting. She responded by whirling around and flipping her dress up, exposing a naked bottom. This brought roars of laughter. I didn't know how to react and I tried to look as if I enjoyed the performance, suppressing my discomfort. Then someone began shouting, "Jimmy, Jimmy, come on out here and play something for us." A moment or two later, an elderly black man, looking somewhat intoxicated, opened a bedroom door and came into the living room. He sat down at the piano and began banging out boogie-woogie music. The dancing woman came over to the piano and sang. Everyone, including me, was clapping and shouting. I had never experienced anything like it.

The world of Hyde Park was exotic and exciting, but I needed to earn money to continue living there. My part-time job driving a school bus paid only a small salary, which barely covered my rent. A furniture store on the South Side was looking for a part-time collection agent and I was willing to try it. The store's customers were black people who were paying for their furniture in weekly installments. My job was to go to their apartments and collect the installments. I was given an old car and a stack of cards with the payment records of each customer. The manager told me to expect that many would stall, give excuses, and tell me to come back next week. My job was to be stern and warn of repossession, although the manager made it plain that repossession was the last thing the store wanted.

The black ghetto was an intimidating place for a young white man. Apart from the rent party, I had never knocked on the door of a black home and I didn't know what to expect. What I found was poverty and humanity. Usually, the occupants were a mother and her children. They were expecting the weekly collector and there was no hostility. Some of the women told me they didn't have the money for the payment then and asked me to come back the following week. The poverty that I saw choked off any thought of talking tough to these people. One family was so wretched that I opened my wallet and gave the woman a dollar. Apparently I was too softhearted for the manager, and after two weeks he let me go.

Meanwhile, my deep ambivalence about law school made my studies more and more perfunctory. I skipped classes, sat through others barely concentrating, and in one course never opened the casebook the entire semester. I knew I was playing with fire, but somehow hoped I could cram for the comprehensive year-end exam and pass my courses.

One of the few friends I made in class was Lawrence Friedman. He was nineteen, a year younger than me. Lawrence was a polymath. While staying at the top of the class, almost effortlessly, he wrote fiction, composed music, played the bassoon, and studied Arabic and Old French. Lawrence came from a middle-class Jewish family in Chicago and had worked as a proofreader for the Yiddish newspaper *The Forvitz* (Forward). He not only spoke and read Yiddish, but he also knew four or five other languages. For some reason we became close friends. He volunteered to tutor me and I accepted gratefully.

In an act of extraordinary kindness and generosity, Lawrence devoted hours to teaching me the essentials of each of our courses. He could boil down the most complex areas of law to clear and easily understood ideas. He was my savior. Bolstered by his tutoring, I was able to pass my exams. Lawrence M. Friedman went on to become one of the most distinguished legal scholars in America, writing the first history of American law. Today he holds an endowed chair as a professor of law at Stanford University Law School.

As the summer of 1950 approached, I had to decide what to do during the hiatus from school. I wanted to travel to Europe, but that was out of the question. Not only did I have no money for travel, I needed to earn money for school. Then I hit on an idea: why not combine travel with work? Select some far-off, exotic part of America, travel there, get a job, and work all summer? I had read about the beautiful, even mystical Pacific Northwest. It seemed like the kind of place I was looking for, and Seattle was the city to go to.

In 1950 Seattle was a small city, of no importance nationally. I drove there with a friend, but I had no idea what I would do after I arrived. En route, listening to the radio, we learned that the North Koreans had invaded South Korea and that American troops were going into battle. The Korean War had begun. It seemed remote and disconnected from me, but two years later I would be drafted into the Army because of that war.

My friend and I found rooms near the University of Washington, and after a few half-hearted efforts at finding a job in a law office, I hired on as a construction laborer, working on the addition to the university football stadium. The job required climbing to the top of scaffolding within the structure and working "high." Initially I was terrified to stand on a narrow plank wielding a crowbar, but I overcame those fears and ultimately worked there confidently all summer.

Meanwhile, I met a fellow tenant of my rooming house, a Bolivian architecture student. I initially tried out my limited Spanish, and he responded warmly to my overture, though it was soon obvious that our conversation would continue in English. We struck up a friendship. He was working for an architect that summer, and he invited me to see some of the homes his employer had designed. I never dreamed houses could be so exciting: floor to ceiling glass walls, outdoor decks, clerestory lighting, daylight basements, skylights, river-rock fireplaces...and views.

View. That was a word rarely heard in Chicago. Except for along the narrow strip of the city's lakefront, there was no view of anything in Chicago but other buildings. But in Seattle vistas of lakes, mountains, and forests were framed in the windows of many homes. Mount Rainier loomed like a watchful god. The snowcapped peaks of the Olympic Mountains formed the city's western horizon and the rugged peaks of the Cascades sat to the east.

That summer in Seattle was magical. Drinking and partying with South Americans, dancing and singing to Latin music, joining a party where some of the revelers—boys and girls alike—dove naked from a houseboat into Lake Union, discovering real Chinese cuisine, and experiencing the snowfields of Mount Rainier in August—all of it stirred me profoundly. That summer opened my eyes to a different kind of life, making Chicago seem drab by comparison. I had visions of living in Seattle. But my mom and dad were rooted in Chicago and I really knew no one in this new city. The dream would have to be shelved.

That fall I began my third and final year of law school, and I met the girl I would marry. I spent so much time with Lenore (who preferred to be called Lennie) that I dangerously neglected my studies. What was more, by the end of spring semester it was clear that I could no longer afford to live on campus, and I moved home with my parents and once again became a commuting student.

I needed to find a job, one that paid enough for my tuition and books. Driving a cab offered an easy solution, though it meant working nights and trying to study during any free time. Cruising the streets of Chicago from late afternoon till the early hours of the morning was an adventure, but exhausting. Working long hours I did manage to accumulate enough money for school, but it all came to an end one night at two-thirty in the morning when three men hailed my cab. Twenty minutes later they had me over the back of my seat, choking me while they rifled my pockets and stole my day's earnings. The next day I quit.

My precarious grip on my courses finally resulted in a failing grade for one subject on the comprehensive exam, federal income taxation. This meant that I didn't graduate with my class that June. Instead, the administration allowed me to take two courses during the summer, and I managed to get respectable B's—the best grades I ever received in law school. I earned my JD in the summer of 1951.

Looking back at law school, I see it with the clarity that hindsight brings. I received excellent training in legal analysis and writing. I was forced to engage in rigorous analytical thinking, an important requirement for a lawyer. Grudgingly, I am forced to admit that the dialectical teaching method equipped me for a lifetime of legal practice.

Yet I lived the entire three years in a state of profound internal conflict—I wanted to flee from an intolerable situation but could not disgrace and disappoint my parents. It seems clear that my attending law school was my father's desire, not mine, and this probably contributed to my ambivalence. But I think the more important reason for my disaffection was the school's approach to law. None of the courses addressed the large questions that excited me. Instead, they called on the student to immerse himself in narrow ideas: the doctrines constructed to resolve disputes over property or to settle issues of liability for accidental injury, which all seemed mere jargon devoid of social significance. When the curriculum did take up larger questions, the emphasis was on the ideas of free-market economists such as Milton Friedman, George Stigler, and Frank Knight. Suggestions that government had a constructive role to play in addressing societal problems were treated with disdain. The whole experience was stultifying.

I came away from my legal education with no love for the law. It was a tool that, in the hands of a well-motivated lawyer, could be used to achieve justice. My passion for justice remains powerful, and I have tried to use my skills and knowledge of the law to combat injustice. But law for its own sake never fascinated me, and my law school experience made me view it with distaste.

As my studies ended in 1951, I needed to decide whether or not to pursue a career in Chicago as a practicing lawyer. My dismal law school performance had robbed me of confidence, and instead I felt drawn to my first love, international relations. I wanted to test myself in the tough academic world of the University of Chicago and this time succeed. So I enrolled in a master's program in international law. I also took the Illinois bar exam, but made only half-hearted efforts to prepare for it. Predictably, I did not pass, which only further convinced me that I was not suited for the law.

To gain acceptance to the master's program, I had to suggest a thesis topic, and I proposed exploring the implications of dividing sovereignty. That issue arises if a national government shares some of its inherent sovereign authority with a supranational body or other government, yet retains sovereignty over the areas not ceded. My proposal was accepted and I began my studies thinking they would apply only to the international sphere, with no idea that they would have practical application in America. Yet this question of sovereignty was precisely what would form the basis of much of my law practice twelve years later, representing tribal governments.

Lennie and I married in the summer of 1952 and I took up my new studies. My self-confidence returned when I received a B in international law and A's in my political science courses. Lennie and I were living in a small apartment in Hyde Park when the draft notice came: I was to report for induction into the army in September. My studies ended, never to be finished. The Korean War was on and I became a soldier.

I was assigned to the U.S. Army Signal Corps and was sent to Fort

Gordon, Georgia, for basic training. It was a shock: the constant yelling and cursing of the training cadres, the sleep deprivation, and the endless marching and drilling. This could not be me. Basic training seemed like an alternate reality. Afterward, I was sent to the Signal Corps school at Fort Monmouth, New Jersey, for training as a telephone and teletype repairman. When I learned that as a married soldier I could live off-post, I promptly rented a little house in Long Branch, New Jersey, and Lennie joined me. We spent a pleasant eight months living in a house with only one entry door, quite different from the Chicago apartment buildings where we had to open an outer door, traverse a dingy foyer, pass through another door, and climb the stairs to our apartment. It was while we lived in Long Branch that our first child, Jeffrey, was born.

The army assigned me to the Signal Corps depot in Sacramento, California, where I expected to do the work I was trained for. But shortly after arriving, I was stunned to learn that no soldiers worked at the depot. It was staffed entirely by civilians and they didn't want military personnel intermingling with them. So why were we here? I asked. No one could give me a satisfactory answer. It seemed the military base was a holdover from World War II, when soldiers actually did work in the depot. The result was that a company of highly trained soldiers, with skills and experience in repairing communications equipment, whiled away their time working on their cars, making bookshelves, and trying to "look busy." Another company was assigned there for our support: motor pool, mess hall, and headquarters, an expensive waste of money and manpower.

After several weeks I was assigned to what was called Troop Information and Education, administering education programs and providing Saturday morning training movies and lectures—a task I was far better suited to than repairing communication equipment. Lennie and I rented a small house in Sacramento off-post and lived a comfortable life there, with me going into the base every day, performing my duties as a lecturer and education administrator. It was while we were there that our second child, Martin, was born.

My two-year sojourn in the army turned out to be a way station on the road to Neah Bay. The year in Sacramento gave me time to consider soberly whether I was going to make a career of the law. I briefly considered the foreign service, but ultimately concluded I was not enthusiastic about a civil-service job. With a wife, two small children, and a law degree, practicing law seemed the logical thing to do. This decision led to another momentous choice—I would go to Seattle to establish a career there. Two years of living in houses convinced Lennie and me that we wanted no part of life in Chicago—climbing stairs to an apartment, taking the El to a downtown law office, and coping with the rough edges of big city living. No, now was the time to seize the dream of living in the Northwest. I would take a leave and go look for a job with a law firm in Seattle. That is where we would make our home.

FOUR

Becoming a Lawyer

IN SEPTEMBER OF 1954 I WAS DISCHARGED FROM THE ARMY, AND Lennie, our two boys, and I drove up the West Coast in our 1947 Hudson. I was on my way to the life of a lawyer. I began as a law clerk for an attorney named Jerry Hile. I knew little about Hile, but several Seattle lawyers told me that he had a good reputation. What they didn't tell me was that he was rumored to have some kind of problem—no one was sure what.

Hile was a partner in a downtown Seattle firm, but he was leaving the firm, he told me, to set up an office in West Seattle. It seemed he had a flourishing practice and wanted to hire one seasoned lawyer and one neophyte, the latter to serve as a law clerk. I, of course, was to be his law clerk. During my interview he struck me as a bit strange—slightly talkative, a little grandiose—but what did I know? Aside from my week of interviewing lawyers while I was job hunting, I had never met or talked to practicing lawyers. I attributed his manner to the difference between Chicago stuffiness and Seattle informality.

I reported to Hile's downtown office for my first day of work. He was still practicing out of the offices of his old firm, but told me he had rented "beautiful" quarters in a new building in West Seattle. West Seattle is an area almost geographically separate from the city—a large peninsula jutting into Elliott Bay, the harbor of Seattle, connected by bridges that span waterways. It was filled with working-class homes and served by a central business district called the Junction—an area of modest stores whose undistinguished facades spoke of the lower middle-class customers who shopped in them. It was in this district that Hile's office would be located.

Hile told me he had hired an older lawyer who would join us in a week or two, but I had not yet met him. The new firm's rented office space was still being outfitted, and Hile invited me to come along and inspect our future quarters. As we drove up to the building, I saw that it was a storefront office, with a large plate-glass window giving a full view of the interior. We walked in and Hile pointed out the reception area and the secretary's station in front of the window. Then he led me down a corridor to the attorneys' offices. There were only two, and in the rear was a large back room where the toilet and the rear door were located. I was alarmed.

"Where will I work?" I asked.

"Oh, we'll put a desk back here for you."

Some beginning to a law career—a storefront neighborhood office and a desk in the back of the store. What would my father think of this?

About a week later the seasoned lawyer appeared. He had been a lieutenant commander in the navy and he retained the officiousness of that rank in all his dealings with me. There were few law books in the office, and Hile told me I would be doing all my legal research at the King County Law Library, a bus ride away in downtown Seattle.

There was precious little dignity in my first year as a lawyer. I had to pass the Washington State bar examination—the next one was six months away—and until then I could only do legal research, write memos, and draft a brief or two. My wardrobe consisted of one suit and two white shirts. I had no briefcase and used an expanding manila envelope to carry my files and a legal pad. Hile was so penurious that he wouldn't pay for janitorial service. Instead, my duties included emptying the wastebaskets and, on Saturdays, washing the front window. I performed these tasks without objection, self-conscious only when the local merchants made joking remarks as I stood outside washing the window.

I settled into a routine. Hile would give me an assignment and I would take the bus to the law library. There I searched the cases for legal authority to support our clients' positions. Gradually, I learned the language of the cases and Washington law. I refamiliarized myself with the principles I had studied in law school and learned the intricacies of

Washington's procedures for beginning and prosecuting a lawsuit. At the same time, I was attending a bar exam preparation course at night. My salary was a meager two hundred dollars a month, so inadequate for my family's basic living expenses that we lived hand to mouth. Without help from my parents and Lennie's, we could not have survived. My parents came to Seattle to see us and their grandchildren. As I expected, my father was disappointed at the undistinguished legal career his son had established. Before he left, he bought me a briefcase.

As I waited for the bar exam, I noticed something strange at the law office. My employer was closeting himself in his office more and more. Most of the time, the door to his office was shut and when I spoke to him his responses were brusque and impatient. Once, I opened his office door and saw him reading a paperback and eating a candy bar. He was clearly embarrassed and I hurriedly gave him my message and left.

After I passed the bar exam—laying to rest my fears that I could not master the law—I assumed I would receive a salary increase, but Hile said nothing about it. In fact, nothing changed. My routine didn't vary. I continued to travel by bus downtown to the law library, doing research and writing memos. Then one day, Hile stopped coming to the office. He called our secretary to say he had the flu. Two weeks went by. Clients were calling and his cases were awaiting action. I was growing more and more uncomfortable over his prolonged absence. My assignments were almost all completed and I had little work to do. The secretary became increasingly uncomfortable putting off his clients with assurances, and after the third week a crisis developed. The lieutenant commander announced he was leaving to join a law practice elsewhere. That left only the secretary and me. I had never spoken to a client, never spoken in court, and had never taken responsibility for a case in litigation.

Matters came to a head one day when the secretary looked at me gravely as I came to work. "We've got a serious problem," she said. "Mrs. Vance, one of Mr. Hile's clients, called me this morning and she's very upset. She has to go to court tomorrow and she's pleading with me to have one of the lawyers go with her if Mr. Hile can't. You're a member of the bar, can't you go with her?"

I was horrified. Go to court? What was it, a trial? The secretary was not able to enlighten me. She didn't know what the court proceeding was about. My mind raced. What could I do, refer her to another lawyer?

If she had a date in court tomorrow, I doubted that any lawyers would take the case on such short notice. I would have to talk to her. I called her and tried to sound confident.

"Did you receive some papers telling you to be in court tomorrow?" I asked. She had. "Tell me what the papers say." She read to me: "Order to appear for examination in supplemental proceedings." My worst fears were realized. I didn't know what these proceedings were and had never heard of such a thing. "Mrs. Vance, please be patient while I check on this and I'll call you right back," I said in what I hoped was a confident tone.

There was no time to run downtown and research this, so I called a lawyer I had met in Hile's old firm, Dave Harris, and explained the predicament. He reassured me that this was not a trial. It was a routine hearing in which a creditor brings a debtor into court to question him about his assets. "Usually," Harris said, "no lawyers appear with the debtor. The judge allows the creditor's attorney to take the party into a jury room and question him there. There's really nothing for the debtor's lawyer to do."

I was vastly relieved. So I wouldn't have to go to court after all. But when I called our client and gave her what I thought was reassuring news, her response was agitated.

"Didn't Mr. Hile tell you about our case?"

"No, I don't know anything about your case," I said. And she proceeded to tell me about the deep trouble she and her husband had gotten themselves into.

"My husband Dick and I operated a small mortgage business. We collected payments on mortgages and real-estate contracts and we were supposed to forward the money to the party holding the lien. Well, things got a little tight a year ago and we had to use some of that money for our own investments. We thought we could pay it back, and we intended to, but we couldn't. When the mortgage companies began to notify their borrowers that they were in arrears, we tried to stall, but in the end it caught up with us. We knew we were in trouble and that's why we came to see Mr. Hile. Mr. Ziontz, I can't answer questions about what money we have and where it's deposited. I'm afraid we're going to go to jail."

This simple debtor's hearing had just taken on grave implications. I needed time—time to research the law. I told Mrs. Vance to come in at five that afternoon, buying as much time as I could. I found the legal procedures spelled out in the Washington statutes, which we had in our office. Maybe there was a privilege against self-incrimination? Aha! Yes, there it was. But wait, there was another section authorizing the judge to grant immunity, and if he did, she would have to answer. The problem was that her answer could incriminate her husband. This was getting too deep for me. I had no confidence that I knew what I was doing. The hearing was the next morning. I would tell Mrs. Vance about the privilege, tell her to claim it and then deal with the consequences.

When Mrs. Vance arrived in the office that afternoon she was tense and fearful. "Mrs. Vance," I said, "I've looked into the law and I think there is a way to protect you, but I can't guarantee that it will work. When you go up on the witness stand you're going to claim the privilege against self-incrimination. Now you're going to have to be very careful. You have to answer routine questions, like your name and address, but when the other attorney starts to get into financial information, I will nod to you and then I want you to say, 'I decline to answer on the ground that my answer may tend to incriminate me.' Or, you could just say, 'I claim my privilege against self-incrimination.' Either way, that stops the questioning. But I have to tell you that the law allows the judge to grant you immunity from prosecution, and if he does, then you'll have to answer the questions."

Mrs. Vance looked somewhat relieved and then asked, "Could you write that down and I'll try to memorize it tonight?" I did and she left. I hoped I sounded more confident than I felt, because the next day I would actually have to stand before a judge and push the levers that operated the legal system. The possibility of unforeseeable consequences left me so tense that I spent a sleepless night.

The next morning, Mrs. Vance and I entered the courtroom. The benches were occupied by hapless debtors and lawyers representing their creditors. The lawyers looked bored, some reading newspapers. After a number of these debtors were marched off to the jury room to be questioned, our case was called. Mrs. Vance was sworn and took her seat in the witness box. The judge gave her the same little speech he had given the others, offering her the option of being questioned in the jury room. At this point I stood up and uttered the first words I had ever spoken in a courtroom.

"Your honor, there are complications in this case that require a hearing before the court." There was a look of surprise on the face of the creditor's lawyer. He had expected a routine hearing.

"All right," said the judge. "Proceed with your interrogation of the witness, Mr. Williams." After a few preliminary questions, Williams moved to the object of the proceeding, asking for the location of the Vances' bank accounts. Mrs. Vance dutifully stayed silent and I nodded to her.

"I claim my right against self-incrimination," she announced in a tremulous voice.

The judge was taken aback. Williams looked nonplussed. He was not prepared for anything like this. Neither were the lawyers sitting in the spectator's benches. They all put down their newspapers and began listening intently. After several more questions produced the same response from Mrs. Vance, the judge stopped the proceedings.

"Gentlemen," he said, "Please come into my chambers. I think we need to have a conference." I had never been in a judge's chamber before and had to make an effort to appear composed. The judge asked me directly, "What's this all about, Mr. Ziontz?"

I explained the reason for Mrs. Vance's claim of the privilege, and he immediately understood there were good legal grounds for it. He turned to my opponent. "How about that, Mr. Williams?"

Williams had no answer. He had never encountered the claim of privilege against self-incrimination in this kind of proceeding and was at a loss. But the judge got up and pulled a volume of the Revised Code of Washington from his bookshelves. I had been afraid of this. Now he would find the section authorizing him to grant immunity. So I anticipated him and told him where to find it. After a moment of reading, he looked up and asked, "Can't I grant her immunity?"

I had to improvise. "Yes, you can, Your Honor, but you can only immunize her from state prosecution, not federal. Some of the mortgages involved were federally insured and there is a risk of federal prosecution. Besides, her testimony could incriminate her husband, who was her partner in this business. Your grant would not extend to him."

The judge was troubled and he pondered his next step. Then he came up with a Solomonic solution. "I will grant her immunity, but I will order that her testimony be given at a closed hearing and the court reporter will be ordered to seal her notes, to be disclosed only upon a direct court order."

My tactics had succeeded only in blocking criminal consequences temporarily, with no guarantee that Mrs. Vance and her husband would be permanently protected. It was the best I could do, and Mrs. Vance seemed satisfied. Apparently the prosecutor later found other evidence of the Vances' embezzlement, because I heard several months' later that Mr. Vance had pleaded guilty to the crime and was sent to prison. My first venture into the world of law had led me into deep waters.

The waters would quickly get deeper. I was a raw novice and I had no one to turn to for help or advice. Hile discouraged direct phone communications. His wife said he was seeing a doctor, but she had no idea when he would be able to return to work. The lieutenant commander had moved out, and I took over his office space. I began to examine the stacks of files and documents on Hile's desk. What I saw sent a chill through me: a jury trial was only a month away. I knew next to nothing of trial procedure and was only vaguely familiar with the complexities of the rules of evidence. Looking further through Hile's disorderly desktop revealed something even more terrifying: he had three cases on appeal, two to the state supreme court and one to the federal Ninth Circuit Court of Appeals. As far as I could tell, Hile had done nothing beyond filing the notices of appeal. The cases had to be researched, and no doubt there were deadlines to be met. I knew nothing about appeals.

My year of apprenticeship, however, had drilled me in the discipline of legal research—finding out the rules of law and procedure and applying them to the situation at hand. So I plunged in, trying to grasp the necessary steps. The most immediate threat was the jury trial. I had only a month to prepare.

I was fortunate—the case was ideal for a beginner like me. The facts were simple. Our client, a police sergeant, had been rear-ended while his car was stopped at a traffic signal. He had suffered a neck injury—a "whiplash," then a relatively new term. I had no idea of physiology or anatomy or how to present medical evidence. I did have the doctor's reports, which described our client's complaints and the diagnosis. Good. Now, how would I present this to a jury? From the law library, I obtained the multivolume treatise *Modern Trials* by a famous personal-injury lawyer, Melvin Belli. Belli gave an easy to understand explanation of what he called "demonstrative evidence," and after reading most of these volumes I felt confident that I could present our case.

My opponent was a veteran of the insurance-defense bar. He was smooth and polished. Still, I was able to put on our case with confidence. Thank you Mr. Belli. When I stumbled occasionally, the judge helped me navigate through the shoals of evidentiary procedure. I adopted the Belli approach to trial practice: hide nothing and aggressively put all the facts into evidence. The liability of the defendant, a sailor on leave who didn't attend the trial, was clear. My confidence and my candor apparently persuaded the jury to announce a generous verdict in our favor. My confidence soared.

I turned my attention to the pending appeals. Two were run-of-the-mill state law cases. The federal case, however, was highly unusual. We represented a Seattle businessman named Harold Bauer who had been charged with illegal possession of gold bullion. Mr. Bauer, it seems, found himself in need of immediate cash and resorted to buying gold illegally in California with the aim of reselling it in Canada at a substantial profit. Private possession of gold bullion was illegal under federal law, and while the official price of gold was thirty-two dollars an ounce, Canadian buyers paid forty dollars and more for the bullion.

I had researched the law on possession of gold bullion for Hile and what I found was not a straightforward criminal statute, but a 1933 presidential executive order, a 1917 act of Congress, and a 1934 congressional act, all dealing with possession of gold bullion.[1] Bauer was charged with violating a presidential executive order, a felony.

This strange legal concoction was the product of hasty action taken by Franklin D. Roosevelt to deal with the crisis of the Depression shortly after he took office. One of his first acts was to declare a national bank holiday and then to take the country off the gold standard. To accomplish this, he needed to ban private possession of gold. Searching for statutory authority, the government lawyers found the Trading with the Enemy Act of 1917. This law contained a provision authorizing the president to prevent private hoarding of gold by executive order, but the statutory language authorized such drastic action only "in time of war." The administration rushed a bill to Congress amending the act with the words "or national economic emergency." Congress passed it, and Roosevelt promptly issued an executive order declaring a national economic emergency and banning the private possession of gold. Violation was a felony, punishable by ten years in prison and a fine of twice the value of the gold.

The executive order had withstood challenge in several cases decided in the 1940s, but Bauer's offense had occurred in 1954. While Jerry Hile was still on the case, he had insisted that there must be cases holding that an emergency order ceased to be effective when the emergency had ended, and I did the research to find them. Hile filed a motion to dismiss. The trial judge denied the motion, and the unfortunate Mr. Bauer went to trial.

I sat in the courtroom and watched as twenty-seven bars of gold bullion were introduced in evidence, with expert testimony that they met the statutory definition of bullion: 99.99 percent pure. Bauer had no factual defense, and he was convicted and sentenced to five years in prison. Bauer was released on bail pending his appeal, on condition that he not leave Washington. Hile was now absent and it was this appeal that I had to undertake alone.

I began with more legal research, looking for some authority holding that the Depression of 1930 had ended. I found it: there were state court decisions striking down emergency legislation based on the Depression beginning as early as 1937. Armed with these and other arguments, I wrote the brief. A three-judge panel of the Ninth Circuit convened in Seattle to hear oral arguments. I walked up to the podium and addressed them confidently. In my argument I stressed the serious implications of a law enacted to deal with an emergency being enforced twenty years later, long after the emergency had ended. The judges seemed intrigued with the issue. My opponent, a U.S. Justice Department attorney sent from Washington, D.C., was passionate in his opposition. Upsetting the executive order would lead to wide-open trafficking in gold and would seriously disrupt the U.S. monetary system, he argued. My answer was that Congress had enacted a statute to forestall this, the 1934 Gold Reserve Act, which provided for forfeiture of the gold illegally possessed and a civil penalty.

The decision of the Ninth Circuit was a victory of sorts. The court ruled that if the economic emergency of 1933 had passed, the executive order had no effect. But the judges declined my invitation to follow the state court decisions holding that the Depression was over. They instead remanded the case to the U.S. District Court to take evidence on the issue.[2]

I was elated. There was no way the government could show the continuation of the Depression to 1954, the year of Bauer's transgression. All that was needed was a method of proof, and I found a professor of economic history at the University of Washington who would deal the fatal blow to the government's case. But the government was not going to confront that issue. Instead, I received a motion seeking to permit the testimony of Secretary of State John Foster Dulles, by affidavit, and, indeed, his sworn affidavit was attached. It was a lengthy document reciting a long series of national emergencies and ending with a dramatic claim that the Soviet Union was seeking to undermine the U.S. monetary system by acquiring gold. The affidavit flatly declared that overturning the executive order would seriously threaten U.S. interests. Wow! What had this neighborhood lawyer from West Seattle gotten into?

Naturally, the affidavit concerned me, but I didn't think it would win the case for the government. After all, the executive order rested on a discrete foundation—the economic emergency of 1933. If the government could tack on different and later emergencies, not related to the emergency designated by Congress, extending the emergency from the 1930s to the 1950s, what was the meaning of the "emergency powers" condition contained in the act of Congress?

Instead of the court showdown I was expecting, I got a call from the assistant U.S. attorney representing the government. "Do you know where your client is?"

My heart sank. Over two years had elapsed since the trial. Had Bauer violated the terms of his probation? "No," I answered, "I don't." I was completely unprepared for the news.

"He's in the federal penitentiary in Terre Haute, Indiana."

"What's he doing there?" I asked. The government attorney told me that Bauer had pleaded guilty to several counts of mail fraud in Indiana. The attorney was anxious to avoid a hearing on the emergency powers issue and offered a deal. If Bauer would dismiss the appellate proceedings, he would see that Bauer's sentence on the gold bullion charge would run concurrently with the mail fraud sentence. The attorney even suggested that the government would be willing to make some concessions to avoid the expense of transporting my client back and forth from Indiana, accompanied by U.S. marshals. I told him I couldn't agree to anything without consulting my client, and he offered to arrange for me to talk to Bauer. When we spoke, Bauer said he would drop the appeal if the government transferred him to the federal penitentiary at McNeil Island in Washington and also gave him some time off for good behavior in consideration of the benefit they were receiving. The deal was struck, and thus ended the Bauer case.

The case clearly had serious implications for the government, and I had innocently stirred up a hornet's nest. In the process, I learned a lesson: don't be afraid to be audacious in arguing a legal theory. My oral argument had gone very well, and the three-judge panel of the Ninth Circuit Court of Appeals didn't intimidate me. I had gained confidence and priceless professional experience.

The *Bauer v. United States* decision didn't come down until 1957. By that time I had argued two appeals before the Washington Supreme Court, winning one and losing one. All the while I was scrambling to run a law practice, knowing little about how much to charge, sending out bills, setting up files, and managing a caseload. I lived in dread of making mistakes, and every day brought new unknowns. Living on my meager earnings put severe strains on Lennie, who had to operate a household that was constantly short of money. I needed a higher salary badly. Hile's practice was generating money and, though I had no idea how much, it was enough to pay the office's bills. I had kept the practice together during the eight months of Hile's absence, so I felt justified in asking for a raise. I went to his home and, though I was highly uncomfortable confronting him about a topic that he clearly found distasteful, I made my case. He raised my salary to $350 a month.

The precise nature of Hile's disability continued to be a mystery, until one day his wife came to the office. He was manic-depressive, she said, and was being treated by a psychiatrist. She begged me not to disclose this, because Hile expected to return to practicing law, and public knowledge of his mental illness would impair his ability to practice. I agreed to keep the knowledge confidential.

Now I understood why he had seemed so pale and withdrawn when I had to go to his house to discuss some pressing issue. I also understood why he had closeted himself in his office and seemed to resent my intrusion on his privacy. So, I was working for a manic-depressive lawyer. I was to learn how difficult this would make my life after he returned, some eight months later. But by then I was no longer a law clerk. I was a lawyer.

FIVE

Seven Years of Lawyering in West Seattle

DURING JERRY HILE'S ABSENCE, CLIENTS CAME TO ME WITH EVERY imaginable kind of legal problem: wills, divorces, leases, contracts, real-estate transactions, bankruptcy, personal-injury claims, criminal cases, traffic cases, and even federal income tax returns—the subject I had failed in law school. Confronted with this variety, I was forced to research and analyze new areas of law constantly. Few young lawyers have the opportunity to learn the practice of law so directly in such a short time yet without the benefit of guidance from an experienced lawyer.

Hile returned to the office in November of 1956. He was subdued, not at all like his former ebullient, confident, even bombastic self. But this didn't last long. After two or three months I began to notice his energy level increasing dramatically. He was once again attracting clients. I was concerned that many retained him because of his sweeping assurances that they had a wonderful case and couldn't lose. I didn't always share his optimism, but after suggesting that a case might not be as clear-cut as he anticipated, I couldn't argue in the face of his emphatic rejection of all doubt. I retreated to my office and my own cases and left him alone. After all, he was a lawyer of many years' experience.

Unfortunately, it became impossible to ignore his increasingly bizarre conduct as his assertions became more and more irrational. He insisted that his illness had been caused by negligent dental work. He often worked the entire night without going home to sleep. The most serious problems resulted from his increasing belligerency. I often heard him shouting over the phone, talking to opposing attorneys with language that was often shocking. A lawyer simply does not tell his opponent, "You're a stupid asshole," and worse. When I tried to gently tell Hile that I thought it unwise and unprofessional to talk to a colleague that way, he smiled slyly and said it was just a tactic to intimidate the fellow—he knew what he was doing.

One of the most bizarre episodes involved Hile's feud with a young lawyer named Preston Niemi. I knew nothing of their case, but I heard Hile shouting at him on the phone: "Niemi, you're a yellow belly, nothing but a yellow belly!" Matters came to a head when Hile received a call from the clerk for a superior court judge advising him to be present at a hearing the next morning. This was highly unusual, because ordinarily attorneys simply receive notices of hearings from their opponents and ignore them at their peril. When Hile told me about the call, I knew something odd was going on. So I decided, in the interest of protecting him from his own recklessness, to attend the hearing with him.

Driving to the courthouse, Hile seemed agitated, smiling malevolently every time he mentioned his young opponent. I tried to calm him down, but to no avail. Entering the courtroom he spotted Niemi, a tall, lanky young man, sitting at the side of the room. Hile took a seat in the front row and immediately began taunting him, whispering loudly, "Yellow belly." Niemi was clearly upset.

The hearing concerned Niemi's motion for an order of default—Hile's failure to file an answer to a complaint in a lawsuit within the time allowed. The courtroom was crowded with attorneys waiting to argue their motions. When the judge called out Hile's case, he and Niemi strode forward to the bench. Niemi could barely control himself as he recited the history of his dealings with Hile on the case. I remember his words.

"Your Honor, I have never received such abuse from any attorney I have ever dealt with. His answer to our complaint was two weeks overdue and out of courtesy I called him to remind him and ask when I could expect the answer. I got a stream of insults. He called me a horse's ass, Your Honor, and said I would get the answer when he was goddamned good and ready. So when I said if that was his answer I would file a motion for default, he said, 'Just try it, yellow belly.'" At this point,

Niemi's voice was quavering with rage.

"I filed the motion for default and noted it up for a hearing. I didn't get any response, so I came down to court for the hearing. But when I looked at the docket list it said the motion was continued for two weeks. I asked the clerk how this had happened and she told me Mr. Hile had called that morning and said he was sick and needed a two-week continuance. He never called me about a continuance, but there was nothing I could do but wait two weeks for the next hearing date. Two weeks passed and I still didn't get his answer, so I went down to court for the hearing on the motion. But again the clerk told me that Hile had called in that morning to say he was sick and asked for another continuance. I called him and he was in his office. When I began to tell him I was tired of the runaround, he began screaming that I was an asshole. He kept calling me a 'yellow belly' and said I was afraid to fight him. That's when I went to the presiding judge and got an order for him to appear today."

Niemi by now was struggling to maintain his composure, and he was losing it. "Your Honor, I have never had to deal with an attorney like Mr. Hile in my career. He's so abusive I can't talk to him. When he calls me a horse's ass and yellow belly…" Niemi was unable to continue.

A chuckle ran through the attorneys sitting in the courtroom. But the judge didn't see the humor. When Hile began to pontificate about dentist appointments and toothaches, the judge interrupted him. "Mr. Hile, I've heard enough. Your answer will be filed by three o'clock this afternoon or I'll sign the order of default."

With that, the hearing was over. As Hile and Niemi were leaving the courtroom, Hile hissed: "Yellow belly!" Niemi had had enough. He squared off with Hile in the corridor, raised his fists and said, "You want to try me? C'mon, right now!" I grabbed Hile and pulled him away before any punches were thrown and urged him to leave. With his mad little smile he said, "Okay, Al. I have to go to the law library anyway." I was relieved to have avoided a physical confrontation between the two. But the relief was short-lived.

The law library was two floors down from the courtroom. The men separated, but a short time later they encountered each other as Hile was leaving the library and Niemi was entering. Niemi stepped to the side to go around Hile, but Hile confronted him. "Niemi, you're nothing but a god-damned yellow belly and you know it!"

Niemi grabbed Hile's lapels and pulled him toward the door. "I've had enough of this! Let's go out in the hall and we'll see who's the yellow belly," he snarled, and the two of them went into the corridor. I ran after them and found the two circling each other with fists raised. Hile was rotating his fists like a caricature of an old-time boxer. Niemi looked like he meant business.

Another attorney who had heard the commotion came along. I wrapped my arms around Niemi, while the other attorney held Hile. Niemi struggled to break free and I struggled to hold him. He was too big for me to hold, and if a police officer had not arrived at that exact moment, there would have been a fight, with potentially disastrous consequences for Jerry Hile.

The officer seemed confused about who had started the fracas and, perhaps because I looked so disheveled, grabbed me. Bystanders soon cleared this up and the cop said, "I think the two of you should go into the prosecutor's office and straighten this out." One of the deputy prosecutors ushered us into the office. After a few minutes of angry exchange between Hile and Niemi, the prosecutor chided them. "You should both be ashamed of yourselves. This is no way for attorneys to act. I don't care who said what to who, there is to be no more fighting. Is that agreed?" Hile actually seemed relieved and said, "Sure." Niemi also agreed, and we all left.

This episode left me deeply troubled. What was Hile capable of? What escapade would he pull next? What about my career? Could I keep my promise to Mrs. Hile to conceal his illness? Maybe I should go to the bar association and report him, but that would destroy his career. I was saved from that dilemma by Hile himself withdrawing from our law practice—this time for nearly a year—after another precipitous decline into depression.

I became more comfortable as a lawyer. I joined the West Seattle Democratic Club and my circle of acquaintances grew. Attorneys downtown thought of me as "the guy from West Seattle." Some of my friends were members of the American Civil Liberties Union, and I joined, believing this would help me translate the idealism of my youth into action. In the 1950s, the ACLU in Seattle was a tiny band of true believers, branded as radical by the local press, the city government, and the business community. Later I served on the board of the Washington

State affiliate, getting more deeply involved in civil liberties issues.

Jerry Hile had been gone for months and I was operating the practice alone. I called on Hile again and told him we needed a new arrangement. He proposed a formula: He would receive all the fees from his old clients and from any new ones who asked for him. For me, there would be no more salary. Instead, I would have to live on the income from clients who came to see me. He would underwrite the cost of maintaining the office so that he could eventually return to the practice. He thereby relieved himself of the obligation to pay me a salary. I was to be self-supporting. As time went by, fewer and fewer clients asked for Hile—most asked to see me. My income increased.

This time Hile was gone almost a year. When he came back, he acted normally for several months. I was amazed by how quickly he accumulated clients and cases. He was gregarious and knew a lot of people, and he struck up conversations easily with almost anyone. He radiated confidence and many were attracted to a lawyer who was enthusiastic about their case. Hile had an exceedingly agile mind and was quick to grasp the essentials of any set of facts and bring to bear an extraordinary legal intelligence. If only he had been mentally healthy, he would have been an outstanding lawyer.

Sadly, a growing practice just excited his mania. I could by now recognize the early signs: grandiosity, abnormal energy, running at high speed in everything he did, irrational belief in his infallibility—he couldn't lose any case he undertook. He began talking seriously about running for the U.S. Senate. He was heading for a fall.

The fall came after another bizarre incident. Hile had become highly agitated over a woman client's case. Her boyfriend had tried to set her apartment on fire. Instead of going to the police, she went to Hile. He immediately decided the boyfriend was insane and filed a petition to have him involuntarily hospitalized. The boyfriend was arrested and taken to the county hospital for a psychiatric evaluation. The following morning, according to the law, a hearing was held to determine whether he should continue to be hospitalized. The attending psychiatrist gave his opinion that the man was not psychotic, but was simply an alcoholic.

Hile was in attendance, and when the hearing judge, a court commissioner, announced he would discharge the man, Hile became enraged. He got a stay of the order of discharge while he appealed to the King

County Superior Court. Hile next filed a motion to disqualify the court commissioner on the grounds that the oath of office signed by this civil servant didn't conform to the exact words required by law—an absurd technicality. Judge Wright, the presiding judge of the superior court (and the judge who had heard my baptismal court case), decided to take a personal hand in the matter. He scheduled another hearing at the county hospital the next morning and said he would preside himself, thus avoiding the issue of the sufficiency of the court commissioner's oath.

I hadn't followed the case closely, but when Hile returned from the first hearing he was enraged. He was so agitated about the new hearing scheduled for the following morning that I felt I had to go with him to try to prevent a scene. When I arrived at his house, he was wearing old paint-stained pants and a plaid lumberjack's shirt. His wife had been pleading with him to put on something more appropriate for a court appearance. He was adamant, saying he had a dentist appointment that afternoon, and if the judge didn't like his outfit, that was too bad. I joined in and urged him to change his clothes if he didn't want to preju-dice the judge against him. That seemed to work, and Hile put on a suit and tie. But he was still acting highly agitated and I tried to get him to calm down. His response has stuck in my memory all these years: "Don't worry about a thing, Al. I'm as silent as a cathedral inside."

We arrived at the hospital and entered the hearing room. Hile had insisted on having a court reporter present to transcribe the proceed-ings. The only other people present were a deputy prosecutor assigned to these mental health hearings, the psychiatrist who had evaluated the patient, and the judge. The judge told Hile that under the statute he had no standing to participate, but that out of courtesy he would allow Hile to make a brief statement. For Hile, making a brief statement was like squaring a circle. He began to orate and the judge cut him off. "That will be enough, Mr. Hile. I understand your position and now I want to hear from Dr. Karth." Hile responded, "Very well, Your Honor, but I want to make a statement for the record," and he began to orate again. This time the judge bluntly told Hile to sit down and be quiet or he would have him removed. I noticed Dr. Karth pass a note to the judge. The judge glanced down at it and nodded. The doctor then recited the details of his examination and his findings and said unequivocally that the man did not suffer from any psychosis, only alcoholism.

Judge Wright said, "I will enter an order discharging the man immediately." Hile jumped up and asked for a stay to allow the filing of an appeal. "The request is denied and the hearing is concluded," Judge Wright brusquely announced. When we left the room and went to the elevators, Hile and the judge arrived together. Hile began to harangue the judge and grabbed the lapels of his coat. I could see the judge's face reddening and I stepped in, gently pushing Hile away. It was clear that Hile's mental problems could no longer be glossed over. I told the judge that Mr. Hile was not entirely in control of himself.

I called the judge some time later and we had lunch. I explained my dilemma, and he was sympathetic. Then he said, "Do you know what was in the note Dr. Karth passed to me at the hearing? It said, 'This attorney is clearly mentally ill.'"

Hile's outburst was followed soon after by another crash into depression. It was a relief to be alone again in the office. I had come a long way from the fearful young neophyte I had been two years earlier, when Hile had first left me to cope with the practice alone. The year was 1957, and it would be portentous. One day I received a phone call from Jack Gordon, the manager of the local bank branch where I had a modest checking account. "Al," he said, "I'd like to refer a client to you." Gordon had never referred a client to me in the two years I had used his bank. I felt momentary elation.

"This gentleman is an Indian," Gordon continued, "and he has some kind of problem with Indian property. He asked me about it and I don't know anything about Indian property and I referred him to you." I immediately understood why Gordon was referring this client. I was a well-known liberal, a member of the ACLU and an activist in the Democratic Party. The banker no doubt thought this was a good match for me. Time would prove him right in ways neither of us could foresee.

I knew nothing about Indians, had never met an Indian and certainly had no knowledge of the law concerning Indian property. But I was accustomed to plunging into unknown areas of law and researching my way through a problem.

Within an hour, a large middle-aged, paunchy man came to my office. He was Pat Wilkie. The problem involved his son, Pat Wilkie Jr., whom he referred to as Shine (short for Sunshine). Shine had inherited an allotment from his grandmother on the Quinault Indian Reservation on the Olympic Peninsula, and the Bureau of Indian Affairs had contracted with a logger to cut the timber, the proceeds to go into the grandmother's trust account, held and administered by the BIA. The grandmother had died and the BIA was relying on a power of attorney she had given to authorize the logging. Shine, it seemed, didn't want the BIA to log the timber. He wanted to do it himself and keep the proceeds. I had never heard of an "allotment," and I didn't know why the BIA would be cutting timber that belonged to an individual. But I assured Pat Wilkie Sr. that I would look up the law and determine what needed to be done.

In the law library, I could find no legal textbooks about Indian law. The only information I found was in Title 25 of the United States Code. Title 25 is a compendium of all U.S. statutes dealing with Indians. It is a hodgepodge of archaic provisions dating back to the nineteenth century, often containing terminology that is impossible to understand without a background in federal Indian policy. Since I couldn't make sense of the statutes, I turned to the court decisions in the accompanying annotations. Thus I made my first acquaintance with the little known and arcane field of Indian law.

I gradually absorbed the language of Indian law and discovered what an allotment was. It derived from an 1887 law that divided tribal lands and distributed them to individual members.[1] In my reading, I also came across a surprising find—early decisions referred to the sovereignty of the tribes. I knew about sovereignty. To learn that under the law Indian tribes were sovereign was an eye-opener. It put Indians in a new light. From my limited knowledge of tribes in America, it certainly didn't seem that they were treated as sovereigns. While this didn't bear on the problem of Shine and his timber, it was an important doctrine and I would not forget it.

I developed a legal position in Shine's case: we would challenge the BIA's logging plan on the grounds that, with the demise of the owner of the allotment, the power of attorney ceased to be effective. I wrote a letter to the BIA challenging their plan, and they promptly replied with a legal opinion citing several court decisions trumping my argument. Once consent to cut timber on an allotment was given, the death of the owner did not revoke the consent and the BIA was entitled to conduct a timber sale, the proceeds to be held in trust for the allottee or his heirs. After reading the cases, I concluded that it would be hopeless to bring an action challenging the BIA. Mr. Wilkie and his son Shine were resigned to my conclusion and accepted it, expressing their appreciation for the work I had done.

Pat Wilkie Sr. was a member of the Turtle Mountain Band of Chippewas in North Dakota. He had come to Seattle during World War II to work in the shipyards. He had met a woman who was a member of the Makah Tribe, and they had married. Nell Wilkie had several children by a prior marriage, including Shine, and she and Pat had several together. Their children were all members of the Makah Tribe, though Pat was not.

Over the next three years, I developed a warm and lasting relationship with the Wilkie family. Shine had a child custody dispute that I litigated and won. Shine's little sister was injured when a moose head mounted on a wall swung loose and injured her, and I prosecuted a claim and obtained a settlement. Nell Wilkie slipped at work and injured her back, and I obtained an award for her in a workman's compensation case. But handling a small claim on behalf of Nell and Pat's son Bruce would turn out to have important consequences.

In 1961, after seven years, my West Seattle practice came to an end. Hile returned from one of his cyclical absences and was easing himself back into the practice. One day he came into my office and announced it was time to change our arrangements: he wanted to form a partnership. I wanted no part of the personal and legal responsibility involved in having a manic-depressive partner. In a poignant parting, he told me how much he appreciated what I had done to hold his practice together. Our relationship had lasted seven years. I had grown in maturity and skills, and it was time for me to strike out on my own.

SIX

Creating a Law Firm

LEAVING THE SHELTERED LIFE OF AN EMPLOYEE AND BECOMING AN independent lawyer, solely responsible for paying all the bills and earning enough to support my family, was both frightening and exhilarating. I knew I had to leave West Seattle if I wanted experience beyond run of the mill cases and clients. That meant moving downtown. I rented space from an older lawyer in his suite of three offices and bought furniture from the outgoing tenant. I was ready to begin my own law practice.

I brought some clients with me from West Seattle, but the number of new clients dwindled because I no longer had the walk-in clients of a neighborhood law office. Income dropped, and each month I struggled to earn a livelihood. But after six months or so, new cases came. Old clients referred some, and others came through political activities and friends and acquaintances. At the end of my first year, I had a respectable number of cases and was earning a modest income.

The years 1961 and 1962 were hard ones. Mom and Dad decided to move to Seattle to be close to their grandchildren, but within four months of arriving in Seattle, Dad died, following surgery for stomach cancer. Then early the next year, my mother died and the lawyer I rented from died suddenly, and the other lawyer in the office suite moved out. I was confronted with a choice: look for another office space, or keep the suite and find others to join me. I had had enough of being subordinate to another lawyer. I wanted to start a firm of my own, so I decided to stay put and look for two partners to join me.

My first stop was an old friend who always seemed to know what was going on in the Seattle legal community, Floyd Fulle. Did he know any lawyers who might be interested in joining me? His response took me by surprise. "Me," he said. I didn't know he was looking for a change, but I quickly accepted his offer. He was a good lawyer, a Columbia Law School graduate, and a nice guy. We would be partners.

Several days after meeting with Fulle, I found my second partner in a strange way. I was in the elevator of the county courthouse and was struck by the appearance of the only other occupant, a short fellow with a craggy face, bushy eyebrows, and an Abe Lincoln beard. He was carrying a briefcase and looked like a lawyer. I took the initiative.

"Hi, my name's Al Ziontz, what's yours?"

"Robert Pirtle," he answered briskly. We shook hands. When the doors opened and we stepped out, I decided to find out a bit more about this odd-looking man.

"What firm are you with?" I asked.

"I've been in solo practice for the past year," he answered.

I pressed on. "What were you doing before you went on your own?"

"I spent several years at Perkins, Coie, but I became disillusioned with the practice, being in a large firm, and I decided to leave law, study philosophy and practice only part-time. But I found what I was doing was so much fun that I've been going at it full-bore the past year."

I was impressed. Perkins, Coie was one of Seattle's premier law firms and they represented major clients like Boeing. If Pirtle had been in that firm, he clearly had uncommon ability. Here was my third man. I told him I was looking for another lawyer to join me in a new firm, would he be interested? His enthusiasm was immediate, and we repaired to a nearby coffee shop to discuss the idea.

Pirtle was a dynamo, bristling with energy. "What kind of practice do you have?" I asked.

"My main client is a collection agency," he told me, "and most of my cases are lawsuits against purchasers of vacuum cleaners. I get a percentage of what I collect and it's a heck of a lot of fun!"

I was disappointed. Pirtle's practice seemed shabby, and hounding debtors was not the noble face of justice. Still, if he made a living at this, he must be a hard worker. I decided to take a chance. Early in our conversation it became clear that Pirtle had jumped far ahead of me;

he spoke as if his joining the partnership was a mere formality, and he wanted to know more about Floyd, the office space, the rent, and a myriad of other details.

"Look, Bob," I started.

"Call me Robert," he quickly interjected.

"Okay. Robert. I'll have to discuss this with Floyd, who by the way prefers to be called Frost, and if he's agreeable then we can talk about the details of the partnership."

"Sure," said Pirtle, and the foundation of the partnership was laid. Frost Fulle was diffident when I told him about Pirtle; if I thought he'd be a good addition, that was fine with him.

I had given some thought to the idea of partnership and had come to a conclusion. I wanted a partnership of equals, no formulas for division of fees, no apportionment of overhead, but a relationship that gave us a sense of unity, not division. A few days later, the three of us met and each of us opened his records of income and lists of pending cases and expected fee income. I had the most substantial practice. I think Pirtle and Fulle were expecting some kind of bargaining and a proposed formula for proportionate sharing. When I told them that I wanted an agreement for equal sharing of all income after payment of the firm's expenses, they were surprised at what must have seemed like rare idealism, and they promptly accepted my proposal. The firm of Ziontz, Pirtle and Fulle was born. The year was 1963.

For the first year of the new firm's existence, we struggled financially. We had a mix of cases: Pirtle's collection cases, Fulle's marginal business clients, my real-estate broker client and his numerous deals, together with a miscellany of individual cases. Later we were retained by a large collection agency to prosecute their claims. We were busy, but the practice was not ennobling. For that, I found satisfaction in my work with the American Civil Liberties Union.

I had been elected to the board of the ACLU's Washington State affiliate and later was elected president. In 1964, while I was a board member, we decided to take action concerning the practices of the Seattle Police Department. For many years, the ACLU had been receiving a steady stream of complaints alleging racism and brutality by police officers. Citizen complaints to the police department were routinely rejected as unfounded, and the department seemed completely indifferent to them. We compiled a collection of damning sworn affidavits and submitted them to the Seattle City Council, together with a petition demanding an investigation and corrective action. Copies were released to the newspapers. Then we waited for the response from the city council. The silence was deafening. There was no response—they were going to stonewall. Perhaps they felt that since the ACLU was seen as a radical left-wing organization, they could safely ignore us. But they hadn't taken into account the hunger of the local press for a dramatic story. There were regular articles badgering the council. When were they going to respond?

Finally, the council was pressured into action. Instead of responding to the allegations, they announced that the ACLU would have to prove the allegations, and a date was set for a public hearing. The council had miscalculated. A public hearing would get extensive news coverage and we had dramatic testimony to present.

In January of 1965, the hearing opened before a standing room only audience. I conducted our presentation as I would to a jury. We presented witnesses who had observed firsthand—or had personally experienced—police beatings, racism, and misconduct, all of which had been duly reported to the police department and then ignored. When the hearing concluded, we had presented a case that cried out for official action. Instead, the city council announced it would give the police department a hearing to answer the charges. Predictably, the department trotted out police officers who testified that our witnesses were liars and various officials, including the mayor, who claimed that the department was one of the finest in the nation. As far as the city council was concerned, that ended the matter and they would take no further action.

We called for the establishment of a police review board, but we were ignored. While our hearing had attracted strong press coverage, and even national attention, the press and the public gradually lost interest and the issue faded away.[1] City government was content to allow the police department to run itself as a closed enclave with no outside interference. The hearing did establish the ACLU as a voice in city affairs, particularly on the issue of police misconduct. I became persona non grata with the Seattle Police Department.

But if the department felt smug about deflecting the charges we had brought, this attitude would soon change. The following year an ugly racial confrontation between two off-duty Seattle policemen and two black men led to one of the officers shooting and killing one of the men. This brought days of demonstrations and violence from the black community against the police. The city's comfortable illusions about relations with Seattle's black citizens were shaken. Later that year, the Watts riots erupted in Los Angeles and awakened every police department in America to the reality of black hostility toward the local police, much of it based on real grievances. The era of the "bull cop" was ending. Police departments expanded minority hiring, professionalized their departments by requiring college degrees for their supervisory officers and chiefs, and made serious efforts to reach out to the black community.

I had played a small role in this movement and I was proud of the work the ACLU had done to bring public awareness to a previously ignored and serious problem. There was another, very different problem of injustice and denial of rights that had been ignored in the state of Washington: Indian treaty fishing. This was to occupy a large part of my life in the years that followed.

SEVEN

Indian Fishing Rights:
Joining the Struggle

THAT FIRST YEAR OF ZIONTZ, PIRTLE AND FULLE WAS ALSO THE year of my first meeting with the Makah Tribal Council, courtesy of Bruce Wilkie. Three months after the Makah Tribe hired my firm, several members of the council came to Seattle. The chairman, Quentin "Squint" Markishtum, spoke for the group.

"Al, we're poor, but we're hoping your firm can help us. We don't have decent housing on the reservation and the only jobs are working in the woods for Crown [the Crown Zellerbach timber company]. I drive a log truck for Crown. But working in the woods is hard and dangerous. A lot of our boys want to fish and they know how. But we don't have the boats or the gear to compete with the commercial fishermen. We can fish the Hoko [River] because we won that right in court, but you can't make much of a living from that. The state arrests us if we go to other rivers. It looks to us like they have saved all the fish for the sport and commercial fishermen and there's nothing left for us. Now Bruce, here, has a plan, and we want you to know we're behind him 100 percent."

Bruce began to explain: "A lot of us feel the state is never going to honor our treaty rights unless they're forced to. They've put the Indian in a bad light; they call us poachers and they ignore our treaty. We've gone to the BIA, but they don't want to tangle with the state. So we decided to take matters in our own hands. Hank Adams, a Quinault friend of mine, has been working with me on this and we've got a plan. We call it 'public awareness.' We're going to go public with our story.

We're going to demonstrate on the rivers and let them arrest us, like they always do. But this time we're going to try to have some celebrities with us. So when they make their arrests it will make news nationally. Hank and I have talked to Marlon Brando, and he wants to come up here and help us. Al, we want you to be with us to give us the legal advice and deal with the state officials. Can you do that?" Of course I agreed.

"Good," said Bruce, laconically. A month or so later he called again: "Marlon Brando is coming and we're going to have a fish-in, just like the black people had sit-ins. Meet us at the Puyallup River bridge where Highway 99 crosses the river, just outside Tacoma, Monday morning at eight o'clock. We don't know what's going to happen, so be ready for anything. If we don't go to jail, then afterward we're going to Olympia with Brando to demand a meeting with the fish and game people, maybe with the governor."

Bruce was right about how Indians were seen—or not seen. The tribes were nearly invisible to white America, certainly to the citizens of Washington State. They were perceived as anachronisms, vestiges of a by-gone age, destined to ultimately disappear into the mainstream of American society. When they asserted themselves and claimed rights that inconvenienced or were in conflict with society, their claims were ignored or declared null by the state. This was comfortably justified under the rubric that, as a people, the Indians would have to live under the same laws as the rest of the citizenry.

I spent the next several days reviewing the decisions of the U.S. Supreme Court and the Washington Supreme Court that dealt with Indian treaties and fishing rights. The cases offered some rays of hope. A decision of the state supreme court in 1957 threw out the conviction of a Puyallup Indian named Bob Satiacum for fishing with a net on the Puyallup River. The state had failed to show that its regulation barring net fishing was necessary for conservation of the fish runs. It was because of Bob Satiacum that we were going to the Puyallup River with Brando.

Satiacum, I learned, was a World War II veteran who was angry at the state of Washington's refusal to honor Indian treaty rights. While Washington's Indians had for fifty years fished at night to avoid arrest, Satiacum went out on the river in broad daylight, in plain view of passing motorists, and cast his net in the river. He was challenging the state's legal system and he was prepared to confront the authorities. Satiacum felt deeply that his right to fish was guaranteed by his tribe's 1859 treaty with the United States and superseded state law. He was right, but he was ahead of his time. State officers arrested and jailed Satiacum and confiscated his boat and outboard motor. The case ultimately went to the state supreme court, and he won. Satiacum was determined to continue his fight.

It was March of 1964 when Marlon Brando got in Satiacum's boat on the Puyallup River. A crowd of Indian people and their supporters watched from the riverbank. Everyone saw this as a historic moment. I felt a momentary thrill at the sight of the familiar, classical features of Brando's face. In the boat with Brando and Satiacum was an Episcopal clergyman, who joined the demonstration to show moral support for the Indian's cause. Satiacum, assisted by Brando, set his net in the river. A few minutes later, Satiacum pulled it out and proudly held up a salmon. (We later learned the salmon had been planted to make sure there would be a display; otherwise the net might have stayed empty for hours.) A shout went up from the crowd, and the press snapped away with their cameras. As soon as the boat returned to shore, state Fisheries Department officers arrested all three of the occupants and they were taken away to the Pierce County Jail. I went to the jail to help arrange for their bail, but suddenly, inexplicably, the men were released. I learned that the county prosecutor had called the jailers to advise he was not going to file charges because, as he later told the press, "It was all just a publicity stunt."

A publicity stunt it was, but it worked. Photographs of Marlon Brando under arrest for fishing with Indians were printed all over the nation. The Indian treaty rights struggle had moved from the sports pages to the news pages. From that point on, Indian treaty rights became a major issue in the state of Washington and a major headache to the state fisheries management agencies. It became more and more difficult for state officials to portray the Indian as a lawless poacher, and state government found itself embroiled in more and more court cases as the Indian people intensified their struggle.

Bob Satiacum was not the only Northwest Indian to wage a long-running battle for treaty rights. Billy Frank Jr., a member of the Nisqually

Tribe, was also a leader in the struggle. Billy and other Nisquallies fished from a site along the Nisqually River called Frank's Landing, a small tract of land that had been in Billy's family for two generations. Frank's Landing became the focal point for demonstrations and its name became synonymous with Indian resistance.[1]

Brando's appearance gave enormous encouragement to Indians of the Northwest. After Brando's release from jail in Tacoma, Hank Adams led a group of fifty or so to our next destination: Olympia. The objective was for Brando to speak to the director of either the Fisheries Department or the Game Department and make a direct appeal to honor Indian treaty rights. The next day a meeting was set with the director of the Game Department.

In the state of Washington the Game Department regulated steelhead fishing, while the Fisheries Department had authority over salmon fishing (the departments have since become one, the Department of Fish and Wildlife). The steelhead is a trout that migrates to sea and, like the salmon, returns to its natal streams. Unlike salmon, which stop feeding when they enter freshwater streams, steelhead feed in these streams, which means that sportfishermen can catch them with rod and reel using a lure.

Steelhead fishermen are a breed apart. Because the fish put up a mighty struggle and because they are so difficult to catch, sportfishermen prize the steelhead and the experience of hooking one. The steelheaders formed an organization and obtained special legislation declaring the steelhead a "game fish," not to be bought or sold. Fishing for steelhead was permitted only by rod and reel—nets were prohibited.

Under Washington law, all game, including steelhead, was regulated by the Game Department, a branch of state government that then enjoyed almost complete autonomy. It was funded entirely by sportsmen's license fees and did not depend on appropriations from the legislature. Its policies were set by a board made up of officials from hunters' and fishermen's organizations. This board selected the director of the department. The Game Department was thus a government within a government; it was clothed with state police power and its enforcement officers had the authority to make arrests and seizures to enforce game laws. All the same, it served the narrow interests of a powerful special interest group.

The Game Department was an implacable foe of Indian treaty fishing. Steelhead swim in rivers and streams that for hundreds of years were the traditional fishing grounds of the Northwest tribes. They are winter fish and have always provided food for the tribes in the winter months. But under Washington law, Indians were prohibited from casting a net for these fish, and if they caught one within their own reservation, they were prohibited from selling it. The officers of the Game Department regarded the Indian as a threat to their resource, and they reflected the almost rabid views of the steelheaders, those dedicated steelhead fishermen. The department even produced a propaganda film titled *The Problem of Indian Fishing*, which depicted the Indian as a greedy predator who, left unchecked, would destroy the natural runs of steelhead. It fell to Marlon Brando to appeal for justice to the director of the Washington Game Department.

I joined Brando and a small contingent of Indians in the office of John Biggs, the director. Biggs sat impassively while one after another we presented the case for honoring the treaties and allowing Indians to fish the rivers as they always had. Biggs scowled throughout the meeting, and his response was a curt and dismissive "No." Finally, in a completely spontaneous gesture, Brando fell to his knees before Biggs and implored him to show some compassion. If this made Biggs uncomfortable, he didn't show it. The meeting ended with nothing accomplished, but it was not a useless undertaking. There had been newspaper and TV coverage of the Olympia meetings and of the demonstrations by Indians and their supporters on the steps of the capital. The campaign was just beginning.

That night we held a strategy session at the Olympia hotel where Brando was staying. Hank Adams continued to be the chief strategist. He had arranged for another fish-in, this time at La Push, a Quileute village on the Pacific Coast. Brando would go out in an Indian dugout on the Quileute River with a Quileute Indian, and together they would set a net in the river. Adams had notified the Game Department and the press, and maybe this time there would be an arrest that led to jail time. A small procession left Olympia the next day, and I followed in my own car. I took a room in a local motel, and the next morning went out to the river to observe the event. Brando had spent the night in an unheated cabin of a Quileute fisherman.

I arrived late and Brando was not there. Someone said he'd gone out on the river. Soon, though, he returned, looking terrible. He motioned for me to follow him as he went into the cabin. "Al, I've got the crud," he told me. He had a fever. "I went out on the river with those guys, but there weren't any fish cops or press. After an hour, I said to them, 'Take me back, I'm sick.'"

Later, we learned that the Fisheries patrol went looking for him on a different river, and no press ever showed up. Miscommunication, probably, but the whole venture was a fiasco. Brando had been willing to endure the harsh cold of the river and his growing illness, but finally had to give up. As he changed clothes in the cabin, he said, "Al, I want to go back to LA. Can you drive me to the airport in Seattle?"

I assented, and in a few minutes he had tossed his bag in my car and we were off, driving the long winding road from La Push to Highway 101. Though Brando was obviously sick, he wanted to talk about Indians.

"How did you get involved with Indians?" he asked. I told him about Bruce Wilkie, my passion for the victims of injustice and the empathy I felt toward the Indian people. I described the legal background of the Indian fishing rights dispute and the racism that I felt pervaded the state's dealings with the tribes. Brando listened respectfully.

"So how come these assholes in the state of Washington can treat the Indians this way?" he asked. This evoked a lengthy discourse on the history of the industrialization of the salmon fishery, the powerful influence of sport and commercial fishing interests on government, and the unquestioning acceptance of the state's claim that preventing the Indians from fishing was necessary for "conservation."

Brando was profane: "That's a crock of shit. What about the treaties? How can they get away with treating the Indians that way when they have a treaty?"

"Marlon, it's going to take court decisions to stop them. I don't have any faith that the state court system will do it. The state judges are elected and, frankly, I think they're playing to their constituency. No, it's going to have to come from the federal courts."

"What about the federal government?" he asked. "How come they don't step in and protect the Indian? It's a federal treaty, isn't it?"

"Marlon, you put your finger on a big question. Yes, where *is* the federal government? I think they ducked out of this fight because of some court decisions years ago that said the states can regulate Indian hunting and fishing. Now they don't want to tangle with the states. But listen, Marlon, what you're doing can help change that. National publicity can put this on the agenda in Washington, D.C. How it's going to come about, I can't predict, but I think that with the Indians building up pressure, they're bound to get results sooner or later."

Brando felt deeply about justice for the Indians. Going out on the river was no publicity stunt. He was already world famous and didn't need the publicity. No, he was strongly committed to helping Indian people and was willing to do what he could, even though it meant getting up at dawn in an unheated cabin on the rugged coast of Washington, going out on a river in a dugout canoe in the freezing cold, and risking his health.

As we drove the talk turned to other topics. He knew that I was Jewish and began telling me Yiddish jokes, and I was stunned to hear him break into colloquial Yiddish. His pronunciation was so good that I had difficulty believing it was coming from Brando. "How did you learn Yiddish?" I asked.

"When I first went to New York to study acting, I heard about Stella Adler. She ran a school for actors. So I went to her and she took me on. Stella was a brilliant teacher. What I was able to accomplish as an actor, I owe to her. She had a wonderful family and they took me in. Yiddish was spoken constantly in that house and they had a marvelous sense of humor. I learned from them, and I've always felt a strong empathy with the Jewish people, who've been persecuted throughout history. When the Irgun [a militant Zionist group that took up arms to ensure a Jewish state in Palestine between 1931 and 1948] was fighting to open the door to refugees from Europe to get into Israel, I sent them money. I yelled at the top of my lungs at the failure of the United States to help the Jews of Europe who survived the concentration camps. Maybe my feeling about the Indians has the same roots. I've always felt passionate about a people who are treated like shit and don't deserve it."

This profound humanism went a long way toward explaining Brando and his extraordinary power as an actor. But there was another side to him. He was a perfect mime and told joke after joke, most of them sexual or scatological. Brando seemed obsessed with sex, and his sexual jokes were crude and vulgar, but they were funny, even hilarious. He was an entertainer as well as a skilled actor.

As we drove through the mountains and forests of the Olympic Peninsula, he fell to musing about his acting career. Somehow a rapport had sprung up between us and he spoke candidly. "You know, when I first hit Broadway, I knocked them dead in *Streetcar Named Desire*. Man, I was hot. But that was fifteen years ago. A lot has happened since then, and I just don't have the steam any more." Then he said, "I feel like shit. I must be really sick. Can we stop for coffee somewhere?"

I found a restaurant in Port Angeles and we sat down to coffee and pie. We were talking, just talking, when a couple came over. "Mr. Brando! Would you mind giving us your autograph?" Brando obliged, and soon there were others. Even though he was sick and would have been justified in turning them away, he autographed the papers thrust toward him and even exchanged some conversational banter.

Brando's flight to Los Angeles didn't leave Seattle till seven thirty that evening. "Marlon, you'll have time to kill, why not come over to my house for dinner before you go to the airport?"

"Sure," he said. Now I had to get to a phone and tell my wife who was coming for dinner. I excused myself and went to a pay phone. My eleven-year-old son answered. "Let me talk to Mom."

"She's not here. She went out and said she'd be back in an hour."

I was tense. "Listen carefully, Jeff. Tell Mom that I'm bringing Marlon Brando over for dinner tonight. I want you kids to straighten up the house and dress nice."

Jeff sounded incredulous. "Really? Marlon Brando the movie actor?"

"Yes, Marlon Brando, the movie actor. Now be sure and tell Mom what I told you."

When I returned to the booth, Brando was engaged in conversation with a gaggle of his local admirers. It went on and on. He didn't seem to tire, and I began to glance at my watch. We were still two hours out of Seattle, and driving to my house and then to the airport was going to be a tight fit. Finally, I persuaded him that we had to leave.

While he had been animated during our Port Angeles stop, as we drove on toward Seattle he faded. Finally, he said, "Al, I'm really sick. I'd love to have dinner with you and your family, but I think I better head straight to the airport. It'll have to be another time. I'm feeling worse by the minute." In fact, Brando had pneumonia and had to be hospitalized on his return to California.[2] At the time, however, I could only think about the disappointment my wife and children would feel when I arrived without our illustrious guest. At the airport he gave me his home phone number and asked for my card. "Call me any time. I want to stay in touch on this," he said. We parted as he carried his bag into the terminal.

In the years that followed, Brando called me several times about Indian issues. He was thinking of deeding some land to Indians and wanted to know the best way to do it. My last contact with him was ten years later, in 1974, when he called me about John Ehrlichman. Ehrlichman had been President Nixon's chief domestic affairs advisor and was under indictment and facing serious criminal charges in connection with Watergate. I had known Ehrlichman as a practicing attorney in Seattle when we faced off against each other in a civil trial, but I'd had no contact with him during the years when he was a rising star in the Nixon administration.

I'd actually recently seen Ehrlichman in 1974, when we both happened to be in the departure lounge at Dulles Airport outside of Washington, D.C. Ehrlichman came over and seated himself next to me, asking if I still did Indian work. When I told him I did, he asked me to explain to him the status of Indian land. I thought this a bit strange, but put it down to intellectual curiosity, since he had been a land-use attorney in Seattle. I tried to give him a legal overview of the concept of tribal land, allotted land, trust land, and fee patents, all terms in the lexicon of Indian law. He listened carefully and said he found it most interesting.

When Marlon Brando called, he told me that Ehrlichman claimed he wanted to help Indians. Apparently, Ehrlichman wondered if Brando could help him establish his bona fides with some Indian tribes. Brando said he and Ehrlichman had stayed up till two in the morning talking and he was convinced Ehrlichman was sincere. What did I think? I told him bluntly that I thought the man was a cynical opportunist and that I would be skeptical of his sincerity. He had, I thought, an ulterior motive. What that motive was became clear after his conviction.

When Ehrlichman stood before the judge for sentencing, he pleaded for leniency and said that he was deeply interested in the problems of

Indians of the Southwest (where he was then living), that he had studied the issues they faced involving the status of their lands, and that with his background in land-use law he felt he could help them. He offered to work pro bono for the Indians. The judge, apparently, was not swayed, and Ehrlichman received a prison sentence. I don't know whether Ehrlichman ever did do any legal work for any tribes after he was released from prison. That conversation about Ehrlichman was the last time I spoke with Marlon Brando.

Brando had performed a valuable service to the Indian struggle on Washington rivers. After he left, the struggle went on and other Hollywood celebrities showed their support for treaty rights: Peter and Jane Fonda and the comedian Dick Gregory. All of these celebrities gave national prominence to the Northwest Indians' fight against the state of Washington. But the state was determined to retain control of fishing, and nothing but a defeat in the courts would force it to end over half a century of violating treaty rights.

EIGHT

The Makahs

DURING MY ENTIRE CAREER IN INDIAN LAW, THE MAKAHS RE-
mained the touchstone of my Indian world. Neah Bay was the place
that held the earliest and most important memories of Indian life for
me, and Makah men and women were my teachers and my friends. For
over thirty years I shared the triumphs and setbacks of this small tribe.
I spent countless hours with Makahs over the years at meetings and
conferences, in restaurants, in lounges, in hotel lobbies, and at tribal
gatherings—ceremonies, dances, funerals. Members of the Makah
Tribal Council attended the bar mitzvahs of my two eldest sons, and my
wife and I attended some of the happy celebrations at Neah Bay. There
were countless hours at tribal meetings in the community hall. I came
to know well the firebrands, the traditionalists, the thoughtful mothers
and wives, and the family heads who all spoke before the tribal council.
Ed Claplanhoo, a former tribal chairman, and his wife Thelma remain
close friends, and I continue to enjoy seeing many of my old friends at
Neah Bay.

Everyone at Neah Bay knows every Makah. Families are intermarried, and some family names are found throughout the village: Markishtum, Parker, Johnson, Bowechop, Claplanhoo, Ides, McCarty, Peterson,
Arnold, Hottowe, Colfax, Ward, Irving, Hunter, Cooke. What happened to the men who sat on the council I first met in 1964? All are dead
now. Most of them were older than I was at the time, so their deaths are
no surprise in one way. But, sad to say, many died prematurely. An aura

of death seems to pervade the Makah community and, for that matter, all Indian communities. Alcohol claims many lives in ruined health, and auto crashes take a steady toll. Pat Wilkie Sr. and Pat Wilkie Jr. died prematurely. And Bruce Wilkie, that bright and promising young man who went on to become executive director of the National Congress of American Indians in Washington, D.C., succumbed to the scourge of alcohol. All of these deaths touched me with personal sadness. But it was the death of Squint Markishtum that hit me hardest.

I had formed a close bond with the short little man who was the tribal chairman. He was a plain man, of little formal education, who had spent his life fishing and logging. But he had charm. Squint was wise in his common-sense approach to the tribe's problems. He was married to a pleasant, blond non-Indian woman. They had no children, but I gathered from other members of the council that he was deeply attached to her. Then I heard that she was sick. She had cancer and Squint was driving her to Port Angeles every week for treatment. His habitual jauntiness disappeared. He looked worried all the time. I got word from the councilmen that "things look bad" for her. Then she died and Squint seemed to shrivel up. His attendance at council meetings became perfunctory, and finally he turned over his duties to the vice chairman.

When I saw Squint, he seemed so withdrawn that I felt something serious was going on. I asked another council member, Charlie Peterson, what might be wrong, and Charlie told me, "Well, when an old Indian's wife dies, sometimes he decides he wants to die too. I think that Squint has decided he wants to die." I couldn't believe this. Who can will themselves to die? Then I heard that Squint had been admitted to the hospital in Seattle.

I went up to visit him, and he was sitting up in his bed. "How are you doing, Squint?"

"Not too good, Al," he answered.

"What's the matter?"

"They don't seem to be able to figure it out."

"Can you get out of bed?"

"Sure," and he swung himself around and stood up on the floor.

"Can you take a short walk?" I persisted.

"Yeah," and the two of us walked down the corridor to a bench. Our conversation was forced. He didn't show any interest in tribal affairs, a highly unusual thing for him. After a short while, he indicated he wanted to go back to his room. I told him I would be back in a day or two for another visit. He mustered a weak smile and said goodbye. He seemed like a hollow man.

Two days later I returned to find him in the intensive care unit. I insisted on speaking with the attending physician. "His health seems to have deteriorated," I said. "What exactly is the medical problem?"

"We think there's a problem in his respiratory system, although we haven't found any pathology in his lungs."

"What's his prognosis?"

"Well, I'm not very optimistic, since his condition has deteriorated markedly in the past forty-eight hours. But we're doing all we can."

I went back into Squint's room and stood by his bed. I tried to will him to live. I spoke to him, but he gave no sign of hearing me. I stayed till eleven that night and finally left. The next morning he was dead. Squint's death left me deeply shaken. There seemed to be an almost mystical quality to Indian life in which death was a constant companion. This lent a somber note to the experiences of those of us who came into Indian life from the outside.

But it would be wrong to think of Makah life as gloomy. The people enjoy the pleasures of family, of nature, of fishing and recreation. The schools are bustling with activity. The kids enjoy athletics. Mothers enjoy their children and the young teenagers do what all teenagers do. But life on the reservation differs from life in non-Indian rural communities because of the ceremonies and celebrations that bond members to their tribal identity. Every significant event is marked by festivities in the old community hall, with drumming and singing of traditional Makah songs accompanied by ritual dancing. There is rhetoric and ritual gift giving, a remnant of the old institution of the potlatch.

I have spent many nights in that community hall, listening to the songs and watching the dances. These are social occasions for me, and I end up shaking hands and making jokes with many of my Makah friends. If the event is a party, there is always a gift ceremony. A representative of the family sponsoring the gathering stands at the front of the hall and calls out the name of each recipient. Many times I have been called to receive my gift, usually a small amount of money. And

I have learned to turn to the Makahs in the hall and say, "Klak-ho!" Thank you.

The Makah people are inclined toward friendliness and kindness. They love humor, and they tease and make jokes about almost everything. But they also carry within themselves an acceptance of the ever-present threat of tragedy. Bad accidents, dread disease, and drownings at sea periodically bring sorrow and funerals. I have attended many of these sad events, some in the community hall and some in a church.

The Makah reservation encompasses about ten square miles, small as Indian reservations go. Small rivers and streams flow through the reservation and there are beautiful beaches on the Pacific Ocean side. The terrain back from the coast is quite hilly and heavily timbered. That timber is the main source of revenue for the tribal government and is managed by the Bureau of Indian Affairs to provide a perpetual income. Except for the summer months, the skies are gray and rainfall is an almost daily event. But even during the winter months, there are periods of clear and sunny skies. I have never heard any Makah complain about the weather.

Neah Bay is a fishing village. It looks out on a bay and the docks and marinas where fishing boats are moored. Along the main bayside street are the town's businesses, motels and one or two cafes. You must turn up one of the intersecting side streets to see the main residential areas.

Driving the back streets of Neah Bay you'll find a kaleidoscope of homes: some new, painted and in good condition, many rundown, some derelict and abandoned, some trailers, all intermingled. In many front yards are cars, trucks, fishing boats, and rusting hulks of junk cars, machinery, abandoned refrigerators, and toys. There are lawns and picket fences, but they are few. To the eyes of a non-Indian outsider, the disarray suggests a people with little concern for appearances, and I think this is an important truth about Indian community life. For sociologists or anthropologists, the message is that we Americans are overwhelmingly concerned with appearances, about order and neatness and what others may think of us. Indian people don't necessarily share these values, or at least don't give them the priority that American non-Indian society does.

Neah Bay's population fluctuates, but now averages around 1,500 people, more than twice what it was when I first went there in 1963.

It is distant from large centers of non-Indian population; the nearest large town, Port Angeles, is seventy-five miles away. This separation has served to protect the tribe from many of the pressures of acculturation and has enabled the Makah to maintain their strong sense of tribal identity.

When I first came to the reservation, there was a U.S. Air Force base there. The military had built a radar station on one of the hills overlooking the village, a product of the cold war intended to provide early warning of enemy bombers approaching. The air force personnel who operated and maintained the station occupied a small installation southwest of the village, with barracks and clubs for officers and non-commissioned officers. The base was closed in 1988 after some thirty years of operation. Today its buildings are used by the tribe as its government center.

There is also a Coast Guard base at Neah Bay of long and distinguished vintage. It was established in 1877 under the U.S. Lifesaving Service. Probably owing to its remoteness, it was at first entirely staffed by Makahs under the direction of a "keeper." This was one of the first units in any U.S. military service made up entirely of American Indians. Later, the Makahs were replaced by non-Indian members of the service, which became the U.S. Coast Guard in 1915.[1] The base remains important because of the frequency of mariners in distress in the waters off Cape Flattery and in the Strait of Juan de Fuca. The Coast Guard people have a close working relationship with the tribe, and many of the guardsmen participate as volunteers in community activities—the emergency rescue service, youth programs, and community celebrations. Some have married Makahs. The Makahs, like most American Indians, are highly patriotic. Service in the U.S. military is honored. There is an American Legion Post at Neah Bay, whose members furnish the honor guard at community functions. At community parades, many Makah military veterans wear their uniforms.

The Makah name for themselves is *Kwedechechat*, or People Who Live by the Rocks and the Seagulls. The name *Makah* actually comes from their neighbors, the S'Klallam Tribe. But their established name has become Makah, and they call themselves Makahs. The Makahs have inhabited the corner of the Olympic Peninsula jutting into the Pacific Ocean for several thousand years. Before the 1850s, they lived in five winter villages along the northern coast of the peninsula and south along the Pacific shore some twenty miles.

The Makahs are linguistically and culturally distinct from other Indian groups in the United States. Their language is based on Nootka, while their neighbors to the east and south speak a form of Salish. The Makahs are the southernmost of the Nootka-speaking tribes, the rest living in Canada on the west coast of Vancouver Island. The prevailing view of anthropologists is that at some point Makah ancestors, part of the Nootka-speaking tribes, traveled some fourteen miles across the strait from Vancouver Island and settled in the area of Cape Flattery. The Makahs are interrelated with the Vancouver Island Nootka groups and often travel and visit back and forth. This small tribe is geographically and culturally unique, another reason for their strong sense of tribal identity.

The Makahs were a seafaring people and their food came from the ocean: whale, seal, salmon, halibut, clams, and sea urchins. While other coastal Indians also lived on the products of the sea, the Makahs were the premier whalers of the Pacific Northwest. Their whaling canoes were thirty-six-foot-long dugout cedar logs, manned by skilled crews of whalers. The whaling canoe carried harpoons, seal skin floats, and lengths of line. Whaling was dangerous, and the men who went out to hunt the whale had high status. Taking a whale was a spiritual experience, calling for ritual fasting, bathing, and flagellation to purify the spirit of the whaler before venturing out for the hunt. Whaling was central to the Makah identity. The figure of the whale is woven into the tribe's basketry and displayed in carvings. It is in their songs. I will have occasion to say more about Makah whaling later.[2]

As I came to know Makahs intimately, our conversations grew more candid. At first there were only hints of the resentment they felt at the stereotyping of Indians. Later, the depth of their feelings came to the surface. Charlie Peterson, a respected member of the tribal council, once remarked to me on seeing the model name *Cherokee* on a Piper airplane, "They like our names, don't they." I understood him. Americans exploit the names of Indian tribes when it adds panache to their enterprise, but they show little respect for living, breathing Indian people. Indian people took no pride in seeing non-Indians use a tribal name for their own purposes. Makahs' comments about the disparaging remarks and name-calling they encountered revealed emotional scars. It was something I was familiar with as a Jew.

The effect on me was to try to get the public to see the Indian people in a respectful light. I wrote articles, spoke to interested audiences, and argued passionately for understanding modern Indian life and dispelling the stereotypes of the past. I was not just a tribal attorney—I was an advocate for Indian life and Indian rights.

The Makah reservation and its government have changed drastically since my first visits in 1963. I have described the tribal government then: a five-member council meeting in a tiny office. The councilmen had to work at outside jobs during the day, so meetings were held at night. They met infrequently because there was little for them to do. The Bureau of Indian Affairs was the dominant government for the tribe, and the council was often simply asked to formally approve actions taken by the bureau. The tribe's staff consisted of the tribal secretary who kept the minutes and filed documents in a single filing cabinet and in cardboard boxes on the floor. This was a government in name only. It lacked the framework of a government and the reason was simple—money. Unlike American local governments, the tribe lacked a tax base. The land was nontaxable and the people's income was meager. Unemployment was widespread. Tribal government limped along as best it could.

All of this began to change with the War on Poverty programs initiated under President Lyndon B. Johnson.[3] The Economic Opportunity Act of 1964 offered new hope to tribes. In 1965, I got a call from Neah Bay telling me the council was going to Washington, D.C., for a conference about how they could benefit from the new programs, and they wanted me to go with them. I was excited. We all stayed at the same hotel, one of Washington's least expensive—dingy and rundown, but located near the Capitol.

The tribal participants assembled for a meeting at the U.S. Interior Department and were given a multipage program. That evening and the next day, the council members divided up assignments to ensure that all presentations were covered. Back at the hotel, we discussed what we had heard and went out to dinner. One councilman declined to take part in the social activities—Art Claplanhoo, a soft-spoken, elderly, gentle man. He attended only one presentation, and he seemed content to sit in the hotel lobby the rest of the time.

A week or so after returning to Neah Bay, the council called a general meeting of the tribe to report on the trip. A large crowd assembled in the community hall, and one by one the councilmen got to their feet to speak. One talked about the Community Action Program, another about the transfer of decision-making power to the tribes, another about employment programs. Their reports were plodding and aroused little excitement. There was no applause. Finally, Art Claplanhoo stood up. I thought he had done very little in Washington, D.C., so I was curious what he would say.

Art was a man of few words, and his talk was short. It went something like this: "Well, I went to the housing meeting. They showed us the nice houses the government had built for them people over in Korea. They were sure nice houses. That's about all I got to say." And he sat down. To my amazement, the hall broke out in thunderous applause. What was this all about? I couldn't understand it. Only later did I comprehend Art's message. He was telling the Makahs that the government of the United States could build very nice houses for people in other countries. They could have done the same here. They hadn't. Would they? Wait and see.

It taught me a lesson in communication, Indian style. Non-Indians can be glib and wordy. If a non-Indian had given the report, it would have consumed twenty minutes and been filled with tedious bureaucratese. Indian people seem to have the ability to cut to the heart of the matter without unnecessary verbiage.

In time, the Community Action Program transformed the Makah reservation and enabled the tribe to build a real government. Today, the tribal government consists of the council, a tribal court, a police and fire system, and departments that manage the reservation's physical and social environment. The tribe operates a Head Start Program and a child-care department as well as a tribal health office. There is a Fisheries Department and a Forestry Department, staffed with trained professionals. The tribal government's structure is parallel to non-Indian local governments, and tribal government functions like its counterparts in the non-Indian world with one exception: respect for the tribal character of the community. This is reflected in decision making that keeps in mind the history of the people, their identity, and their responsibility to preserve the tribal way of life for future generations.

One of the principal goals of the Makah Tribal Council is to build new housing to replace old and dilapidated structures and to provide decent living environments for young and old. As new housing has been built, many Makahs have returned to the reservation. Young Makahs who might otherwise have left the reservation have stayed and taken jobs working for the tribe.

Congress has, for the past twenty years, increasingly provided for tribal governments to deliver federally funded services. As a result, federal-tribal interactions have gradually evolved into a true government-to-government relationship. The Makah tribal government today is a far cry from the days of five councilmen and a secretary. Yet, while outwardly the Makah reservation and its people have the trappings of a contemporary society, those appearances are deceiving. The Makahs remain a people who preserve a distinctive and old culture, and they are a people with a history never far from the present. Ozette is part of that history.

NINE

Recovering Lost Property: Ozette, Tatoosh, and Waadah

WHEN I FIRST BEGAN WORKING WITH THE MAKAHS, I HEARD VAGUE allusions to Ozette, but didn't know what it was. In time I learned that it was one of the five major Makah villages, although no Makahs lived there now. While Ozette seemed only a distant memory, many Makahs traced their ancestry to the village, and the oldest Makahs recalled growing up there, about twenty miles south of the reservation along the Pacific coast. In 1967, the tribal council called on me to help them protect the Makah character of Ozette in the face of a proposal to incorporate it into the Olympic National Park. Once the village site became part of the national park, the Makahs would not be able camp, fish, or hunt there. The Makahs had strong feelings about this tiny, 719-acre parcel of land. They saw it as Makah property that others were trying to take from them.

The history of Ozette revealed a familiar pattern of bureaucratic ignorance and stubbornness. U.S. officials had always known that Ozette was a Makah village. After all, one of the signers of the Makah treaty with the United States was Tse Kow Wootl, described in the treaty as a Makah chief from Ozette. But since the boundaries of the Makah reservation did not include Ozette, the Makahs living there were technically landless Indians. This didn't bother the Makahs then at Ozette, who intended to keep living there as they always had, but it seemed to bother the Indian Bureau. The bureau had responsibility for Indian communities that didn't fit into any legal categories. So the Indian agent at

"Osette" requested that a reservation be established by executive order for the Indians living there. By the magic of bureaucratic fiat, they came to be designated "Ozette Indians." Voilà! There was now a new Indian tribe. And in 1893 an executive order was promulgated establishing a reservation for the "Ozette Indians."

But the bureaucrats of the Indian Bureau had no intention of letting the Makahs at Ozette live as they always had. Soon after the Makah treaty was signed in 1855, the government established a school at Neah Bay. While many Makahs wanted their children to be educated at the white man's school, others did not. The government then ordered compulsory school attendance, and parents who did not comply were arrested and jailed by order of the Indian Bureau superintendent. By 1860, the agency had turned its attention to the children at Ozette. No one proposed establishing a school there. Instead, parents were informed that their children must be sent to Neah Bay. This meant that the children would have to live with relatives in Neah Bay and return home only on weekends. Few Makah parents wanted to be separated from their children, but after the government agent threatened arrest, they reluctantly complied. The result was foreseeable—over time, families left Ozette and moved to Neah Bay, and Ozette's population dwindled. By the time the Ozette reservation was established in 1893, there were only sixty-four people living there. By 1905, the number had dropped to thirty-six, and by 1937 only one Makah continued to live there.[1]

Where did they go? Almost all went to Neah Bay. But even after the last Makah left Ozette, the land remained legally an Indian reservation. Under the law, Indian lands don't automatically undergo a change of status when Indians no longer make it their permanent home. Makahs continued to visit and camp at Ozette. But by the middle of the twentieth century, many non-Indians had discovered the beauties of Ozette. In the popular press it was treated as the home of a vanished tribe. Sunday newspaper supplements routinely carried articles with titles like "The Mystery of the Vanished Ozettes." Well, there was no mystery at all. Not only the Makahs, but also anthropologists and historians knew that all the residents of Ozette had gone to Neah Bay because they were Makahs; they had family there and they all spoke the same language.

It was probably inevitable that sooner or later some group would propose taking the Ozette land. The most interested party was the

National Park Service because the Olympic National Park already abutted the Ozette reservation to the south. Many hikers, nature lovers, and members of a park support group called Olympic Park Associates saw absorption into the park as a way of preserving the natural beauty of Ozette while also expanding the park. The Makahs were aware of this threat and beginning in 1941 asked the Bureau of Indian Affairs to transfer Ozette to the Makah Tribe. The U.S. Interior Department refused, but did decide not to add the reservation to the park.[2] The tribe tried again in 1957, and once again the Interior Department's solicitor held that the reservation was created for the Ozette Indians and not for the Makahs. A bureaucratic error had become cast in concrete and could not be corrected.

In 1967, Olympic Park Associates once again asked the Park Service to extend the park boundaries to incorporate Ozette. This is when the tribal council asked for my help, and I set about doing historical and legal research. The history was not difficult to document. The facts were well known. It was the legal consequences that had to be fought, and I was confronted by a history of two solicitors' opinions rejecting the tribe's claims. I tried a different tack. I wrote a lengthy legal memorandum to the Interior Department showing that the Makahs had aboriginal title to the tract as a tribe, that the federal government in establishing a reservation at Ozette in 1893 affirmed that title, and that the use of the term "Ozette Indians" was a misnomer. Then I argued that the Makahs had been coerced by the United States to leave their land, and that title can never be lost, nor property be treated as abandoned when the legal occupant has been coerced to leave. I thought it was a good argument, and I wrote it as a brief citing legal authorities to support my position.

My efforts came to naught. For the third time, Interior's solicitor rejected the claim, saying the Ozette reservation was created not for a tribe but for a class of Indians, namely those Makahs not living on the reservation. The conclusion was the same: the Makah Tribe had no rights to this reservation. But the solicitor did have a suggestion: get Congress to pass a law. The solicitor's decision was released in 1969.[3] And this time, fearing a real threat to Ozette from Olympic Park Associates, the tribe decided to seek help from Congress.

I contacted the office of Washington State's junior senator, Henry M. "Scoop" Jackson. The initial response was sympathetic, but then his staff contacted the Park Service and learned of the Olympic Park Associates' desire to see Ozette made part of the Olympic National Park. The senator told me he didn't want to get in the middle of a dispute between the Makahs and park interests. He strongly suggested we sit down with the OPA and see if there wasn't a way to satisfy both groups. The tribal council reluctantly agreed to a meeting.

Several council members and I met with officers of Olympic Park Associates, a fifty-year-old organization of some three hundred members dedicated to protection and support for the park. The three members who attended the meeting, two women and one man, tried to assure the Makahs that they had the highest respect for Indians, but that absorption into the park was necessary for preserving the pristine beauty of Ozette. When the Makahs responded that Ozette was rightfully theirs, one of the OPA officers said, "But you don't understand. We *love* Ozette." The Makahs received this icily. It was like being told that an interloper really *loves* your spouse and should therefore be able to take possession of her. Several meetings followed, and eventually the OPA saw that the Makahs were not going to let Ozette slip out of their grasp. Understanding that Ozette could not be taken into the park without legislation terminating its status as an Indian reservation, OPA reluctantly proposed a compromise. They would drop their proposal for incorporation into the park if there were some assurances that Ozette's natural beauty would be protected. "Well," one of the OPA negotiators said, "if the tribe was to get it and some of your members moved there, we wouldn't want it looking like a junkyard." The council members drew themselves up and coldly informed her that the tribe respected Ozette and would not allow it to be desecrated. With the understanding that no commercial development would be permitted there by the tribe, OPA announced they were satisfied and would withdraw their opposition to the tribe acquiring Ozette. After that, things moved quickly. On October 22, 1970, Congress enacted Public Law 91–489, declaring Ozette to be part of the trust land of the Makah Tribe. After almost a hundred and fifty years a wrong was righted, and the Makahs recovered their property.

The recovery of Ozette was to have far-reaching consequences for the Makah Tribe, not clearly foreseen in 1967 when the council directed me to fight for the tract. In 1970, a winter storm resulted in an unusually high tide, and wave action washed away an earthen bank up from the beach. Some Makahs came back and reported that artifacts had been exposed. The tribe dispatched a member to stand guard over the site. Dr. Richard Daugherty, an archeology professor at Washington State University, soon arrived and quickly saw that a part of a Makah house had been exposed—there would likely be artifacts inside. He asked for and obtained permission from the tribe to open an archeological dig at Ozette. The Ozette dig soon became one of the richest archeological finds in North America.

Dr. Daugherty, with the assistance of Senator Jackson, obtained financial support from the Bureau of Indian Affairs, the National Park Service, and others. The Makah Tribe gave its approval for the removal of artifacts from the site on the condition that all that was found remain on the Makah reservation. The dig became a beehive of activity, as students and volunteers from around the country set to work to carefully excavate and remove Makah objects from the earth.

Daugherty and the tribe recruited young Makahs to take part in unearthing their own past, and excitement spread as the tribe began to see the dig's first results. The remains of six Makah houses were uncovered, and as the dig proceeded the contents of the houses came to light. A temporary laboratory was established at Neah Bay for the preliminary identification and classification of the objects. The story that the dig told was extraordinary. Ozette had been occupied by the Makahs for over two thousand years. About five hundred years before the storm of 1970, a slide had buried six houses of the village. Sealed by damp clay, the contents had been perfectly preserved—through them we could see how the Makahs had lived, whaled, fished, and carved in the fifteenth century.

News of what the Ozette dig was finding spread worldwide. To show the world who they were and how they had lived, the tribe built a beautiful museum to house the Ozette objects. The museum opened in 1979 as the Makah Cultural and Research Center. It houses over 55,000 objects found at the Ozette site, which show the Makahs to have been whale and seal hunters and skilled carvers and builders of houses, canoes, and marine hunting implements. The University of Washington Anthropology Department worked with the tribe to train Makahs as museologists. Today the museum is unique among the world's museums, staffed by Makah Indians who proudly display the material culture of their own people. The museum contains an authentic Makah longhouse, carefully assembled by dedicated Makahs, recreating the life of their ancestors who lived at Ozette. Since its opening in 1979, the museum has welcomed over 350,000 visitors who have seen the Makahs as a people with an ancient history and a connection to the sea that is dramatically displayed.[4] The long fight to return Ozette to its rightful owners ended in a way that enriches the Makahs and the nation.

The law of damages is based on the principle of making the injured party whole—restoring what was lost by the harm done to them. All Indian tribes have been damaged by the loss of their lands and cultures. Making them completely whole is usually impossible. But restoration of even a part of their loss is deeply satisfying to a tribe and provides a real sense of achievement for a tribal attorney.

Just as Ozette had long been denied to the Makahs, so had two tiny offshore islands, felt by the tribe to be their land but claimed by the federal government instead. Waadah Island sits at the entrance to Neah Bay and Tatoosh Island is just off Cape Flattery. Before the arrival of whites in the Pacific Northwest, the Makahs were the undisputed owners of the entire northwest corner of the Olympic Peninsula, from the Hoko River to the east, along the strait westward, south along the ocean to Ozette, along the shores of Lake Ozette, and inland to the Olympic Mountains. Waadah and Tatoosh islands were a part of that territory.

All their lands and islands were a part of the fabric of Makah life. They were in the tribe's songs, stories, and legends, and they formed the matrix of thought and belief of the Makah people for centuries. When the United States set its sights on acquiring the Indian lands of the Northwest for eventual white settlement, they decided to take most of the Makah lands, leaving them a tiny reservation, much smaller than the present one. Territorial Governor Isaac Stevens met with the Makahs in January of 1855, and treaty negotiations were carried on for four days through a translator. The minutes recite that the treaty was then read to the Makahs and explained to them. They were asked if they accepted the treaty as read, and the minutes say they did and that they signed the document. But events that transpired after 1855 clearly show that the treaty did not conform to the Makahs' understanding of what the bargain was.

The Makahs had used the island known as Tatoosh as a summer

fishing village since time immemorial. To the Makahs, the island was the Stone House, and the chief of the Makahs who occupied the island in the eighteenth century was Tatooche. Early charts show the name of the island as *Tatoosh*. The year following the 1855 treaty, the federal government began constructing a lighthouse on the island. The Makahs were enraged and sent a war party to attack. Construction was halted so that the government could build a blockhouse and arm the workers with muskets. The Makahs withdrew, but did not acquiesce to the work. A lighthouse was completed in 1857, but the following year the keeper reported to the Indian agent that he was unable to keep assistants working there because they feared the Makahs. The Makahs could not be kept out of the lighthouse, had broken into the storehouse, and had struck the keeper and threatened to kill him.[5] U.S. military force was threatened, and relations with the Makahs remained uneasy until 1885. It seems the Makahs did not believe that the government had any right to occupy the island.

Legally, the Makahs were wrong. The Treaty of Neah Bay contains a recital that the tribe cedes to the United States all the lands described in the treaty, "including all the islands lying off the coast." The tribe's vehement objection to the occupation of Tatoosh, which continued for almost twenty-five years, strongly contradicts the recital in the treaty minutes that all clauses were read and explained to the Makahs. At the very least, the translator was not capable of communicating the clause in the Chinook jargon that was used (a trade jargon, not a true language), or else he glossed over the clause regarding the offshore islands. This was not an oversight. The treaty minutes recite: "Kah-tchook, again, 'I do not want you to leave me destitute—I want my house on the Island' (Tatooshe Island, commonly called the Stone House)." Eventually, the Makahs gave up their struggle to retain Tatoosh and it remained federal property.

Waadah Island, lying at the entrance to Neah Bay, was another integral part of Makah lands. There is no record of strife over this island, probably because it remained undeveloped and was not used by the Makahs as a fishing village site. But, like Tatoosh, it was lost. The federal government took title under the 1855 treaty. And thus matters stood for over a hundred years. When I first began my work with the tribe there was no mention of the issue. No doubt, the tribe considered the islands beyond redemption. My ultimate concern with these islands began with a case that was entirely unrelated, the Makah claims case.

In 1969, six years after my firm began representing the Makahs, I received notice from the Indian Claims Commission that unless some action was taken within the next sixty days the Makah claim would be dismissed. I had never heard of the claim and knew nothing of the Indian Claims Commission. I soon learned.

The Indian Claims Commission was created by Congress in 1946 to function as a court adjudicating Indian claims against the United States. The claims were narrowly defined as those arising from failure to pay promised money or inadequate payment for lands taken by the United States. The commission's creation was prompted by a growing sense of discomfort at the repeated accusations that the United States had dealt unjustly with Indians. With the end of the Second World War, in which Indians had served loyally and heroically, Congress decided it was time to make reparation. But the Indian Claims Act made it clear that the only remedy available to the tribes was money. No land could be returned or released.

The Indian Claims Act gave rise to a small group of attorneys who developed a special expertise. These attorneys were almost entirely concentrated in Washington, D.C., and they were attracted to this field of litigation by the lure of huge fees. The statute limited attorney fees to 10 percent of the amount awarded, but for most of the land-using tribes the acreage involved ran into the millions, and so the potential dollar recovery was very large.

In order to prove a tribal claim, a tribe had to establish the precise land area to which it had "aboriginal title." This required hiring anthropologists, historians, and other specialists to dig into historical records and prepare reports. The attorney then had to present proof of the fair market value of those lands at the time they were taken, and the award would reflect the difference between the worth of the land and the amount paid. But the government was entitled to claim "offsets," deductions for amounts paid to the tribes over time that were not an obligation under a treaty. So the government dredged up old records of food and supplies furnished, health services provided, and the like. All of this was presented to a commissioner who made the final decision. Either party could appeal the decision to the U.S. Court of Claims, or ultimately to the U.S. Supreme Court.

This was the arcane world of law I had to deal with in undertaking this newly rediscovered Makah claim. None of the tribal council members in 1969 knew anything about the case, since it had been prosecuted almost twenty years earlier. When I contacted the federal government lawyer assigned to the case, he explained that the claim had originally been filed around 1950 by a Seattle attorney who had since died. The claim was based on loss of Makah sealing rights because of federal legislation banning fur-seal hunting (except for natives of St. Lawrence Island in the Bering Sea), loss of income from salmon and halibut fishing restricted by a U.S.-Canadian treaty, and inadequate compensation paid for the land ceded by the tribe. The commission ruled against the first two Makah claims in 1959.[6] Those claims had been finally adjudicated and could not be reopened. The only claim that remained was one for inadequate compensation for land. This case had been inactive for years, and the attorney who had originally prosecuted it appeared to have lost interest in pursuing it further before he died.

The land claim was economically unpromising. The Makahs were not a land-using tribe, they were a seafaring tribe. They did have aboriginal title to interior lands, but would have to prove the boundary of those lands. Several years were consumed in this effort, engaging expert witnesses and ultimately conducting a trial. The final decision of the commission was disappointing—only about 100,000 acres were found to be theirs. The fair market value of this land as of 1855 would be in the neighborhood of fifteen or twenty thousand dollars. Since the Makahs received the thirty thousand dollars provided in their treaty, and an additional large amount could be claimed by the government as offsets, any damage claim based on inadequate compensation for land would be of little or no value. This was no doubt the reason my predecessor had abandoned the case. But I was determined not to just let the claim go.

After researching the history, I amended the Makah claim to allege that the government had breached its promise to provide the Makahs with the fishing and whaling implements that Territorial Governor Stevens had promised. My effort to open this new avenue was strenuously opposed by the government. Ultimately the commission allowed it. I litigated the claim and we were successful: the Indian Claims Commission ruled that the United States had indeed breached its promise.[7] But the task of proving the resulting loss of income was daunting. It would be almost impossible to prove that Makahs lost income solely because of lack of fishing and whaling implements. The government then gave notice that they would seek to offset any claim with millions of dollars of various kinds of aid they had furnished to the Makahs since the 1855 treaty. There was a good chance the tribe would end up with nothing. I pursued the litigation, hoping I would be able to develop evidence to support the Makah claim. Then I received a call from the government's attorney—he wanted to talk about settling the case.

When we began discussing what the government might be willing to pay, the figure was in the neighborhood of $100,000. I knew the tribe would not be attracted by this offer, so I brought up the subject of return-ing some land to the tribe. We had already reacquired Ozette. Now I raised the issue of Tatoosh and Waadah, islands that had significance to the Makahs and that should rightfully be theirs. The government attorney asked me to submit a legal memorandum giving the law and the history; he promised he would consult with the appropriate agencies to see if relinquishing these islands was feasible. After I submitted the memorandum, he called and said he had spoken with the Coast Guard. The lighthouse on Tatoosh was no longer manned. It was entirely auto-mated and the Coast Guard had no objection to transferring Tatoosh Island to tribal ownership, so long as they could continue to go to the island to service the lighthouse. Similarly, there was no objection to relinquishing federal ownership of Waadah. So it was up to the tribe.

I explained the proposition to the council—$100,000 versus the return of Tatoosh and Waadah. The council decided this was a mat-ter for the tribal membership to decide and called a general council meeting. I appeared before the entire membership in the community hall and explained the issue. I pointed out that there could be strategic importance in the tribe owning these islands and controlling the har-bor of Neah Bay. The vote was overwhelmingly against accepting any money and in favor of the return of Tatoosh and Waadah.

After I notified the Justice Department attorney of the tribe's deci-sion, the wheels were set in motion. On May 15, 1984, Congress passed Public Law 98–282, restoring to the Makah Tribe ownership of Tatoosh and Waadah. It had been almost 130 years since these lands were taken from the Makahs, and it had taken me nearly 15 years to accomplish this step in making the Makahs whole. I had succeeded in using the Indian Claims Act to restore lands to an Indian tribe—a remedy not authorized by Congress. In the process, we had accomplished something else: the Indian Claims Commission made a binding ruling that the United States had breached its promise to provide the Makahs with whaling and fishing implements. Perhaps one day that might prove useful.

TEN

The Lummi Tribe

BEING A TRIBAL ATTORNEY MEANT ATTENDING INNUMERABLE meetings and conferences with Indian leaders. One of the most colorful and nicest I ever met was Sam Cagey of the Lummi Tribe. His sheer physical presence was overpowering. He had broad, powerful shoulders and a massive torso. His hands were large and his fingers were as thick as sausages. His voice was loud and hoarse and his nose broad and mashed. Sam had a marvelous sense of humor and his laughter could be heard throughout a room. But he was a tough and determined fighter for Indian rights.

One day Sam approached me at a meeting and said, "You know Al, some of the people on the council have been talking about needing a good tribal attorney. I think you and your firm could help us with some of our problems. Would you be interested?" At that time our only tribal client was the Makah Tribe, and I thought taking on the Lummis would be a great addition. But I told Sam we'd have to discuss it with the Makahs. He accepted this and nodded soberly. "I understand," he said. "Let us know." I think he respected our sense of responsibility to the Makahs and the need to avoid any conflict between the two tribes.

When I asked, the Makah tribal chairman told me he didn't think there would be a problem. "We don't have any conflicts with the Lummis," he said. "In fact, we get along pretty good with them. But I'm glad you came to us and asked. I'll talk to our council and let you know." A few days later he called and said, "Go ahead."

So in 1968 Ziontz, Pirtle and Fulle was retained by the Lummi Indian Tribe. The Lummi Indian Reservation lies about ninety miles north of Seattle, northwest of the city of Bellingham. Before the landmark case of *U.S. v. Washington* in 1974 changed Indian fishing rights, the Lummis, like all the tribes in the Northwest, were struggling in poverty. Their forebears had been fishermen, and while a few Lummis had fishing boats, most barely made a subsistence living.

The Nooksack River flows through the Lummi reservation before emptying into Bellingham Bay, and Lummis gillnetted on the river. But they also had a unique fishery—a reef-net fishery. In this type of fishery, two canoes are stationed over a reef where the salmon pass on their return to their spawning grounds. The canoes are tethered to heavy boulders sunk down to the seabed, which serve as anchors. The fishermen then suspend a net in the water between the canoes and station a watcher. When he sees a large group of fish passing over the reef, he shouts to his fellows and they quickly haul up the net, usually heavy with salmon.[1] But by the twentieth century, the Lummis had been displaced from this fishery by non-Indians who claimed ownership rights to the best locations over the reefs. This would be challenged in *U.S. v. Washington*. But when the Lummis contacted us in 1968, *U.S. v. Washington* was several years in the future.

Instead of waiting for the day when their treaty rights would finally be vindicated, the Lummis placed their hopes of climbing out of poverty on a bold project conceived by a professor at Western Washington University in Bellingham, Dr. Wallace Heath. Heath was an extremely bright and talented man with many interests. He had a PhD in zoology and a minor in physics and he had become interested in the Lummis.

Wally Heath had learned about exciting work in Hawaii and other places around the world with aquaculture—fish farming. As he toured the Lummi reservation with the chairman, Vernon Lane, he viewed the reservation's extensive tidelands and saw an ideal location for a fish-farming operation. Heath was a man of great enthusiasms, and he backed up his ideas with scientific and logical analysis. Soon, he convinced the tribe to launch a full-blown campaign to create an aquaculture operation on their tidelands.

The Lummis were excited by the idea of operating their own fish farm. The aquaculture project would require enclosing a large area of tidelands, using a dike with gates to allow fresh seawater to bring nutrients to the artificial pond. But the Lummis were not prepared for the strong opposition from non-Indian waterfront homeowners. These landowners complained that the dike would mar their pristine view of the bay. Because the structure would be built in navigable waters, a permit also had to be obtained from the Army Corps of Engineers. The corps was soon bombarded with letters of opposition to the Lummi project, not only from the waterfront homeowners, but from non-Indians in the entire Bellingham area. The corps decided to hold a series of public hearings.

The Lummis felt the opposition stemmed in part, at least, from anti-Indian prejudice, and they were incensed. A public meeting on the project was scheduled by the non-Indian landowners at a downtown hotel. Vernon Lane asked me to come with him. The crowd seemed evenly divided between supporters and opponents of the project. I spoke, explaining the basic right of the Lummi to use their tribal land to better their community. After several of the landowners spoke in opposition, Vernon raised his hand and asked to be recognized. His speech was simple and from the heart.

"I know most of you. I grew up with you. We went to high school together. But when I went to you looking for a job as a carpenter, you wouldn't hire me. And the people of Bellingham have always showed us their prejudice. Now we have to come to you to get permission to build—to build on our own land. I want to tell you we're tired of being held down. We want to make a better future for ourselves and our children and we're going to build this project."

After two more hearings, the Army Corps issued the permit and the Lummis built their project. The fish farm brought the Lummis together as a tribe, and eventually the project gave rise to an oyster-farming operation, a diving school, and ultimately a tribal college. In 1970 the Lummis would continue to fight for their rights, becoming important parties to the fishing-rights litigation in *U.S. v. Washington*.

ELEVEN

Indian Fishing Rights:
Eighty Years of Suppression,
Twenty Years of Confrontation

THE UNITED STATES MADE SOLEMN PROMISES TO THE TRIBES OF THE Pacific Northwest, assurances that they could carry on their fishing without interference. Those promises were forgotten when the newly created state of Washington found Indian fishing to be in the way of a fledgling industry—commercial salmon fishing. How did the treaty promises of the United States become subverted, leaving the Indians to face the power of the state of Washington alone? Perhaps it was the inevitable consequence of white settlement and industrial development of the Northwest, but it was also the product of a racist view of Indians and the reluctance of the federal government to commit its resources to enforce its treaties. What follows is the story of a clash between cultures and between state power and, ultimately, federal law.

The lives and culture of the Indian people of the Northwest have always revolved around the products of the sea. Fishing was the preeminent feature of Northwest coast Indian life. Salmon and steelhead were the staples of the Indian diet, and for the coastal tribes halibut, seal, whale, and shellfish were as well. The salmon, all five species, are anadromous fish: they spend most of their existence in the ocean and then return to their natal freshwater rivers and streams to spawn and die. Their offspring migrate downstream to the ocean to repeat the cycle. The timing of that cycle established the rhythms of Indian life in the Northwest. Salmon runs begin their return to freshwater in the spring and summer, and Indians historically set up temporary fishing camps on the banks of these waters to catch the fish in nets and weirs, or traps. The Indian people lived in permanent villages during the winter, eating mainly smoked and preserved fish as well as steelhead, a winter fish, and returned to their traditional sites along the rivers each spring. They followed the runs, moving from one river to another as each run of fish from that river returned.

Among all the indigenous people of the American continent, the Northwest coast Indians developed a culture extraordinarily rich in its mythology and belief systems, dances, songs, wood carving, seagoing dugout canoes, plank longhouses, woven mats, capes, baskets, and hats. The food from the sea enabled them to lead a bountiful life. Their fishing techniques, implements, and catching devices were highly efficient. Not only did they fish for their own subsistence, they also cured and stored fish and sold or traded it to other tribes from the inland regions and to white traders who visited the area. What we would call a commercial trade in fish was flourishing before the treaties were made with the United States. That commerce was duly reported to the federal government by agents who investigated the prospect of opening the region to white settlement.

Settling the Pacific Northwest meant persuading the Indian people to confine themselves to reservations, but that did not present the same difficulties the government faced with the Plains tribes, who roamed over tens of thousands of acres hunting animals. It did mean that in order to persuade Indians of the region to give up their lands, they had to be guaranteed the right to continued use of their traditional fishing sites so they could support themselves. No conflict was foreseen. There was such an abundance of fish that government planners even thought the white settlers who were coming would rely on the Indian to supply them with fish.

In December of 1853, the governor of the Washington Territory, Isaac Stevens, wrote to the commissioner of Indian affairs suggesting the need to make treaties with the tribes. The following year, Stevens was appointed to make the treaties and given general instructions. He was assisted by George Gibbs, a lawyer who drafted a form of treaty to be presented to the tribes. Stevens immediately organized a small party to conduct the negotiations, which included an Indian familiar with Chinook jargon— not an actual Indian language, but a mixture of English and Indian words used by whites in their dealings with the Indians of the Northwest. Then messengers were sent to convene representatives of the tribes to meet with the treaty party. There followed a series of whirlwind meetings held in five locations within the territory of each of the major groups of Indians.

The treaties that resulted are called the Stevens treaties. Their main object was to get the Indians to surrender all claims to traditional lands and agree to reside permanently on the small reservations set aside for them. Reflecting the government's principal aim, each treaty begins with a clause reciting that the tribe ceded and relinquished all claims to a described area of land and agreed to withdraw to the area reserved to them, described by boundaries. But, following this clause, each of the treaties also contain this provision: "The right of taking fish, at all usual and accustomed grounds and stations, is further secured to said Indians in common with all citizens of the Territory." This guaranty, which seemed to promise so much, was soon made meaningless by Washington State. The critical phrase, "in common with," was seized upon to bring Indians under state laws.

For six or seven years following the treaties, there was no conflict between the Indians and the newcomers over fishing. But the Washington Territory was rapidly filling up with settlers. In 1866 a technological development, the perfection of the vacuum canning process, brought a profound change to the fisheries of the Pacific Northwest. Rail lines connecting the region with national markets had been completed in 1873, and salmon became a valuable commodity. Canneries proliferated up and down the West Coast. In Puget Sound, the number of canneries grew from three in 1894 to twenty-four in 1905. The salmon fishery expanded quickly; by the early twentieth century, hundreds of commercial fishing boats plied the waters of Puget Sound to supply a growing demand for this food fish.

Soon after achieving statehood in 1889, Washington enacted the first in a series of restrictions designed to discourage and ultimately ban all net fishing on rivers. Fishing would be permitted only in marine waters, under state license, at times and places set by state regulation. The Indian net fisheries on the rivers and streams, where returning salmon were intercepted, were far more efficient than hundreds of boats seeking the salmon in open waters. But the state chose to ban the river fisheries because the rivers could not accommodate the thousands who would set nets in front of each other and create an unmanageable problem for the state. Concerns over conservation also arose early on, and the state moved to permit harvesting only before the fish entered their natal streams. Thereafter, the runs were to be untouchable—needed for reproduction. So within thirty years after the Indians and the United States made treaties, the state succeeded in zoning the Indians out of their fisheries.

When Indians attempted to defend their treaty rights in the state courts, their claim received short shrift. Washington courts ruled that "in common with" meant "no different than" other citizens. Some decisions held that any right the Indians might have was trumped by the state's police power to regulate for conservation. Indians continued to fish and to insist that they were protected by treaty, but a U.S. Supreme Court decision in 1916 held that the state of New York could regulate off-reservation fishing by Seneca Indians.[1] Although that decision was based on the fact that under their treaty the Senecas had only a privilege, not a right—unlike the Indians of Washington—the case discouraged the federal government's interest in defending treaty fishing rights in the Northwest. After that, Indians were reduced to trying to evade state fisheries police, sometimes fishing at night or simply hoping they would not be caught. Many were arrested and served jail sentences in addition to forfeiting their catch, their nets, and their boats.[2]

In the 1940s, the federal government came to the defense of a Yakima Indian named Sampson Tulee, who was cited by the state for fishing off the reservation without a license. The case reached the U.S. Supreme Court, which ruled in 1942 that the state could not impose a license fee on an Indian exercising his treaty rights. But in a gratuitous comment it said, "the treaty leaves the state with power to impose on Indians equally with others...such regulations as are necessary for the conservation of fish."[3]

This remark, made in a discussion of the scope of the treaty right and not addressing any issue presented by the case, was dictum and not binding law. But it gave the state of Washington what it sought—a clear path to regulate Indian fishing. It simply insisted that all its fishing regulations were for the purpose of conservation and could be imposed on treaty Indian fishing. For fifteen years it was successful in foreclosing judicial scrutiny of state regulation of Indian fishing.

That state of affairs continued until Puyallup Indian Bob Satiacum decided to throw down the gauntlet in 1954. The inability of the state to make his arrest stick emboldened other Indians, and they began to risk arrest on Washington's rivers. Marlon Brando's entry into the arena, followed by other celebrities, served to intensify feelings on both sides and the demonstrations went on, led by the Puyallups, the Nisquallies, the Muckleshoots, and their supporters. These tribes had traditionally fished on the rivers and they suffered the greatest deprivations from the state's laws.[4]

My clients, the Makahs, were mainly marine fishermen, not river fishermen. In addition, they were not as negatively affected by fishing regulations as the Puget Sound tribes because they had won a court case in 1951 concerning one of the few rivers where they fished with nets, the Hoko River—the state had failed to show a conservation necessity for prohibition of net fishing on that river. They also had two on-reservation rivers that were beyond the reach of state authority. As a result, I did not become personally involved in the courtroom battles over river fishing until 1969. It was not the Makahs who sent me into that struggle, but the American Civil Liberties Union.

The subject of Indian rights was foreign to the ACLU because it did not involve the Bill of Rights—the touchstone of ACLU action. The local ACLU affiliate was guided by policies of the national organization, whose board was largely composed of New Yorkers. They were almost completely oblivious of the Indian treaty rights struggle going on in the Northwest. Ironically, it was Marlon Brando who first brought the issue to their attention when he called and asked them what they were doing to protect Indian fishing rights. Since they had no policy on Indian rights, they had to confess their ignorance and told him they would make inquiries. The national board contacted the Washington State chapter and learned that we had become deeply embroiled in the issue. They also learned that, in the absence of a national policy, the state affiliate had adopted a policy supporting treaty rights on the grounds that they were essential to ethnic survival. The national organization deferred to our state organization, since we seemed to have some expertise in the matter. Our expertise stemmed from myself and a board member named Bill Hanson. We were both attorneys who had immersed ourselves in the legal principles and the justice issues of the controversy, and we helped articulate a policy to guide the state affiliate.

The ACLU entered the fray in 1966 when we joined with the Puyallup Tribe as amicus curiae (friend of the court) in their appeal of an injunction barring them from net fishing on the Puyallup River. I helped write the brief and participated in oral arguments in the Washington Supreme Court. The tribe was victorious, and the injunction was struck down.[5]

In thinking through the deeper implications of the Indian fishing rights struggle, I became convinced that American society did not understand or did not want to understand how threatened Indians felt by the forces of assimilation that confronted them at every turn. To articulate those feelings and to construct a principled basis from which the ACLU could embrace Indian survival as a civil liberties issue, I wrote a paper titled "American Indian Separatism: A Basic Civil Liberties Issue." The article was later reprinted in the *Seattle Argus*, a journal of political opinion, on December 13, 1968, under the title "Separatism Should be Accepted as Future Way of Life."

I wrote that Indian tribal life had persisted despite the efforts of the U.S. government to dismantle it. Perpetuation of a tribal way of life was a basic right that should be protected. For the American Indian, I wrote, survival as an Indian was as basic as individual freedom was to the rest of us. This meant acceptance of the right of a people to develop and retain their identity outside the American mainstream.

That these views reflected the feelings of Indians was confirmed when two years after the article's publication, Janet Mc Cloud, a fiery leader of the Puyallup Tribe, reprinted it in its entirety in a newsletter she circulated in 1970.[6] Her newsletter was prompted by a 1969 fishing rights victory in a case won by a group of Indian protesters. I represented the defendants as an ACLU volunteer attorney in that case. The ACLU had responded to a request for legal representation by a group of Indians facing criminal charges brought after a melee at Frank's Landing during a "fish-in." The incident had actually occurred on October 13, 1965, but the trial was delayed pending decision in cases then before the U.S. Supreme Court. When those decisions did not dispose of the issues, the judge in the state District Court in Olympia set the trial date for January of 1969.

My clients in the case were Don and Janet McCloud, Alvin and Theresa Bridges, Nugent Kautz, Don George Jr., and Suzanne Satiacum, Bob Satiacum's wife. These people were among the leaders in the battle on the rivers. A group consisting of two Indian fishermen, two television newsmen, three Indian children, and a dog launched a small outboard boat from Frank's Landing and set a net in the center of the Nisqually River. Almost immediately, an assault force of state Fisheries and Game officers sprang from hiding places, launched high-powered boats, and raced to the Indian boat. The Indian who was operating the boat tried to head back to shore, but it was seized almost as they touched shore. Between forty and fifty Fisheries and Game officers were waiting. As the Indians tried to get out of the boat, they were grabbed and manhandled by the state officers. A group of Indians and their supporters watched, and many of them interceded to stop the brutal handling of the Indians. A melee ensued: state officers struck Indians with long-handled flashlights, clubs, and blackjacks. The defendants were charged with illegal net fishing and obstructing an officer.

In January of 1969, I stood before a jury in a Thurston County District Court and gave my opening statement. The spectator section was filled with Indians, many from other states. The state called four officers, who testified that the defendants had set a net in the Nisqually River in violation of state law. Then they described how they were set upon when they tried to effect a lawful arrest.

When I cross-examined the officers regarding their use of weapons, I was surprised to hear them deny the possession or use of any weapon. I questioned them carefully to ensure that their denials were explicit and vehement—no long flashlights, no nightsticks. When the state rested, I called a local news photographer who had closely followed the fishing rights conflict and introduced photographs he took of the confrontation. In photograph after photograph, officers were shown hitting Indians with nightsticks and long police flashlights. Then I called one of the Nisqually men who had snatched a blackjack away from one of the officers after he tried to hit one of the demonstrators with it. I introduced the weapon into evidence and then handed it to the jury to inspect. It was a mean-looking object. Several jury members experimentally smacked their palms with it and were immediately aware of its potential for injury. The weapon had the name of one of the officers inscribed on it, and I called the officer to the stand and asked him whether it was his. He could hardly deny it. Sheepishly he admitted it was his, saying, "Yes, that's my slapper." I asked him why he used the word *slapper*, and he said, somewhat embarrassed, because it was used to "slap" people.

I proceeded with the testimony of the men and women who were charged, about their oppression at the hands of the state of Washington when they tried to exercise their treaty rights. One of the most forceful and eloquent witnesses was Janet Mc Cloud. When she took the stand her anger was evident: "When we went out on the river, we wanted to expose to the world Washington State's policy toward the Native people who once owned all this land. We wanted everyone to see the racism that we have to put up with when we try to exercise our treaty rights. And yes, we wanted to expose the Gestapo tactics of the fish and game wardens. What were they doing? They were trying to silence our voice. They made a mockery of freedom of speech."

Other Indian witnesses spoke eloquently about the injustices they had suffered, the arrests, the seizure of their fish and their nets, the confiscation of their boats and even their motors. As for the charge of illegal netting, one of the defendants explained it was a torn old net, virtually incapable of catching fish, put in the water to make their point.

When both sides rested, I addressed the jury in closing argument and emphasized the fundamental right of the Indians under the U.S. Constitution to express their grievances, and I lambasted the state for the violence of its reaction and the lies of the officers on the witness stand. The jury was out only a short time and returned a verdict of not guilty for all defendants on all counts.[7]

The Nisqually case was only a minor skirmish in the larger fishing wars. It didn't dampen the aggressive tactics of the state enforcement officers, but it hardened the determination of Indian tribes to continue the fight. The Indian cause was gathering more supporters, many of them non-Indians. And there were more clashes between Indians and enforcement officers.

On September 9, 1970, over two hundred police stormed an Indian fishing camp on the Puyallup River. They tear-gassed the protesting Indians and their supporters, arrested dozens, and bulldozed the camp. Many were arrested, charged, and jailed. Four were later convicted and four others were acquitted. The white juries surprisingly accepted the

Indians' defense of speaking out for their treaty rights and acquitted them.[8]

Meanwhile, the Fisheries Department remained deeply committed to regulating all fisheries in the state and preventing any fishing with nets on the rivers. They were determined to ensure that the salmon fishery was conducted only in marine waters, where the thousands of Washingtonians—sport and commercial fishermen—could fish. The department's management of the resource was based on the principle that when the non-Indian fishery had taken all the fish above the number estimated as necessary for spawning, all the remaining fish were untouchable, with no allowance for any Indian fishing in the bays or the rivers. This left no room for treaty Indian fishing rights. In the Fisheries view, this was "conservation" and justified everything the department did.

The state maintained that their management was based on science, holding up the Fisheries and Game departments as bastions of science and casting the Indians as irresponsible villains. The state also succeeded in persuading the public and many judges that river fishing was antithetical to conservation, because nets could theoretically intercept all the fish returning to spawn, though the Indians had never done so.

The press and the public accepted the state's reasoning so completely that there was no appreciation that the Indians had fished the rivers for thousands of years and had never destroyed any runs. Neither was there any public knowledge that tribes established their own regulations to conserve fish runs and enforced them against their own members. The state succeeded in hiding the real truth: their management system was designed to allocate *all* the salmon to the non-Indians, leaving nothing to the Indians. The press failed to inform the public of the full truth and simply reiterated the official line that Indian fishing was a threat to conservation.

The one place where the ugly truth of allocation was impossible to hide was the Columbia River salmon fishery. The Columbia is a broad major river, flowing hundreds of miles and supporting huge runs of salmon. The states of Oregon and Washington had joint jurisdiction over the river fishery. The Columbia is so huge and the runs of salmon so large that this was the one river where commercial fishing in a river with nets was allowed. But here again the Indians were cheated by the states. The Indian fishing sites were upriver. The states allocated most of the harvest to the downstream non-Indian fishing areas and treated the remainder as "escapement," needed to perpetuate the runs. Not only was the blatant violation of federal treaties hard to hide, but the fundamental unfairness of the allocation was in plain view. The Columbia River became the focus of litigation between the Columbia River tribes and the states of Oregon and Washington over federal treaty rights. This was the setting for the first case in modern times in which the federal government attacked the states for denial of those rights. The case was *U.S. v. Oregon*, and its companion case was *Sohappy v. Smith*.[9] The cases were precursors to one of the most important decisions ever made in the field of Indian law, which would come in *U.S. v. Washington*.

TWELVE

The Big Bang:
U.S. v. Washington *Begins*

TWO RIVERS WERE THE FOCUS OF ALMOST ALL THE LITIGATION over treaty rights in the state of Washington: the Puyallup, which empties into Puget Sound within the city limits of Tacoma, and the Nisqually, which flows from the Cascade Mountains into Puget Sound east of Olympia. Members of both the Puyallup and Nisqually tribes fished on these rivers in defiance of state law. A third tribe, the Muckleshoot, also challenged the state on the Green River, south of Seattle. These tribes were small and their reservation lands were pathetically tiny. They were also very poor and could not afford substantial attorney fees, but they had a little money and many supporters, Indian and non-Indian. They operated "smoke shops," selling tax-free cigarettes, and fireworks stands, which only made money during the summer. Today the Muckleshoots operate a huge casino and hotel complex and have grown wealthy, but that came after long years of suffering and poverty.

The fishermen from these tribes tangled with the state of Washington, and the resulting legal battles ultimately ended up in the U.S. Supreme Court not once, but four times over a ten-year period. The Court grappled with whether the state had regulatory authority over Indian fishing. If the state could regulate Indians, were there any limitations on its regulatory actions? If the state could impose regulations deemed necessary for conservation, what was the standard for the balance between conservation and treaty rights?

Twice, in cases now called Puyallup I and Puyallup II, the U.S.

Supreme Court refined its rule.[1] But none of the cases ruled on by the Court involved an overview of the entire state regulatory scheme. Worse, in none of them was any independent biological testimony offered to clarify the distinction between conservation and allocation. Perhaps the greatest shortcoming of the Court's decisions was that they all involved individual Indian fishermen on a specific river. In no case was the picture complete. Missing was the history and anthropology of the Northwest tribes, as was the record of what the tribes had said and understood about the treaties they had signed. A clear, factual description of the entire fishery in Puget Sound and the Strait of Juan de Fuca was also missing, along with how the state managed that fishery. Finally, in none of these cases was the federal government a party. That would be remedied in *U.S. v. Washington*, the case that would end the state's eighty-year effort to keep Indian fishing off the rivers and under its authority.

In all the years of Indian struggle against the state of Washington, there was one nagging question: why was the federal government absenting itself from the conflict? After all, the issue was the protection of rights guaranteed by the United States in federal treaties. But the federal government had chosen to avoid clashing with state authority, leaving Indians to fend for themselves in the state courts. This would change in part because of fundamental shifts in the country's political landscape after 1960. A civil rights revolution was being fought in the South. In the cold war with the Soviet Union, the United States was accused of oppressing its minorities. Most important, the Indians of the Northwest were no longer content to accept the status quo, and their demonstrations had attracted national attention. By the late 1960s the treaty rights conflict had escalated and become violent, with Indians being shot and clubbed. The administration in Washington, D.C., began to take notice of a dispute that was becoming an embarrassment to the federal government—and they finally took action.

There are conflicting accounts of precisely how the federal government decided to bring litigation against the state, and I cannot give an authoritative answer to the question. I can only list some of those I know to have been key parties. Perhaps the most important actor was a little-known federal attorney, George Dysart. Dysart was legal advisor to the Interior Department in the Portland office of the regional solicitor. In his post he had long been witness to the injustices suffered by the Indians of Washington and Oregon at the hands of those two state governments. But his authority was limited to advising the area office of the law on questions referred to his office. He could not bring a lawsuit against the states—only the U.S. Justice Department had that authority. But he could ask the department to bring a lawsuit. To do that required that he submit a litigation request, which he did. Dysart wrote a lengthy and analytical request describing the history of state violation of Indian rights. With respect to Oregon, he zeroed in on the blatant illegality of allocating Columbia River salmon runs to the downstream non-Indian sport and commercial fishermen to the detriment of the Indians upstream. As for Washington, he described the state's discriminatory zoning of the fishery, which left little for Indians. Sometime around 1967, Dysart asked that the Justice Department bring lawsuits against both states to adjudicate and vindicate Indian treaty rights.[2]

Dysart's request found sympathetic ears at Justice, and the department granted authority to the U.S. attorneys for the western districts of Oregon and Washington to bring lawsuits against the respective states. The first suit filed was against Oregon, titled appropriately, *U.S. v. Oregon*. Because of his expertise, Dysart was appointed special assistant U.S. attorney and he joined the prosecution.

The position taken by the United States in *U.S. v. Oregon* was that the Stevens treaty required the state to allow a "fair and equitable share" of Columbia River salmon to pass upstream to the tribes' usual and accustomed sites. That was the ultimate ruling of the U.S. District Court in Portland, but the decision was limited to the Columbia River–fishing tribes and did not govern Washington fisheries elsewhere. Nevertheless, Washington's governor, Dan Evans, adopted the Oregon decision as state policy and ordered the Fisheries Department to change its management regime to make available a greater volume of fish to Indian fishermen and to allow nets in some rivers. The Game Department, which was not under the direct authority of the governor, didn't budge. "No Indian net fishing" was their credo.

While *U.S. v. Oregon* was a victory for Indian treaty rights, the Justice Department had a much bigger target: the regulatory system for all fisheries of western Washington—Puget Sound, all the rivers that flow into the Sound, the Washington coast, and the adjacent ocean waters and the Strait of Juan de Fuca. The task of crafting a suit that would apply to these waters fell to U.S. Attorney Stanley Pitkin, of the western district of Washington. Pitkin was a young, energetic, and idealistic government lawyer. His aim was to bring a case before a federal judge that would encompass all issues in the Indian fishing rights struggle and end the long, ugly history of denial of rights. The principal responsibility for drafting the suit, for trial preparation, and ultimately for the trial was given to a young special assistant U.S. attorney, Stuart "Stu" Pierson, who had been sent out from Washington, D.C.[3]

U.S. v. Washington was filed in September of 1970 by the United States as plaintiff, but also on behalf of seven named tribes, including the Makahs. The Makahs, like the other tribes named, were unwilling to entrust their rights to unknown federal attorneys, and so they directed me to intervene. Two other tribes, the Lummis and the Quileutes, later asked me to represent them as well. In the end, a total of fourteen tribes joined as co-plaintiffs. The government attorneys had no objection. No longer would a lone Indian fisherman have to face the power and resources of the state; the state was now facing a powerful adversary, and it was on the defensive.

At the outset, the tribes had little confidence they would prevail, and they were fearful of losing everything. Their fears deepened when the case was assigned to a Tacoma U.S. District Court judge named George H. Boldt. Boldt had a reputation as a very conservative judge. He had become notorious during the trial of a group of radical protesters in 1970, the Seattle Seven. He held several of them in contempt and jailed them. Now the fate of Indian fishing rights was in his hands, and the Indians and many of their supporters were worried. Indeed, Hank Adams, a leader in the struggle from the beginning, went to Washington, D.C., to ask the government to drop the lawsuit, believing it did not represent the best interest of the Indians.[4] But the case went forward, and all the attorneys involved felt we had to do our best to win.

During our first pretrial meeting with the judge, Pierson outlined the scope of the case he wanted to present. It was nothing less than the entire ethnohistory of all the co-plaintiff tribes, the history of the treaties involved, and a complete description of the salmon resource and how it was managed and harvested. The aim was, for the first time, to present a complete picture of all the issues, including the location of the usual and accustomed fishing grounds of each of the tribes. Boldt didn't appear fazed, indeed he was enthusiastic about the challenge of this massive case. In retrospect, this shouldn't have come as a surprise. Boldt had made a reputation adjudicating complex antitrust cases, and he seemed to relish the prospect of getting his teeth into an issue that had become a growing cancer in the Pacific Northwest.

Legal cases make the law and the news. The focus of news coverage is on the parties to the suit, the issues, the court, and its decision. Often, the media praise the courage and the perseverance of the litigant. But the real story is usually elsewhere. Lawyers are the ones who decide whether there is a case, who undertake the arduous work and shape the facts and the law that is ultimately presented to the court. In a large complex case, the trial is the story of two teams of lawyers struggling against each other. This is the nature of the American adversarial sys-tem. The victory of one team may be as much a product of its intellec-tual and human resources as of the merits of its arguments.

In *U.S. v. Washington*, the plaintiff's team included as many as nine lawyers, though only four of us were actually in court every day of the trial and conducted most of the witness examinations. On our team the "laboring oar," as lawyers call it, was carried by Assistant U.S. Attorney Pierson. Pierson was a dynamic and very bright young lawyer. He had a quick, incisive mind and the ability to wade through mountains of facts. Pierson was also a hard worker—always prepared, never caught off-balance. Besides his intelligence, he brought an aggressive and con-fident manner to the case. Another lawyer on the government team was George Dysart, one of the principal instigators of the litigation. Dysart had acquired so much expertise from his years of dealing with the law and complex facts of Northwest Indian fishing that he was appointed special assistant U.S. attorney in this case, just as in *U.S. v. Oregon*.

David Getches and John Sennhauser were bright public-service law-yers. Getches was a staff attorney at the Native American Rights Fund based in Boulder, Colorado. He went on to become a law professor and an internationally known expert on Indian law and water rights. He was a careful advocate with an intellectual approach to the case. Sennhauser was a "movement lawyer" and worked for the Legal Services Center in Seattle, a federally funded program providing legal help to the poor. His courtroom demeanor was more emotional than Getches's, and he made his social identity known by wearing sandals and sporting a pony tail, a novelty in 1973. Together they spoke for the Muckleshoot, Squaxin Island, Sauk-Suiattle, Skokomish, and Stillaguamish tribes.

But the most important member of the plaintiff's team was not a lawyer at all. She was our expert witness: Dr. Barbara Lane. Dr. Lane was an ethnohistorian, a scholar who used her anthropological background to study the documents recording the history of ethnic groups. Dr. Lane taught at the University of British Columbia and had studied the history of the Native people of Hawaii. She had become interested in the Native people of the Pacific Northwest and had developed a broad knowledge concerning their precontact life and their postcontact history. Her work and testimony would prove crucial to the outcome of the suit.

Our opponent, the state of Washington, was unable to speak with a single voice. There was a doctrinal split between the Fisheries and Game departments, so they asked for and received court permission to present two positions, using separate attorneys. The Fisheries attorney was Earl McGimpsey, a practical lawyer. The Game attorney was Larry Coniff, an ideologue who believed deeply in the views of his client, that recognizing treaty fishing rights would inevitably decimate the steelhead population and end sportfishing for this game fish. Coniff had long been a dedicated foe of Indian treaty rights and had spoken around the state on the subject, as well as appearing in the courts wherever Indian treaty rights were at issue.

From the perspective of the attorneys for the tribes, *U.S. v. Washington* was a simple struggle of good against evil. The Indians had been the underdogs for eighty years, and the state of Washington was their implacable foe. But the tribes and their trustee, the federal government, also did not present a unified front.

At the outset, the federal government decided to base its argument on the *U.S. v. Oregon* decision: like Oregon, they would argue, Washington had a duty to regulate the fishery so as to provide the Indians with "a fair and equitable share" of the resource, while also having the right to regulate for conservation as was reasonable and necessary. But the federal government's initial position on the scope of the Indian fishery was constrictive. It initially viewed the treaty right as limited to fishing for subsistence only. This would deny the Indians the right to sell their catch commercially. When Barbara Lane learned of this, she was troubled. She had seen ample historical documentation that the Indians had sold their harvest commercially prior to making the treaties—to other Indians and later to whites— and that it was understood by the United States and the Indians that this activity would not be impaired by any treaty agreements. When she related this to George Dysart, he was initially skeptical, but was convinced when he reviewed the historical materials she brought him.[5] Consequently, the United States took the position that the treaty right to fish included the right to sell fish, in other words, to earn a livelihood from fishing just like white commercial fishermen.

The tribes' position conflicted with the federal position. The tribes contended that the state had no right to regulate Indian fishing at all. The treaties, they believed, guaranteed them the right to fish as they always had—free of any outside interference. The tribes pointed to their own fishing regulations and insisted they were fully protective of the resource. The state, they charged, had used the mantra of "conservation" as a device to prohibit Indian treaty fishing. Instead, they argued the state had a duty to ensure that enough fish reached Indian fishing grounds to provide the tribes with a livelihood.

There were two additional claims, which I filed on behalf of the Lummi Tribe. The first was for the validation of the tribe's right to return to their traditional reef-net sites and to conduct this unique type of fishing. We alleged that these sites had been usurped by non-Indian fishermen operating with state licenses. The second was an environmental claim. The Lummis fished the Nooksack River, which flowed through their reservation and emptied into Bellingham Bay. But upstream farms and industries contaminated the river with manure, insecticides, fertilizer, and chemicals. The result was a decline in the runs of Nooksack River salmon. The state had never acted to protect the water quality of the river and, indeed, had issued permits authorizing such discharges. So, on behalf of the Lummis, I asked the court to require the state to take the appropriate action to protect the fish habitat. If the state allowed the continuing degradation of the habitat, the treaty right to take fish would become an empty right.

This environmental claim was later severed from the main case by

Judge Boldt for separate adjudication in what came to be known as Phase Two. Phase Two was to have a long and tortured history. After an initial holding that the treaty did indeed obligate the state to protect fish habitat, the ruling was reversed by the Ninth Circuit Court of Appeals in 1985. The court balked at a broad rule in the absence of a specific factual showing of state failure to protect the habitat. That, in turn, led to another round of litigation over what came to be known as "the culverts." The tribes charged that the state had constructed thousands of culverts channeling spawning streams under highways in a manner that blocked fish from reaching their spawning grounds. That issue was finally decided by the U.S. District Court in Seattle in 2007. The court upheld the tribe's claim that the state could not act in a way that destroyed fish habitat, and the court ordered the state to reconstruct culverts to permit fish passage or to take other corrective measures. This ruling came thirty-four years after the initial decision in *U.S. v. Washington*. But we are getting far ahead of our story.

In the main case, the Fisheries Department acknowledged that a treaty right existed and argued for a quantification of the Indian share at one-third of the fish originating in the rivers that were usual and accustomed Indian fishing grounds. The Game Department, on the other hand, argued that the Indians had no rights greater than non-Indian fishermen. The department particularly objected to the taking of steelhead with nets and selling the fish, a practice that Game found abhorrent and argued was detrimental to recreational use.

THIRTEEN

U.S. v. Washington: *The Trial*

U.S. V. WASHINGTON WAS FILED IN SEPTEMBER OF 1970, BUT PRE-trial depositions and preparation of biological and ethnological reports consumed more than two years. The case did not come to trial until August 27, 1973.

We gathered in the courtroom of Judge Boldt in the federal court-house in Tacoma on that August morning, and I took my place at the counsel table as one of four attorneys for the plaintiffs: Stu Pierson, rep-resenting the U.S. government; David Getches and John Sennhauser for the Muckleshoot, Squaxin Island, Sauk-Suiattle, Skokomish, and Stillaguamish tribes; and I was representing the Makah, Lummi, and Quileute tribes. Behind us sat Michael Taylor for the Quinault Tribe, James Hovis for the Yakima Tribe, Lester Stritmatter for the Hoh Tribe, and William Stiles for the Upper Skagit Tribe. Strangely enough, the Puyallup and the Nisqually tribes did not have private attorneys repre-senting them, though the federal government named them as co-plain-tiffs and represented their interests.

The atmosphere at the plaintiff attorneys' table was tense. Everything was at risk and we had deep misgivings about the judge. But though I felt apprehensive, I welcomed the showdown. The fishing rights struggle had produced in me feelings of real hostility toward the state of Wash-ington. Like Janet McCloud, I saw every officer wearing a Washington State uniform as a symbol of oppression and racism. I recognized this was irrational, but I had become emotionally caught up in the Indian cause and it affected me deeply. So as I sat in the courtroom waiting for the trial to begin, I felt a rush of adrenalin. I was ready. For the past nine years I had prepared for this moment; I knew the history of state aggrandizement of the fisheries, I knew Indian people and their history, and I knew the law. No longer would the state of Washington be able to overpower Indians with its bullying tactics. This would be a fight unlike any other the state had waged against the Indians.

The trial began with opening statements by each of the attorneys.[1] Stu Pierson rose to speak for the federal government:

> May it please the court, the United States filed this suit for two basic purposes; first, to reaffirm the principles which protect the exercise of the Indians' treaty rights to fish against improper state regulations. The second purpose was to examine and establish specific standards which will guide the parties, the Indian tribes and the State and the United States as well, in circumstances where the state asserts a need or a power to regulate fishing by tribes who claim treaty rights to fish outside the reservation boundaries.
>
> There really are two temporal frames of reference, the first one is the time of treaties and we will go into that to examine the promises made and the meaning of the terms. The second temporal frame of reference is modern times. We have an exhaustible anadromous fishery source; I think all the parties are interested in conserving it. It is a question of how it will be conserved, who will take from the resource and how they will take it.
>
> Our legal frame of reference comes from a line of many decisions.

And here Pierson cited the U.S. Supreme Court decision in *U.S. v. Winans*, which established that the treaty right to fish is a reserved right.[2] He went on:

> Later, in the Puyallup case in 1968, we are told that the state, by an appropriate exercise of police power [regulated Indian off-reservation treaty fishing]...There are three standards in

that decision; the state regulation must not discriminate against the Indians, must meet appropriate standards, and it must be shown to be reasonable and necessary for [conservation] of the resource. Although there is some conflict among the parties about this...it is the view of the United States that the burden to show that the regulations are reasonable and necessary is on the State.

Lastly, the important frame of concentration for the United States in this case is how have the state agencies regulated the exercise of the privilege of non-Indians to fish outside the reservation boundaries. In our view, that privilege must be regulated and controlled so as to provide the Indian Tribes and their members a fair share of the resource...

It is the view of the United States that because the Tribes' treaty rights to fish are distinct, are based on Federal Law, and are in the nature of a reservation for the future and present needs of the Indian Tribes, the State may exercise its police powers to regulate the exercise of the Tribes' rights only when it can show that their exercise of that right will threaten preservation of the fish runs. In our view this may not be done till taking the Tribes' statement of their own needs and the state has limited all non-Indian fishermen within its jurisdiction to at least a share equal...to that of the Indians...

There lurks in the back of every case involving a conflict between state power and Indian treaty fishing rights, the non-Indian assumption that Indian Tribes and their members cannot be trusted to regulate the fishing and management by their own members...Our proof will show that for over 150 years the preservation instinct and practice by these treaty tribes...has been at least as effective in preserving [the resource] as the State's regulation of the non-Indian fishery."

Pierson attacked the state's claim that the growth of the commercial fishery following treaty times somehow limited the Indians' rights: "The law is clear that no subsequent events after the treaty can qualify the right. The proof will show," he said, "that there was no intent by either of the parties to the treaty to limit the Indian's fishery to subsistence and that, in fact, all of the tribes had trade and bartering activities going on at the time of the treaties." Pierson further suggested to the court that the Indian share should not be some immutable percentage, but that it should fluctuate with the needs of the Indians and the status of the resource. As for the Game Department, Pierson said, "[It] has consistently, continually and obdurately violated the Tribes' treaty rights in the face of not only U.S. Supreme Court decisions, but in the face of specific directives from the State Supreme Court."[3]

When David Getches spoke, he provided a broad perspective. The rights of the Indians do not change, he said, "merely because people wear different clothes, travel about in different conveyances or speak a different language. Cultures borrow from each other. This culture that we are in has borrowed from the Indian culture, and the Indian culture has borrowed from it, and it has altered no legal rights as between those parties."[4]

In my opening statement, I pointed out the high stakes in the case: the welfare of almost eleven thousand Indian people. "The evidence will show," I said, "that all of these people remain to this day...involved with fish and dependent upon fish...so that for us as attorneys for the plaintiffs, there is a grave responsibility." And I pointed to the state's inherent bias in favor of their constituency, "the sports fishermen, tourists, the entire economy of the state":

They are representing those interests. They would like to add another class to their constituency, namely, the Indians and... the Indians don't wish to be included under that vast umbrella... This is no mere contract dispute...it is a dispute involving human rights, involving the very life, not mere property rights, of the Indian people. For that reason, a second factor is involved which is peculiarly appropriate to a United States District Court Judge. That factor is the national honor of the United States.

Never before, in the entire history of litigation in this area, has any court ever been presented with a full record, which is going to be presented in this trial, dealing with what the State is actually doing in the nature of conservation, namely management of a resource, a management program which became necessary when a commercial industry sprang up and threatened to destroy the resource, and management for the purpose of distribution.

The Indian Tribes should not be viewed as one small body of the citizenry of the State to be included within the State's allocation, rather they have the same status as governments recognized by treaty and they are on the same plane as the State of Washington, as a government entitled to the dignity and status of a governmental unit.

In an effort to dissuade the court from placing complete regulatory authority over Indian fishing in the hands of the state, I urged:

The State comes before the court asking the court to give it the full mantle of authority—give it the policeman's badge, and it will do a good job of being fair to all parties. History is to the contrary…What the Indians would face if the State's position were accepted is to be told they are entitled to a percentage and they would be sent out of this courtroom and told that hereafter they would have to argue their cause in state administrative hearings. Go present your case to them. They will hear you and they will decide whether they want to make any adjustments in the regulations or not.

We believe the court will come to the conclusion that the Supremacy Clause is dominant and the State does not get that mantle of authority. [The treaties] were not a contract to be assimilated into the white culture…Without that fishing right these people could not survive, and they knew it and they would not enter into such treaties if they did not have a reserved right.[5]

The Game Department's lawyer, Larry Coniff, then rose and began by attacking the rulings of prior court decisions that Indians had a reserved right: "Since at the time of the treaty, Indians were not citizens and not wishing them to be excluded from their accustomed grounds, the United States merely granted them the right to fish off their reservations. But the right was for an equal opportunity, in other words, the same right as the non-Indian had and nothing more."

As for the steelhead, he asked the court to "recognize it as a game fish, that is, a fish to be caught for sport and personal subsistence only." He went on to propose a bizarre solution to his client's legal dilemma: "The Fisheries Department should substitute a fair share of salmon to make up for an equivalent share of steelhead." In other words, the steelhead should remain untouchable; take the Indian's fish out of someone else's share.[6]

Earl McGimpsey then spoke for the state's Fisheries Department. He urged the court to rule that the treaty right was limited to subsistence fishing only and did not extend to commercial fisheries. Off-reservation, McGimpsey said, the state is sovereign and has preeminent power to regulate; tribal regulations could not conflict with state regulations. McGimpsey's argument was directly counter to mine. He acknowledged that the state could accept the *Oregon* principle of "fair share," but he argued that this principle could only apply to a river where the fishery consisted of one stock, not to marine fisheries of mixed stocks of fish. Finally, McGimpsey urged the court to set a fixed percentage as the Indians' fair share.[7]

After our opening statements, Judge Boldt made his own:

> I will render a decision that when reviewed by the Circuit Court
> and the Supreme Court, as I expect and hope will be the case,
> that we may have provided all of the information that is obtain-
> able on these questions, that we will have made fact findings
> on all issues where there are genuine issues of fact, relevant or
> possibly relevant, and that we will give to the reviewing courts
> a record on which, perhaps for the first time, these issues and
> controversies that have plagued this area, from shortly following
> the execution of the treaties, with increasing vigor, sometimes
> violence, throughout the years, can be resolved.[8]

In keeping with the broad scope of the case he outlined, the parties were ordered to prepare a joint biological statement detailing all facts regarding the biology, status, management, and harvest of the salmon and steelhead resources in Puget Sound and Olympic Peninsula waters. While this entailed a great deal of work and agreement among state, federal, and tribal biologists, it generated surprisingly little controversy. After all, these facts were not much in dispute, and the biologists who presented the data were professionals.

More contentious was the historical and linguistic evidence con-cerning what the language in the treaties actually meant. It was here that Barbara Lane's work was critical. Her report on the tribes' ethno-history, fully documented, showed that each of the treaties covering the fourteen tribes contained substantially the same clause: "The right of taking fish, at all usual and accustomed grounds and stations, is further secured to said Indians, in common with all citizens of the territory."

The tribes spoke or understood little English at the time of signing, and the treaty language was translated for them using Chinook jargon, a language of Indian and English words used by traders. Federal law required that in any dispute over treaty language, the meaning must be construed as the Indians would likely have understood it. Fortunately, minutes were kept of the treaty negotiations and these provided an invaluable record of the nature of the promises made by the U.S. repre-sentative, Isaac Stevens. Using these records, words of Chinook jargon, and the historical positions of both the United States and the Indians, Dr. Lane was able to outline how the treaty language would likely have been understood by the Indians.

She gave evidence that the United States had intended, and the Indians had understood, that Indians would continue to fish as they always had, selling their catch as before. The single most important point established by Lane was that the phrase "in common with the white citizens" was intended and understood to mean simply that the Indians could not exclude whites and that both peoples would share equally in the fishery. This also fit with the meaning of *common* found in the Webster's dictionary of the time and was consistent with the United States' treaty-time understanding of what they had sought to achieve.[9]

Dr. Lane's report went on to describe the culture and fishing prac-tices of the Northwest Indians, delineating geographically the "usual and accustomed" fishing grounds of each of the tribes in the case. All of her findings were heavily documented, showing the source for each of her conclusions. Where the historical record was thin or nonexis-tent, she said so. Where she had to make a judgment, she described the factors that led her to her conclusions. Dr. Lane's testimony was chal-lenged by the state's attorneys in depositions and in the trial. The state had engaged an anthropologist of their own, Dr. Carrol Riley. He was unable to specifically contradict anything Dr. Lane had said and was reduced to calling her conclusions "over formulated."

Dr. Lane's report of the extent to which Indians had carried on commerce in fish before the treaties and the variety of techniques they had perfected all found their way into the final decision of the court. One of the most critical points was, of course, the meaning of the treaty clause securing to the Indians the right to fish at all their usual and accustomed places, and her research was accepted by Judge Boldt as authoritative.[10]

The pretrial work generated hundreds of documents, containing several thousand pages of material that would be submitted into evidence as exhibits. The documents and the witnesses would describe the entire 120-year history of Indian-white relations, the movement of salmon and steelhead during their life cycles, the culture and practices of each of the fourteen plaintiff tribes as they related to fishing, and the schemes of the state to control or prohibit Indian fishing. The trial itself consumed just over three weeks, from August 27 to September 17, 1973. A good deal of time was taken up by Fisheries Department testimony concerning the intricacies of managing the salmon harvest. Barbara Lane was also on the witness stand for substantial periods, giving her anthropological and historical testimony.

Perhaps the most important part of the trial was the testimony given by the Indian witnesses. One of the first was Hillary Irving of the Makah Tribe. On September 10, 1973, Mr. Irving took the stand.

"Mr. Irving, are you a Makah Indian?"

"Yes, I am a full blooded Makah Indian." He was, he said, a member of the tribal council and a technical adviser to the tribe's Fisheries Committee, which recommended regulations to the council each year. He described the Makah fishery:

There are approximately 60 Makahs who are steady fishermen, but in the summer that expands to 150. On reservation there is a set net and a drift net fishery. Off-reservation there were net fisheries on the Lyre, Pysht and Twin Rivers and also at the mouth of the Elwha. But we are prevented from fishing in those areas today by state regulation and have a net fishery on the Hoko only because of a court decision. On the ocean there are 8 boats, three of which are gillnetting in the Straits. During the salmon season in the summer there are outboards from 6 to 24 feet. The larger boats use trolling gear. One boat is a 54 foot tuna boat. The tribe went to the SBA for a loan for the larger boats and there are eight 36 footers.

In response to the question of where the tribe claimed exclusive fishing rights, Irving answered, "Within the boundaries of the ceded area we claim exclusive rights, but outside of that we respect state regulations."

Then I asked: "How far out to sea did the Makahs go to fish?"

"Offshore, in historic times the Makahs did whaling and sealing as far north as the Bering Sea by canoe. The Makahs used sailboats which were towed by tugboats and sailed 200 miles offshore. There are two Makahs still alive who took part in whaling and there are 14 or 15 who took part in the seal hunt. The Coast Guard wouldn't allow them to go out sealing in an open boat; the government would not allow them to seal by paddle and canoe."

"To what extent do the Makahs rely on salmon for their diet today?"

"Today, I think it's practically the same as of the writing of the treaty," replied Irving. "It's still our food just like it is for the rest of the citizens. It's our main meal and I think that the tribe as a whole is used to it and we can't get away from it and we use it for all our ceremonies and potlatch, whatever you call it. As for the commercial fishery, we now depend on that because there's nothing there but logging and salmon is the only way we can survive." Irving testified that he was seven years old when he started fishing, and all the money earned went for clothing and groceries. "There was no road to the village at the time so you had to get groceries for the whole winter at one time."

He described fishing with his father till 1933, when, "the State started arresting us on our purse seining." Irving and his father had fished as far east as the Lyre River without harassment until about 1933, when the state seized their boat and they lost all the fish they had caught. When his father saw the state Fisheries officers approaching, he brought the boat to shore and told Irving to get off, because he didn't want him to miss school if they were arrested.

At this point Judge Boldt interceded, saying, "That is an interesting thing. You were in the boat and your dad put you out, got you away so that you wouldn't be prevented from going to school?'"

"Yes sir," said Irving. "I never...I couldn't make it past the eighth grade without cheating."

"Is that as far as you went?" Judge Boldt asked.

"Yes sir."

Then, injecting some levity into the proceedings, Judge Boldt said, "I wouldn't be surprised if the rest of us had that same problem."

I continued to question Irving, asking him about the tribe's relationship with the state's fisheries agencies. Irving replied that he could "get along with the State Fisheries Department but I can't get along with the Game Department for the simple reason they think they own the steelhead...When the Makahs are fishing for steelhead, we find our nets are cut loose and holes are chopped in our boats or skiffs, and that has happened often. In one incident they started shooting at our fishermen. We made a complaint to law enforcement but got no assistance."

Asked whether there were any problems with the sportfishermen, Irving described a heavy sport fishery off the mouth of the Hoko River and then, obviously emotional, he said, "I think that is one of the things, I don't care to talk about, talk about sportsmen, so-called sportsmen. I will say they fish at the mouth of the river so heavy that it is terrible, it doesn't even look right to any fisherman."

Describing the interactions between the sportfishermen and the Indians, Irving said:

Our people are law-abiding. I have to say they are law-abiding
and they respect law on land or on sea—go by the rules of the
road. We have to watch out for the little boat, and the sportsmen, they see you catch a fish in an area; they will come over
and—like flies—and you are beat. You can't even fish there
any more as a commercial fisherman. You have to understand a
36-foot boat, it has to have room to maneuver, and our outrig-
gers are so far spread out that you have to be careful how you
maneuver, so once the sportsmen get in there, they don't respect
you one bit.

Responding to a question by the state attorney for Fisheries whether the Makahs would abide by a state regulation that allocated a certain percentage to them and whether that would be a fair recognition of the treaty rights on those rivers, Irving answered, "No, I don't. For the simple reason that your treaty says we can fish so long as the tide went out, came in." Then Irving was asked, "Do you feel under the treaty that you would be entitled to all the fish in those rivers?" And he responded, "Well, prior to the treaty didn't we have all those fish?" Irving said he would be willing to accept a fair share if it was established by the court, but not if it was established by the state.

On the subject of steelhead, Irving explained how the Makahs used the fish: "The steelhead was just a commodity that was for food between the winter months December to March. When the Makahs wanted fresh fish they went out and got steelhead."

The Fisheries attorney then asked Irving whether the Makahs could actually manage the fishery. After all, the state could predict run sizes and the Makahs couldn't. Irving fired back: "I feel we can do a better job than the state, because...we live right there and we see what is going on."[11]

Another Makah, John Ides, testified that he has been a fisherman since the age of thirteen and had owned and operated boats in different fisheries from that time on. The Makah Tribe began regulating their fisheries in the 1930s, he said, because the state was claiming they had no fishing rights on the Hoko or Sekiu rivers, or on any off-reservation rivers. When asked how the Makahs felt about conservation, Ides answered, "Well, I believe that the attitude of the Makah, and always has been, that he must have a run, a perpetual run, of salmon at all times. He will regulate. Conservative enough minded to be able to regulate his fisheries." Asked whether the Makahs would be willing to accept state regulation, he answered, "No. It has never worked."[12]

Billy Frank Jr., a member of the Nisqually Tribe and a long-time fighter for Indian fishing rights, then took the stand and described the oppression suffered by treaty fishermen at the hands of Washington State. Frank's boats, motors, and nets had been confiscated by the Fisheries and Game departments, including fish being taken with the nets. State officers had thrown grappling hooks into gillnets, tearing them out of the river with pickup trucks. State officers had gone upriver in jet boats to take nets, using knives to cut the nets and to cut off Frank's anchors. If a net was snagged, the officers would cut away the free part and leave the snag in the river. This had been going on since the early 1960s, with the most recent instances in 1971 and 1972. The state, Frank said, had never undertaken any judicial proceedings that justified taking and keeping Indian property. And though his property was taken and destroyed, Frank was never charged with any offense in connection with this fishery.

When the state's attorney asked whether off-reservation fishing was prohibited, Frank said, "Off-reservation fishing when the chum are running is prohibited by the state and I've been in jail enough times to say it probably is." Asked if a court-dictated percentage of the salmon catch for commercial purposes would be a fair recognition of treaty rights, Frank said, "No. It depends what the court would order."

"Do you have any idea what you would consider fair?"

"I figure 100%."

"Do you believe your tribe is entitled to all the fish in the Nisqually River?"

"No. I believe there should be some escapement."

Frank testified that there were still tribal ceremonies consisting of cooking fish and having dinner together, with some Indian dancing. Such ceremonies were usually in the spring, "when the Indian eats his first salmon and has a dinner with his people. I would say at the end of the winter would be a good time for the Indian—that is, if he wasn't locked up in jail every time he got through fishing like I was." As to other ceremonies, Frank said, "We used to celebrate the 4th of July, but we don't do that anymore," leaving his listeners to draw their own conclusions about Nisqually feelings concerning this national holiday.[13]

Benjamin Wright, a member of the Puyallup Tribe, painted a similar picture. He too had had a net and a boat confiscated by the state, his gear taken and his boat shot full of holes as well as motors stolen. He didn't know who took his gear, but none of it had ever been returned, and there had never been any court proceedings to determine who was entitled to it. A majority of the Puyallups went to work when they weren't being arrested by the state for fishing. But the jobs were part-time, low paying, and dead ends. Most Puyallups would rather fish. "I don't know exactly how [the non-Indian commercial fishermen] feel about fishing," Wright said, "but I believe this is a way—part of our life. Fishing." He then echoed John Ides's views about state allocation of the salmon resource: "We don't have any faith in the State Department of Fisheries or Game. We would have to have someone other than the state [make the allocation], such as the Judge."[14]

Witness after witness took the stand and painted a clear and powerful picture of a people oppressed and denied their rights. Forrest Kinley, a member of the Lummi Tribe and a former tribal chairman, presented a broad view:

> The general citizenry of the State of Washington has got to realize that it's been so long since the Indian has had any opportunity to develop his fisheries, that we really feel were ours when the treaty was made, that was made between our people and the non-Indians. We give up our land without any restrictions. But when it came to hunting and fishing, we wanted exclusive rights in certain areas. We felt that we were giving the citizens a right to fish in common with us. All right, the non-Indian has developed and made good money and made a good economic base on fisheries. Now this is the type of thing that our people know. I think that we are the best fishermen. We've always lived with nature and we have dealt with it. I think that we can deal with nature. We can deal with the fishing problems. I think that we should be given a chance to build our economic base around our fisheries, and we have never been given this chance in the state of Washington. We have been harassed in our accustomed fishing grounds. The non-Indian has made millions off of our fisheries; we have made nothing.

Then he placed the entire history of government dealings with Indians in perspective:

> I think that you take a look at your own track record towards Indian people, that throughout the history of the United States, that the United States government…has tried to build a glove to put us into, that they've tried to make farmers out of us, they've tried to make executives out of us, and various other things, and they have tried to fit us into them, and we haven't been able to fit into any of these programs because there is a

cultural value difference between what you value and what I value as an Indian, and I think that you can see the change that is being done now, that our people have lived with nature and now you take this ecology and everything else, that they [the public] finally realize that we did have something, and you have turned around and you are trying to follow some of the ideas that we tried to present to you years ago. So I think that...we need an economic base to where the type of work that we do, that we enjoy, and our people enjoy—hunting and fishing, and they respect, you know, nature itself.

Judge Boldt then asked Kinley what he meant by "establishing an economic base for Indian people," and Kinley answered:

What I would like to see is, that we bring our income to our tribal members up to the same middle bracket that the rest of the nation is on. And I don't think it should be done by trying to educate us, by making teachers out of us, we are expert fishermen. We are expert with other types of things. We know how to manage fish. We have proven this. When the white man came, there was abundance of everything, and I think we could put it back in that shape if we was given an opportunity.

Then, in a surprising demonstration of empathy for the dislocation of white fishermen that restoration of treaty fishing would cause, Kinley told Judge Boldt, "Changes should be done in stages; we just can't go chop other people's livelihood. They have done this to us, but I don't feel—my personal opinion is that this has got to be taken in stages."[15]

When Muckleshoot tribal member Bernice White took the stand, she expressed what many Northwest Indians felt: "I don't believe the State or the Superior Court had any right to stop the Muckleshoot Indians from fishing...because Washington State, at the time of the treaty was not a state, it was a territory. The treaty was made with our people with that understanding that we retained this right. So we don't have to come to the state. The state has to come to us. It is our right and it is our rivers and our Sound."

Then she provided personal insight into the poverty and degradation that had been visited upon her people: "Many of the people in my tribe are on welfare. It is something that you don't like, but if you have a large family, you are not working, you have to accept this. You are always looked down upon and your children aren't dressed right, you're not eating right…and so you are more or less degraded by being on welfare. But there is no other choice for our people, they lack education and there is no employment. We have no natural resource. The only thing we can look towards is the fish."[16]

Another Muckleshoot member, Louis Starr, described the plight of his tribe: "The rivers themselves have changed…as the people…make their dams bigger, take more water into the city…make the pipes bigger, drain the rivers. We can no longer fish in the Green River or the Cedar River and up above the White River where they used to fish, is drained dry now. We were left there with nothing…And as for fishing, we have to beg around to get a chance to fish."[17]

Distrust and animosity toward the state, resulting from its oppression of Indians, was expressed repeatedly. Chris Penn for the Quileute Tribe, in answer to whether he was aware that net fishing for steelhead outside reservation boundaries was prohibited by the Game Department, said, "I don't think we made no treaty with the state Game Department… we're still going under our treaty rights is what we are doing."[18]

Joe de la Cruz, chairman of the Quinault Business Committee, described how he had asked the Fisheries Department for an off-reservation fishery. The department, he said, told him they would consider it. But they never responded. The state had instead repeatedly tried to infringe on the Quinaults' sovereignty, and for that reason, he said, "We are very leery of any type of marriage with the state of Washington."[19]

Excerpts don't adequately convey the quality of the story told by the Indian witnesses, but their words had a powerful impact on Judge Boldt. I don't think he had ever heard directly from Indian people. He seemed taken with the forthright and respectful manner of the tribal witnesses. It touched his deepest feelings of love for the country and its laws. Though, like me, he had been born in Chicago, he had spent most of his life in Washington, and he was clearly disturbed that his beloved state was acting in a lawless and oppressive way toward America's indigenous people.

The state officials who testified were unable to defend a system that denied Indians a fair share of the resource, yet they insisted that only the state was capable of managing the fishery. The history of state oppression and denial of rights haunted their case.

Finally, mention must be made of the issue raised by the Lummis: the usurpation of traditional reef-net sites by non-Indians. The contemporary reef-net fishermen opposed the Lummi claim, and their witnesses testified that the modern reef netters did not fish the historical Lummi sites. I called a Lummi elder who testified that the sites were identical and could be located by the anchor boulders used by the Lummis. Then I called two witnesses, one Lummi and one non-Indian, both professional divers. They testified that they had investigated the sea bottom and had found the boulders exactly where the elders had described them, and exactly where the modern reef netting took place. The boulders, they explained, were totally unlike any natural rocks or seabed and were obviously sunk there. This proof went unrebutted.

FOURTEEN

U.S. v. Washington:
Closing Arguments
and Judge Boldt's Decision

CLOSING ARGUMENTS IN *U.S. V. WASHINGTON* WERE SET FOR DEC-
ember 10, 1973, more than three weeks after the last day of the trial.
There was an air of excitement in Judge Boldt's courtroom when the day
came. All of us were aware of the momentous implications of this case;
we had come to the final act in this three-year-long drama.

The federal government's position was argued by George Dysart, the
special assistant U.S. attorney. He began with the basic tenet of treaty
language construction: the treaty must be construed by the court so
as to carry out the intentions of the parties to the treaty—the United
States and the Indians. The language should therefore be construed
in the sense it would naturally be understood by the Indians and in a
spirit that generously reflected the obligation of the United States to
protect the interests of a dependent people. The treaties, he reminded
the court, were not a grant of rights to the Indians, but a grant of rights
from them, "with a reservation of those rights not granted"—language
taken directly from U.S. Supreme Court decisions.

In making the treaties, the tribes did not surrender their existence as
political entities, Dysart pointed out, nor did they surrender all vestiges
of internal sovereignty. Each tribe retained regulatory control over its
members, and the state was wrong in claiming the role of *parens patriae*
for the entire fishery resource and for all entitled to harvest it. But he
opposed the tribes' argument that they could not be regulated by the
state, saying this issue had been settled by the Supreme Court's decision

in *Department of Game v. Puyallup Tribe*. Instead, he asked the court to set a strict standard of justification for any restrictions imposed without tribal concurrence.

As to the "in common with" language, Dysart argued that U.S. intention had been to reserve to the Indians what they had had from time immemorial: fishing where and as they had always fished. Modern conservation requirements presented new problems, but the state was wrong in assuming it could dictate to the tribes the conditions of their fisheries. The U.S. Supreme Court had only recognized a limited sphere of police power for off-reservation harvesting. In view of evidence that the tribes had successfully self-regulated, there was a heavy burden on the state to show why the tribes could not regulate themselves off-reservation. As to limiting the Indians' on-reservation catch, that was at odds with the "in common with" language, which applied only to off-reservation fisheries.

Dysart urged that the state should first determine escapement requirements and then limit the Indians only to conserve the resource and provide a fair share for non-Indians. Finally, he accused the state of fostering an atmosphere of repression and hostility, arguing that justice required that all the gear seized from Indians without judicial determination be returned to them or its value paid.[1]

David Getches, speaking for the Muckleshoot, Squaxin Island, Skokomish, Stillaguamish, and Sauk-Suiattle tribes, argued that any reduction in harvest for conservation must come out of the non-Indian share; there should be no ceiling on the Indian catch unless and until Indians were monopolizing the fishery. Conservation must be narrowly defined as true preservation of the resource. The tribes' ability to successfully self-regulate was demonstrated by the fact that no on-reservation fishery had ever been destroyed by Indian fishing.[2]

In my closing argument on behalf of the Makahs, Lummis, and Quileutes, I tried to place the case in a historical and legal context. My clients had become co-plaintiffs, I explained, because they disagreed with the federal government's premise that the state had regulatory power over Indian fishing. Under the Supremacy Clause of the U.S. Constitution, the laws of the state of Washington, I argued, were invalid as applied to Indians because they conflicted with the federal treaties.

At the time of the treaty transactions between the Indians and the

United States, the Indians were a thriving people with a highly developed culture, living a settled village life in an abundant economy oriented toward the products of the sea and the rivers. In fact, this defined their culture; it was who they were and what they were.

The overriding interest of the United States at the time of the treaties, I said, was to acquire land and open it up for white settlement free from the threat of conflict with Indians. The United States was interested in making a deal for land acquisition and it knew in advance that the Indians would not agree to leave their ancestral territory unless they were assured the continued right to fish. If the Indians were confined exclusively to small territorial reservations, then the federal government would have to support the tribes because, removed from the foundation of their economy, they couldn't survive. So the fishing-right guaranty was as much a benefit to the government as it was to the Indians. By preserving Indian fisheries, the government also believed that these treaties would benefit the incoming white settlers. The Indians could supply them with fish, as indeed they had been doing, in some cases for ninety years before the treaties were made in the mid-nineteenth century.

I reiterated that the treaties themselves were between a powerful, sophisticated, legally trained people and an unlettered people. So a long-standing legal principle of interpretation applied: the language of the treaties must be construed most favorably toward the unlettered people. I then addressed the "in common with" clause. Its purpose, I said, was to ensure that, while the land territory set aside for reservations was for the exclusive use and occupancy of the Indians, the fishing areas were not. The treaties included promises of benefits: schools, doctors, and farm implements. But, while the United States unilaterally offered farm implements, there was no evidence that the Indians wanted to be acculturated. They signed, they felt, for preservation of their way of life.

It was undisputed, I said, that the fishery resource was abundant at the time of the treaties, and no one had any thought of future conservation needs. The Industrial Revolution had not yet touched the fishery. Further, federal agents who visited the Northwest found that the Indians were engaged in extensive commerce in fish and whale oil. They were involved in activity beyond subsistence fishing.

That historical salmon abundance soon declined. I described the industrialization of the salmon fishery brought about by the perfection of the vacuum-canning process and the subsequent proliferation of canneries, together with the completion of the railroad that opened Washington fisheries to national markets. The result, I said, was that more and more of the commercial fishery moved away from the riverbanks to the open saltwater in order to accommodate the proliferation of commercial fishing boats and their gear, leaving the Indian fishery largely in river mouths and along the rivers and streams. The Indians' fishery was gradually supplanted by the industrial saltwater fishery because of the vast amounts of capital invested in the non-Indian commercial fishery. As early as 1914, that fishery threatened to destroy salmon runs, and to prevent that the state legislature imposed restrictions on fishing.

I then described the origin of the state's campaign to stamp out treaty rights. As the Indians came into conflict with the burgeoning commercial fishing industry, they were steadily driven off their fishing grounds or given restricted access. The treaties were ignored. I cited state supreme court decisions of the early twentieth century that dismissed Indian treaty claims in disparaging racial terms, and I quoted the language of the state supreme court in *State v. Towessnute*, in which a Lummi Indian had defended his right to fish by citing the Isaac Stevens treaty. The court said:

> The Indian was a child and a dangerous child, to be both
> protected and restrained. In his nomadic life he was to be left
> so long as civilization did not demand his region. When it did
> demand his region, he was to be allotted a more confined area
> with permanent subsistence. These arrangements were the
> announcements of our benevolence, which, notwithstanding
> our frequent frailties, had been continuously displayed. Neither
> Rome nor sagacious Britain ever dealt more liberally with their
> subject races than we with these savage tribes, whom it was
> generally tempting and always easy to destroy and whom we
> have often permitted to squander vast areas of fertile land before
> our eyes.

The state supreme court then denied the Lummi Indian's treaty defense.[3] "So as early as 1916," I told Judge Boldt, "We see the Indian embattled and losing and in fact, from that date on the Indian has been forced to engage in a kind of guerilla warfare with the state, risking arrest, jail and confiscation in order to exercise the rights he believed were his under the treaty."

The issue before the court, I argued, was not the scope of the Indians' treaty right. Rather, the question was the state's claim of authority. I objected to both the federal and the state positions, because both assumed that the state would absorb the Indians into its management system and thereafter state regulation would govern the scope of the treaty right. I rejected the argument that the U.S. Supreme Court had granted the state police power over the Indians as simply another class of citizens to be regulated according to what the state deemed necessary for conservation. I said that in its previous decisions the Supreme Court had been handicapped in its understanding of what might constitute conservation because it had never been presented with the full scope of the state's management scheme.

In looking at the overall Puget Sound area, we could see, I told the court, that while the state claimed to be acting in the interest of conservation, it was in fact allocating a resource among interest groups, "much more akin to the Texas Railroad Commission allocating underground oil than to the National Park Service preserving wildflowers." I emphasized the language of the U.S. Supreme Court in Puyallup II, which said that limiting Indian fishing had to be based on the need to conserve the species, and that if the species was threatened all fisheries would have to be shut down. This left the state with the limited power to prevent species extinction, and that was the meaning the U.S. Supreme Court gave to the word *conservation*.

I closed by saying that the court had four choices. The position of the tribes I represented was that the treaty fishing right was a federally reserved area of jurisdiction and the state had no authority over it. Another possible position was that the state could claim limited authority—the position of the Puyallup decision —for example, an emergency would justify an extension of state police power. Further authority could be granted, another argument went, if the state compiled proper conservation data showing the need for restriction of Indian fishing in an integrated management system—then the state could impose regulations on the Indians. Finally, there was the state position, which I viewed as extreme and unjustified by legal precedent: that the state had total and complete regulatory authority, and that the state has no reason to treat Indians any differently than other citizens, except to set up a special category for them and to follow whatever guidelines this court may set.

Absent evidence that the Indian fishery was destructive, I urged, there was no basis for the imposition of any state regulation. While the state rejected tribal regulation, it had failed to show a single instance of a tribe failing to regulate responsibly. The state had not shown that Indian fishing was destructive or in need of state regulation for species preservation. There was no basis for even emergency imposition of power.[4]

Earl McGimpsey then made his closing argument on behalf of the state Fisheries Department. He disputed our claim that the state had no authority to regulate Indian fishing, arguing that conditions had changed drastically since the time of the treaties and that the treaties had to be interpreted in light of contemporary conditions. Though the state had authority, he said, he did acknowledge that an equitable apportionment must be made among the various user groups. The rule should be "fair share." This did not, he said, mean a guaranteed portion. The problem faced by the Fisheries Department, he said, was their inability to determine how many fish were required for escapement, that is, to reach the river fisheries. The state proposed giving the Indians a fair share of the fish that would normally reach the Indians' usual and accustomed river fishing grounds; the court should determine in a given year a percentage of these returning fish. To do this, the state said, the court should determine where Indians have received at least one-third of the fish produced in a particular fishery, and that would establish that Indians have received their fair share. McGimpsey explained that the state's rationale for the one-third principle was the need to divide the resource among three groups: the commercial fishery, the sport fishery, and the Indian fishery. Where there were mixed stocks in marine waters, accommodations could be made to compensate for the fewer numbers of Indian fishermen compared to non-Indians by granting the former extra fishing time.

McGimpsey insisted that it was not practically possible to divide regulatory control between the state and the Indian tribes. The state, he maintained, "has the pre-eminent right to regulate Indian fishing in its territory," and he disparaged tribal regulation as unscientific and self-interested. The Fisheries Department was willing to set up an "Indian only" fishery and to try to assure significant numbers of fish in it, but "we cannot stand by and submit to the submission of our regulatory authority to a panel of Indian and State representatives. That is a decision to be made solely by the Federal Court and a special master to be appointed by the court."[5]

The Game Department attorney, Larry Coniff, was obdurate: there simply was no treaty right to fish for a game fish with a net. The game fishery was an "equal opportunity" fishery, and since the steelhead run was supported by fees paid by sportfishermen, Indians should not be permitted to take any of the fish with nets. The department argued that the steelhead run could not support a commercial net fishery and so it had to be prohibited.[6]

This was a foolish argument. Under the law developed in U.S. Supreme Court decisions, there not only was a treaty right, never extinguished by Congress, but the Supremacy Clause of the U.S. Constitution made federal treaties the law of the land, "anything in the constitution or laws of any state to the contrary notwithstanding." Put in its kindest light, Coniff was simply making the best arguments he could for a hard-line client.

When closing arguments ended, Judge Boldt made his own closing remarks: "I seriously believe this kind of a case should have been brought fifty years ago, so that these issues might have been resolved long ago. Much damage, both physical and spiritual, has been caused to the Indian and non-Indian people of this area for want of adjudication of these issues in the way our constitution provides, that is, in a court and not by demonstrations, violence and the like. It is this lack of adjudication that has largely produced a deep bitterness on both sides."

He went on to say that he did not expect his decision to erase all of the bad feelings quickly, and that it is going to take some time to change attitudes, but, he said, "I am hopeful that all will come together as citizens in common, acting like brethren in that wonderful relationship."[7] His expectation that it would take time for the parties to forge new relationships and attitudes proved to be farsighted. Perhaps he was a bit naive, but the judge's comments reflected his deep idealism about this country and its potential for brotherhood between ethnic groups.

Judge Boldt released his 107-page decision on February 12, 1974, five months after the conclusion of the trial.[8] It was a bombshell. He adopted the position urged by the government that Indians were entitled to up to one-half of each run of fish that passed through their usual and accustomed fishing grounds. He adopted one position I had urged, ruling that any tribe may exercise its governmental powers and regulate the fishing of its members without any state regulation. He did impose a requirement for a substantial structure of tribal government and qualified fishery management experts to carry out the management function. On the other hand, he rejected my argument that the state had no regulatory power over off-reservation fishing, saying that this argument had been foreclosed by U.S. Supreme Court decisions granting the authority to regulate such fishing, within the strict limitations laid down in those decisions. The judge was fully aware of the Indian attitude toward such state regulation, expressed by every Indian witness: "State regulation of off-reservation fishing is highly obnoxious to the Indians and in practical application adds greatly to already complicated and already difficult problems and may stimulate continuing controversy and litigation, long into the future."[9]

In this, as in many other predictions Judge Boldt made about the consequences of his decision, he was prescient. But he did his best to narrow the areas of conflict by laying down a strict standard the state had to meet before imposing any closure or limitation on fishing for conservation reasons. Reading his published decision as well as observing his demeanor on the bench during the trial, it was clear that he had given great weight to the testimony of the Indian witnesses. It almost seemed as if he were encountering the Indian people of the Northwest for the first time, hearing them talking about their lives and culture. He was highly respectful toward each witness and in his final decision he incorporated what they had told him.

The Boldt decision, as it would come to be called, addressed a number of other issues involving narrower questions, and I will not go into them here. What is important is that Judge Boldt foresaw that there *would* be other issues, and he retained jurisdiction to decide those issues at a later time. In the meantime, the Indians had won a huge victory and the state of Washington had suffered a major defeat. As for the Lummi claim to reef-net sites, Judge Boldt handed the Lummis a clear victory as well, ruling that the current reef-net fishermen had usurped the Lummi grounds and could not lay claim to any ownership of those grounds. Curiously, though the decision gave the Lummis the right to displace the non-Indian reef netters, they chose not to do so. Perhaps they shared the feelings expressed by Forrest Kinley: "We just can't go chop other people's livelihoods."

When Judge Boldt's decision was released to the public, there was an angry outcry from non-Indian fishing groups: sportfishermen and commercial fishermen. Fifty percent to the Indians? Outrageous! There were fewer than 1,500 Indian fishermen compared to almost 6,000 non-Indian commercial fishermen and 300,000 to 400,000 sportfishermen.[10] The sport and commercial fishermen had been led to believe, by state agencies and by the press, that Indians could not lay claim to rights greater than any other people. The general public knew little about treaty history and Indian rights; these were not subjects usually covered in schools and universities. There was an overriding belief that in America no one was entitled to special privileges. After all, wasn't this supposed to be an egalitarian society?

As the implications of the decision sank in, the wrath grew. If the decision stood up, the fisheries of Washington would be turned upside down, the feeling went. Many commercial fishermen would suffer substantial cuts in their income, and some might have to abandon fishing altogether. Such a result was unthinkable to the sport and commercial interest groups. And what started as a murmur of protest grew to a groundswell of attack against Judge Boldt and his decision. Many swore they would never abide by it. Soon these feelings manifested themselves in open hostility against Indians in communities where there were many fishermen. The atmosphere was volatile.

In that atmosphere, the voice of the Washington State Attorney General's Office was heard, not urging respect for the decision of the court, but inflaming the protesters further. The attorney general was Slade Gorton, a man who, as a matter of principle, was opposed to Indian rights. As a highly intelligent lawyer, he knew that it was hopeless to deny the validity of Indian treaty rights. But as the state's lawyer, he and his assistants were stung by the decision. While they had to advocate the position of their client agencies in court, the decision concerning litigation strategy was up to them. And they decided to fight the Boldt decision.

In one disgraceful episode, a contingent of white fishermen descended on the state capital in Olympia to protest and they were addressed by Assistant Attorney General Jim Johnson. Johnson told the crowd he agreed that Judge Boldt's decision was an aberration, and he assured them that the attorney general's office intended to appeal. What's more, he told them he was confident the decision would be reversed. We will hear of Mr. Johnson again, fighting Indians in Minnesota. In 2004, he was elected to the Washington Supreme Court, campaigning on the claim that he was an expert in constitutional law with a long string of victories. He never mentioned *U.S. v. Washington.*

The hope that the Boldt decision would be overturned was dashed when the U.S. Ninth Circuit Court of Appeals upheld the decision in every respect in 1975.[11] Washington State tried to take the case before the U.S. Supreme Court, but that effort failed when the Court refused to hear the case in 1976. It seemed the issue was closed. But it wasn't.

Judge Boldt had issued court orders requiring the Fisheries Department to implement the decision, but the state regulations put in place to comply with the decision were openly defied by commercial fishermen. State enforcement was half-hearted at best. Then a group of commercial fishermen brought suit in Thurston County, and the state court judge upheld their contention that, under state law, the state had no authority to apportion fish for any purpose other than conservation. The case then went before the state supreme court, which not only held that the state had no authority to enforce the Boldt decision, but that recognizing special rights for the Indians would violate the Equal Protection Clause of the U.S. Constitution! Thus, the state's highest court threw down the gauntlet, refusing to recognize the authority of the federal court in *U.S. v. Washington.* After this decision, the state said it could not and would not enforce Judge Boldt's rulings.

With the abandonment of law enforcement on the waters, the fishery became anarchic. Commercial fishermen put their nets wherever and whenever they pleased and took as much as they could. But they had not reckoned with the iron will of George H. Boldt. He was not about to allow his decision to become an empty promise. After all, it had been affirmed by the Ninth Circuit, and that decision was final. He was a deep believer in the rule of law, and he determined he would take whatever steps necessary to enforce his decision.

Boldt's reaction to the lawlessness on state waters was breathtakingly audacious. He put the entire fishery under federal supervision and ordered federal agencies to take over enforcement. The U.S. Coast Guard and National Marine Fisheries Service soon had their vessels out on the water. Violators were hauled before a federal commissioner and heavily fined. The lawless fishing stopped. But the resistance to the decision did not. Boldt's prediction that it would take considerable time for attitudes to change was borne out. There was smoldering resentment among all the non-Indian fishing interests and continuing public ridicule of the decision in *U.S. v. Washington*, together with animosity toward the Indians of the Northwest. This would not end until the U.S. Supreme Court spoke, five years later.

The Bolasny family, with my mother, Rose, in the back row, second from left. Chodorkov, Ukraine, ca. 1913. Photographer unknown.

My father, Harry Ziontz, the man at far left behind the bar in his tavern in Chicago, 1935. Photographer unknown.

My mother and father with me when I was seventeen, at a family wedding. New York, 1945. Photograph by Paulette Studios Brooklyn, New York.

Standing in front of the Seattle rooming house where I stayed in the summer of 1950. I had just returned from my job as construction laborer working on the University of Washington football stadium. Photographer unknown.

Marlon Brando holding up a salmon caught by net in the Puyallup River, in a canoe with Robert Satiacum, March 1964. Photograph courtesy of the *Seattle Post-Intelligencer* Collection, Museum of History and Industry, Seattle.

Bruce Wilkie, standing next to a local school bus.
Neah Bay, Washington, 1969. Photograph by Alvin Ziontz.

Judge George H. Boldt on the bench in the U.S. District Court. Tacoma, 1977. Photograph by Michael Gesinger.

The author in his living room. Mercer Island, Washington, 2000. Photograph by Lenore Ziontz.

The author's wife, Lenore "Lennie" Ziontz, 2007.
Photograph by Alvin Ziontz.

Paul Gronholt purse seiner captain. Sand Point, Alaska, 1986. Photograph by Alvin Ziontz.

Wanda Boswell and Billy Joe when they visited our home in the summer of 1990. Their newborn infant died because Elk River, Minnesota, jailers refused to seek medical care for Wanda when she was incarcerated. Photograph by Alvin Ziontz

Arapaho man dancing at the Arapaho-Shoshone pow-wow. Wind River Indian Reservation, Fort Washakie, Wyoming, 1994. Photograph by Alvin Ziontz.

Harmony Dancing Rain Spoonhunter, Arapaho-Shoshone, queen of Eastern Shoshone Indian Days. Wind River Indian Reservation, Fort Washakie, Wyoming, 1994. Photograph by Alvin Ziontz.

Northern Cheyenne woman dancing at a pow-wow on the Northern Cheyenne Indian Reservation near Lame Deer, Montana, 1996. Photograph by Alvin Ziontz.

James Black Wolf, Northern Cheyenne holy man. Northern Cheyenne Indian Reservation, Lame Deer, Montana, 1996. Photograph by Alvin Ziontz.

Rose Medicine Elk, Northern Cheyenne, at the Wendell Turkey Shoulderblades Senior Center. Northern Cheyenne Indian Reservation, Lame Deer, Montana, 1996. Photograph by Alvin Ziontz.

Phillip White Man, Sr., Northern Cheyenne, Keeper of the Chief's Drum, in his home on the Northern Cheyenne Indian Reservation, near Lame Deer, Montana, 1996. Photograph by Alvin Ziontz.

Florence White Man, Northern Cheyenne, wife of Phillip White Man, Sr., in her home on the Northern Cheyenne Indian Reservation, near Lame Deer, Montana, 1996. Photograph by Alvin Ziontz.

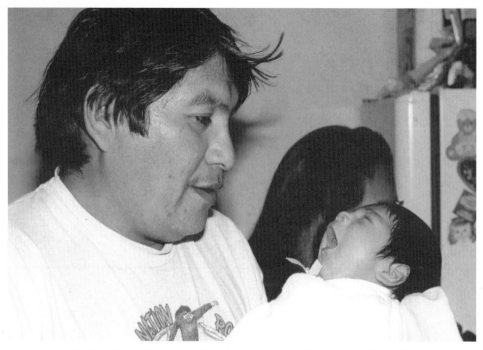

James Walks Along, Northern Cheyenne, with his eleven-day-old son, Jaidell, on the Northern Cheyenne Indian Reservation, near Lame Deer, Montana, 1996. Photograph by Alvin Ziontz.

Northern Cheyenne Halloween celebrants. Northern Cheyenne Indian Reservation, Lame Deer, Montana, 1996. Photograph by Alvin Ziontz.

The author receiving a Northern Cheyenne blessing from Danny Foote, member of the Northern Cheyenne Tribe. In the background are Steve Chestnut and members of his family. Northern Cheyenne Reservation, 1996. Photographer unknown.

The Alden family. *Seated left to right:* Joe Alden, Charlene Alden, and Crystal Alden. *Back row, left to right:* Leslie Alden, Henry Wilson, and his wife Shannon Alden Wilson. *Front center:* the Aldens' son, JP. Northern Cheyenne Indian Reservation, 1996. Photograph by Alvin Ziontz.

Steve Chestnut wearing a ceremonial Northern Cheyenne war bonnet and vest presented to him by the tribe, 1994. The framed photograph is of former Northern Cheyenne tribal president Allan Rowland (deceased). Photograph by Alvin Ziontz.

Makah whaling crew harpooning a gray whale for the first time in seventy years, May 17, 1999. Photograph by Mike Urban, courtesy of the *Seattle Post-Intelligencer.*

Makah singers celebrating the tribe's successful whale hunt, May 1999.
Photograph by Alvin Ziontz.

Makah women celebrating the tribe's successful whale hunt, May 1999.
Photograph by Alvin Ziontz.

Makah tribal elder and former chairman, George Bowechop (deceased), at
the tribal celebration of the whale hunt, May 1999.
Photograph by Alvin Ziontz.

The author speaking at Makah Treaty Day celebration. Neah Bay, Washington, May 14, 2005. Photograph by Lenore Ziontz.

Makah tribal member Micah McCarty dancing at Makah Treaty Day celebration. Neah Bay, Washington, May 14, 2005.
Photograph by Alvin Ziontz.

Makah singers and drummers at Makah Treaty Day celebration, Neah Bay, Washington, May 14, 2005. Photograph by Alvin Ziontz.

Makah youth dancing at Makah Treaty Day celebration. Neah Bay,
Washington, May 14, 2005. Photograph by Alvin Ziontz.

FIFTEEN

The U.S. Supreme Court Has the Last Word: Consequences of the Boldt Decision

IN 1976, THE U.S. SUPREME COURT REFUSED TO HEAR THE STATE'S appeal of the Ninth Circuit's confirmation of Judge Boldt's decision. But then the Washington Supreme Court ruled that the state had no right and no duty to enforce the federal decision. So a new suit challenging the legality of the Boldt decision's enforcement orders was brought, and this time the U.S. Supreme Court was highly interested. The new case presented a direct conflict between the federal courts and the Washington state courts. The Supreme Court agreed to hear the appeals from the decisions of the lower courts, and the Boldt decision was now in the hands of the ultimate authority.

My law firm led the Indian defense of the Boldt decision, and Mason Morisset, one of my partners at that time, argued the case for the tribes. Slade Gorton argued for the state of Washington. The United States was represented by Louis Claiborne, a veteran of the Justice Department's solicitor's office, and Phillip Lacovara argued for the non-Indian fishermen.

The decision of the U.S. Supreme Court came down in July of 1979, driving a stake through the heart of resistance to the Boldt decision. The designated title of the case was awkward, *State of Washington v. Washington State Commercial Passenger Fishing Vessel Association.*[1] The named appellant was an industry group representing sport charter fishing boat operators. The case was decided by a six to three majority, with Justices Stevens, Burger, Brennan, White, Marshall, and Blackmun voting to affirm and Justices Rehnquist, Powell, and Stewart dissenting. The Court reviewed every issue decided in *U.S. v. Washington* and, with a few minor exceptions, upheld all of Judge Boldt's rulings. In the majority opinion, Justice Stevens quoted the 1975 decision of the Ninth Circuit: "The state's extraordinary machinations in resisting the 1974 decree have forced the District Court to take over a large share of the management of the state's fishery in order to enforce its decree. Except for some segregation cases...the District Court has faced the most concerted official and private efforts to frustrate a decree of a federal court witnessed in the century."

This was a historic condemnation of Washington's actions coming from the Supreme Court of the United States. In my view, the responsibility for the state's conduct, which provoked this extraordinary denunciation, falls squarely on Washington State Attorney General Slade Gorton. It was Gorton who led the state's legal campaigns against the Indians and whose failure to support enforcement of the Boldt decision led to the complete breakdown of law enforcement on state waters. Gorton never appeared in court personally in any of the Indian litigation in the lower courts, but his hostility to Indian rights became so well-known that he was often called an Indian fighter. I had occasion to engage in a public debate with him on the subject of Indian rights at Western Washington University in Bellingham. It was very polite, but the tension between us was palpable.

Nearly thirty years have passed since the monumental Supreme Court decision bringing an end to the Washington Indian fishing wars, and one can now see some of the results. They have been far-reaching. The Boldt decision and its subsequent enforcement have transformed the relationship between state and tribal governments. No longer invisible, tribal governments have become co-managers of the fishery resource, sharing power and responsibility with the state. There has been a growth in cooperation and information sharing, to the benefit of both state and tribal governments and the public. The regime has not always been without conflict, but there is a framework for solving problems without the confrontational politics of the 1960s.[2]

The increased capabilities and stature of tribal governments are not the product of the Boldt decision alone. Tribes throughout the nation have developed their government structures, which are increasingly accepted in the American family of governments. In Washington, the Boldt decision laid the groundwork for tribal-state cooperation not only in the management of fisheries, but in other areas such as environmental protection, wildlife habitat, land use, and water management.

Perhaps the single most important consequence of the decision was that it enabled the Indian people of the Pacific Northwest to return to fishing as a way of life. In a rare instance, part of Indian culture that had been taken away was recovered. Many Indian fishermen obtained the capital to purchase modern powered fishing boats, and while many still fished with nets in the rivers, the majority moved into marine waters. Some acquired large forty- to sixty-foot purse seiners and even sailed them up to Alaska. Though Alaska was not a treaty fishery, for Indians the Boldt decision had opened up the prospect of becoming modern fishermen (an outcome that the decision specifically contemplated). Indians who had fished using only small skiffs with outboard motors adapted to modern gear in an amazingly short time. Many, particularly the young men and women, mastered skills involving electronics, engine repair, hydraulics, pipefitting, and boat maintenance. They learned the business skills necessary for operating a large capital item— a fishing boat—often valued in the hundreds of thousands of dollars. They developed the discipline to manage finances, making boat and insurance payments and paying suppliers. They mastered the complexities of fishing regulations, since made far more complex by the application of federal regulations to the ocean fishery.

I observed these changes from a personal vantage point. In 1977, my firm helped establish the first fleet of modern boats for the Makah Tribe by obtaining federal financing to construct ten thirty-foot combination troller-gillnetter boats. The tribe was the borrower, ultimately responsible for repayment of the federal loan, and it set up a contract program with tribal members who wanted to acquire boats. Each participant committed to make regular monthly payments to the tribe and to maintain the boat in good condition. The success of each fisherman was entirely up to him. The first group of Makahs who acquired boats encountered difficulties. A number fell behind in their payments. Some even argued they shouldn't have to repay the tribe at all. But the tribe stood firm. All who failed to meet their payment obligations had their boats repossessed, and new applicants took their place. Not all were diligent fishermen. Some fished harder and smarter than others and prospered, but all in all most learned how to succeed as commercial fishermen.

The Makah Tribe, like most tribes in the Northwest, developed a fisheries department and employed a fish biologist. The tribal fisheries department promulgated regulations for its fishermen based on the best fish data available. Indian fishermen who violated the regulations were cited by the tribal fishery enforcement department and fined by the tribal court. Northwest tribal fisheries departments began daily contact with the state and federal fisheries agencies, exchanging data on run size and numbers of fish caught. Never before had there been such a comprehensive system of reporting on the fish resource from every river and stream and from the ocean. Contrary to the dire predictions of old-line state fish managers, co-management not only worked, it provided better management tools than before.[3]

The Boldt decision also brought a new spirit to Indians in the Northwest. Losing the central activity of Indian life over the prior eighty years had left Indian people, especially the men, without a sense of purpose, and this contributed to social problems: alcoholism, violence, and family disintegration. The return of fishing began to relieve these problems. It would be nice to say that they disappeared, which sadly is not the case. But I did see real changes. Many teenagers I knew in the Makah Tribe, a number of them high-school dropouts, became deckhands on boats owned by other members of the tribe, and then they learned the skills of a boat captain. When I encountered them years later in meetings of tribal fishermen, they were in their late twenties or early thirties, and I was impressed by their mastery of the regulatory regimes and overall fishing skills. Why had their earlier school experiences been so unsuccessful? I believe it was because these men, then teenagers, didn't see high school's relevance to their lives. These same dropouts had since matured, and nothing was now more relevant to their lives than fishing and how to succeed as fishermen. I feel that over time, with new opportunities in the fishing industry such as switching to species other than salmon and fishing in different areas like Alaska, new generations of Indians will find their lives more meaningful and purposeful than their parents did. Judge Boldt would have been pleased.

The expansion of the fishing industry on the Makah reservation was duplicated on almost every reservation in the Pacific Northwest. The number of Indian fishermen grew from about 1,400 prior to the Boldt decision to 4,000 by 1985.[4] From a pre-Boldt share of 5 percent of the salmon harvest, by 1986 the Indian share had increased to almost 50 percent.[5] A corresponding increase in income spread throughout Indian communities. Some Indian fishermen, those who were enterprising and skilled, became very prosperous. Most have enjoyed a modest increase in livelihood. Indian fishing alone did not (and does not) provide enough employment to solve the poverty problem on all reservations, but fishing income has resulted in better housing and a generally higher standard of living.

Another effect of the Boldt decision was the growth in reservation populations and tribal enrollment. In one stroke, membership in a Northwest Indian tribe became valuable. All tribes restricted treaty fishing rights to enrolled members who resided on the reservation—with membership came fishing rights. After Boldt, these rights made a decent livelihood possible, and many urban Indians returned to their reservations. Many small and moribund tribes found their membership rolls growing exponentially.

But the news has not been altogether good. Prior to *U.S. v. Washington*, the tribes were unified in their fight against state power. In the years that followed, tribes became pitted against each other, competing for a share of the fishery. This led to litigation, tribe against tribe. I took little part in that phase, turning over this responsibility to two of my partners. That conflict has continued to the present day and no permanent solution is in sight. Meanwhile, the salmon resource has undergone a precipitous decline due to environmental degradation and overfishing. As a result, some tribes, particularly the ocean tribes, have shifted to other species such as halibut and black cod, since the treaty right was not limited to salmon.

Despite the difficulties, the lives of the members of Northwest fishing tribes have improved markedly. Indeed, the effects of the Boldt decision will be felt for generations to come. While the Indians were the winners, there were inevitably losers. Many non-Indians who had fished commercially for a lifetime left the industry. To ease their hardship, the federal government instituted a boat buy-back program. This had actually been proposed before the Boldt decision, by economists and fisheries biologists who saw the fishery as overcapitalized, with far too many boats chasing after a declining resource.

The Boldt decision and its Supreme Court affirmation righted a historic wrong. In the process, it changed the perceptions of the white citizenry about Indians and Indian tribes. Indian history is now an established part of the state's public-school curriculum. Signs showing the location of reservations are part of the public highway system. Indians are no longer hidden.

The Indian court victory in U.S. v. Washington was only one of many such victories throughout the West. In the latter half of the twentieth century, the Indians had lawyers—and good ones too. There's nothing that brings respect and power like being able to go to court and win. But I will close the discussion of U.S. v. Washington on a less exuberant note. The Nixon administration, whose attorney general, John Mitchell, authorized the suit, was surprisingly supportive of Indians. Mitchell, a conservative, had no known sympathies for Indians. In all likelihood, the suit was authorized at a lower level on the basis that it was strongly advocated by the Interior Department and was consistent with the president's strong support of Indians and with the nation's international posture. If this suit had been proposed during the administration of George W. Bush, with John Ashcroft and later Alberto Gonzalez heading up the Justice Department, I am doubtful that it would have been pursued. And it almost certainly would meet a different fate in the Supreme Court of Chief Justice William Rehnquist—Rehnquist was one of the dissenters in the *Passenger Fishing Vessel* case that affirmed Boldt—and his colleagues Antonin Scalia and Clarence Thomas who replaced those justices that voted to affirm the decision. There would be no Thurgood Marshall to see the justice of the Indians' claims, and I have little confidence that either John Roberts or Samuel Alito would be receptive to Indian treaty rights.

So, perhaps U.S. v. Washington should be seen as a product of its time—an era of growing support for civil rights, of growing judicial willingness to apply protective legal principles to Indian cases, and of growing Indian militancy. Few tribes would be willing to gamble their rights with the present-day Supreme Court. And while there are many courageous federal judges, there is unlikely ever to be another George Boldt. For me, he stands as a symbol of judicial integrity. I hung a portrait of

Judge Boldt on my office wall in 1980. It still hangs there over twenty-five years later, though I have retired and the office is occupied by my partner Marc Slonim. It has become an icon.

SIXTEEN

The Confederated Tribes
of the Colville Reservation

THE REPUTATION OF WHAT WAS THEN KNOWN AS ZIONTZ, PIRTLE and Morisset for vigorous defense of tribal sovereignty led another major tribal client to retain our firm, the Confederated Tribes of the Colville Reservation. They are known as, and call themselves, simply Colvilles. The Colville Indian Reservation is big—1.4 million acres in north-central Washington. The reservation was established by presidential executive order in 1872 as the homeland for eleven bands of Indians who lived in what later became Washington State. Those tribes were the Wenatchee, Entiat, Chelan, Methow, Lakes, Okanogan, Moses, Nespelem, San Poil, Palouse, and Nez Perce. The Nez Perce on the Colville reservation are descended from Chief Joseph's band, who were sent to the reservation in 1885 after being incarcerated in Oklahoma during the Nez Perce War of 1877.[1] A large number of Nez Perce also live in Idaho. The word *Colville* has nothing to do with the names of the Indians. It comes from the Englishman Andrew Colville, who was director of the London company that operated a trading post at Kettle Falls. He never set foot in America. His name became attached to Fort Colville that was built at the trading post site, northeast of the present reservation.

The Columbia River flows for more than 150 miles along the reservation, forming its eastern and southern boundaries. Historically, the Indian people had large salmon fisheries on the river and its tributaries. Most of the Indians of the original bands were hunters and gatherers who roamed on horseback over the hills and plains of what is now north-central Washington. They were nomadic and lived in tepees set up where game was abundant.

The Indian lifestyle was heavily impacted in the twentieth century by the giant hydroelectric dams constructed on the Columbia. The largest and most famous was Grand Coulee Dam, built on Colville lands and riverbed. It flooded Indian lands all along the river, wiping out communities and, by converting a free-flowing river to a lake, destroying Indian fisheries and a traditional way of life. A second dam was Chief Joseph, downriver from Grand Coulee. The Army Corps of Engineers' choice of name was ironic. Chief Joseph was the great Nez Perce chief who led his people on a grueling and historic march to escape captivity. He is widely acknowledged to be the speaker of the sad and deathless words, "Hear me my chiefs, my heart is sick and sad. From where the sun now stands, I will fight no more against the white man."[2] The dam bearing Chief Joseph's name also flooded Colville lands, wiping out village sites and destroying a way of life. That the dam that was the instrument of such destruction was given the name of the great Chief Joseph reveals the unwitting arrogance of a society that assumes that its desires trump everything that stands in its way. I am again reminded of Charlie Peterson's remark on seeing the name *Cherokee* used for an airplane: "They like our names, don't they." The body of Chief Joseph is buried near Nespelem on the Colville reservation.

The Colville reservation became a political battleground during the so-called termination era of the 1950s. Under the Eisenhower administration, the U.S. government initiated a program to "terminate" the federal relationship with Indian tribes and end the protected status of Indian lands. The word *termination*, perhaps unwittingly, had dire implications. Not only would the tribes' relationship with the federal government be ended, the tribes themselves would be extinguished as political entities. The policy envisaged liquidating tribal assets and distributing the proceeds to the members. The Indians and their lands would disappear into the general public, becoming governed by state laws and no longer having any political existence.[3] This was the gravest threat faced by the American Indian nation since the removal policy of the Andrew Jackson administration in the early nineteenth century.

Congress began implementing the policy by asking the Bureau of

Indian Affairs to submit a list of tribes it deemed ready to be terminated. The initial list was short and included the Colville Tribe. The Colvilles had around ten thousand members, many of whom lived in cities far from the reservation. Under the Colville constitution, any member could vote in tribal elections, without regard to their place of residence. Many members had little interest in the survival of the tribe or the preservation of a homeland. Instead, they were interested in the money that liquidation of tribal lands would put in their pockets. Even some members who lived on the reservation supported termination. The "terminators," both on and off the reservation, became outspoken advocates for terminating the Colville Tribe. Many were prolific letter writers to the newspapers and to Congress. Their rhetoric called for adapting to modernity and abandoning a hopelessly outmoded way of life. They harped on the theme of individualism as opposed to tribalism, which was derided as socialistic and debilitating to participation in the American economic system. Such language resonated with many members of Congress.

In the 1950s the Colville Business Council (the tribe's governing body) was dominated by terminators, elected with substantial support from off-reservation Colvilles. But those who lived on the reservation outnumbered the off-reservation members, and by the 1960s they had begun to realize the serious consequences of termination. One of the leaders of the on-reservation antitermination forces was a remarkable Colville woman, Lucy Covington. Lucy was the granddaughter of Chief Moses, the last recognized Colville chief, and she had a powerful belief in traditional Indian values. Lucy was a rancher and an articulate and forceful speaker. She decided to wage political war to get control of the council and she succeeded—her indefatigable campaign ultimately turned the tribe around. By 1968, tribal elections had changed the political complexion of the Colville Business Council, the majority of whom now opposed termination.

Lucy wanted the tribe to have attorneys who were equally committed to tribal survival and tribal sovereignty, so in 1970 she contacted our firm. We were invited to meet with the council at Nespelem. After a discussion in which we described our expertise and commitment to tribes, the council voted to hire us. At the time, our firm consisted of three partners and two associates. Our newest associate was a young New

Yorker of extraordinary intelligence, Barry Ernstoff. Barry was a member of the generation of young rebels of the time: his hair was shoulder length, he wore sandals, and around his neck a beaded necklace. While he scorned conventions, his legal abilities were obvious. He was deeply enthused about working for Indian tribes. When we were invited to attend an Indian pow-wow on the Colville reservation, we took Barry with us.

The pow-wow included traditional Indian drumming and dancing by Colvilles in full regalia. The word quickly went around that we were the new tribal attorneys. Barry, with his long hair and beads, attracted more than his share of attention. In those days, many young people were attracted by the idea of Indians and their lifestyle and affected an Indian look, particularly those whose work took them to reservations. The Indians scorned these "wannabes," and the derisive remark "he's gone to the beads" was common. I'm afraid this was how some Colvilles reacted to Barry at the pow-wow. We were introduced to an older Indian man, who we learned was a highly esteemed chief, George Friedlander. He was tall and dignified and wore his gray hair in two long braids that hung down his back. Lucy Covington said she wanted him to meet us. As each of us was introduced, Friedlander shook hands and made some courteous remarks. But when Barry came forward, the chief looked steadily at him and said: "Young man, cut your hair." Barry smiled and simply said, "Pleased to meet you." Fortunately, this did no harm to our relationship with the business council.

We served as the tribal attorneys for the Colvilles for ten years and during that time took three of their cases to the U.S. Supreme Court. The Colvilles faced some of the same issues as many other tribes—hunting and fishing rights and tribal jurisdiction over the reservation. But they had other problems not faced by tribes in Western Washington, namely water rights and the problems caused by the massive hydroelectric dams on the Columbia. They also had issues with the state of Washington over taxation.

Some Colvilles operated small businesses on the reservation using their exemption from state taxes to attract non-Indian customers. On many reservations, Indians sell fireworks during the run-up to Fourth of July celebrations. But these are short-term opportunities. As cigarette taxes imposed by the states began to climb in the 1960s, Indians began selling tax-free cigarettes. They bought their merchandise from out-of-state wholesalers and had them shipped to the reservation. Customers from nearby communities flocked to these "smoke shops," and this raised some hackles. Non-Indian merchants near the reservation were angered at the loss of business, and states were angered at the loss of tax revenue. The state of Washington tried to close down these businesses by coming into the shops and seizing the untaxed cigarettes. Litigation was inevitable.

At Colville, as on most reservations, the shops were operated by individuals, not the tribe. Yet the tribe had an interest in preserving immunity from state laws on the reservation and also in protecting the livelihoods of their members. On the Colville reservation, the state raided a smoke shop operated by Jerri and Leonard Tonasket in the town of Omak, within the reservation boundaries, and seized their cigarettes. The council directed us to sue the state. We did, and lost—in the lower state courts and in the Washington Supreme Court, both of which held that the state had the authority to tax cigarettes on the reservation. We then took an appeal to the U.S. Supreme Court, which granted certiorari.

The case had implications for Indian smoke shops everywhere. My then partner Robert Pirtle argued the case for the Tonaskets, and I represented the interests of the Colville Tribe and filed a brief as amicus curiae. I was granted time by the court to make the argument separately for the tribe. The case involved important tribal interests: the question of tribal sovereignty, the question of the reach of the state's taxing authority, the preservation of the tribe's authority to tax commerce on the reservation, and the right to build an economy based on business activity on the reservation.

I had never appeared before the U.S. Supreme Court and became increasingly tense about the coming challenge. Since I was traveling from Seattle to the East Coast, I left a few days early to visit relatives in New York. There misfortune struck. I fell ill with some kind of virus. Three days before my scheduled appearance, I was lying in bed with a raging fever and a painful sore throat. But I was determined to argue the case. I did everything I could to get over my illness. But when I had to leave for Washington, D.C., I was still sick; I still had a fever and my voice was racked by hoarseness.

The case was argued in December of 1972. Perhaps because of my raging fever, I remember very little of my argument. Robert Pirtle and I argued that the state had no more right to tax revenue from cigarette sales on the Colville reservation than it did to tax cigarette purchases in Idaho. The justices did not ask me any questions, and I was relieved to sit down. The decision, announced in 1973 was a sweeping victory. The Court, in a *per curiam* opinion (without a full written opinion, thus treating the issue as obvious), reversed the holding of the Washington Supreme Court and sent it back to that court with instructions to read the Supreme Court's decisions in Indian tax cases affirming tribal immunity from state taxes.[4] It was a clear-cut victory for Indians, but it held for only seven years. The decision was substantially gutted when the state of Washington adopted a new strategy.

Following the *Tonasket v. Washington* case, the Colville Tribe imposed a tribal tax on cigarette sales, which was a good deal lower than the state tax. The aim was to create a stream of revenue for tribal government and to show a direct tribal governmental interest in preserving the immunity from state tax. The state of Washington, guided by the Washington tribes' perennial antagonist, Attorney General Slade Gorton, was unwilling to abide by the *Tonasket* decision. It changed tack and claimed that even though it did not have the legal right to tax all sales in Indian smoke shops, it could tax sales to non-Indians. The state government also insisted it had the right to tax house trailers and automobiles owned by Indians on the reservation. The dispute ended up in litigation again, and again it went to the U.S. Supreme Court.

This time the case was argued by Steve Anderson, one of the partners in our firm. Steve was a gifted lawyer, but despite his best efforts the result was not a happy one. The Court ruled that while the state could not directly tax Indian merchants, it could tax non-Indians purchasing cigarettes on the reservation. To enforce that power, it suggested that the state could require smoke-shop operators to keep records of non-Indian purchases, and the state could perhaps also intercept deliveries to the reservation. The Court did, however, deny the state any authority to tax Indian-owned vehicles and house trailers on the reservation. A mixed result.[5]

Meanwhile, a very different sort of conflict with the state of Washington arose. In 1971, a Colville tribal member and his wife, the Antoines, were cited for hunting deer during a closed season. They were hunting on the former "north half" of the reservation, a huge area that had been ceded to the United States under an agreement that specifically reserved hunting and fishing rights to the Indians. The agreement was ratified by Congress in 1891, and the Colvilles traditionally hunted and fished there without concern. After the Antoines were convicted in state court, the tribe took up their appeal. In the Washington Supreme Court, the state argued that Congress had no right to infringe on the state's police power, especially since the state had not been a party to the agreement. This kind of reasoning was typical for the state of Washington under Attorney General Gorton. (It would be offered again in the fishing rights cases of the early 1970s and died only after the U.S. Supreme Court affirmed the Boldt decision in 1979.) The position taken by the state in *Antoine v. Washington* was a states' rights position reminiscent of the obduracy of the southern states in the 1960s and 1970s.

The Washington Supreme Court, not surprisingly, upheld the conviction, and the Colville Tribe directed us to try to carry the appeal to the U.S. Supreme Court. Mason Morisset, one of our firm's partners, wrote the petition asking the Court to grant certiorari, and the Court agreed to hear the case. Morisset argued the case, and the decision, announced in 1975, was a sweeping rejection of the state's claims. The Court upheld the Colville Tribe's rights under the 1891 executive agreement to hunt and fish on the "north half" free of state regulation.[6]

Besides resisting efforts of the state to collect taxes from tribal members and defending Colvilles who were arrested for hunting and fishing under federally reserved rights, the Colvilles were concerned with the impacts that hydroelectric dams on the Columbia River were having on tribal lands. The Indian people of the Colville reservation had paid a heavy price for the construction of two massive dams on the Columbia, the Grand Coulee and Chief Joseph. Grand Coulee was built by the Bureau of Reclamation as a multipurpose dam for electric power generation and irrigation and was completed in 1941. Twenty-five years later, the U.S. Army Corps of Engineers built Chief Joseph Dam downstream from Grand Coulee. More than twenty thousand acres of Indian lands were submerged or made unusable with the construction of Grand Coulee. The dam created a huge reservoir, Lake Roosevelt, and substantially destroyed the spawning grounds of Columbia River salmon, which had been a food and cultural support of the Indians of the reservation. Chief Joseph Dam had flooded even more lands and raised yet another barrier to migrating salmon.

In 1981, the Army Corps of Engineers proposed raising Chief Joseph by ten feet to increase its generating capacity. The Colvilles asked me to assist the council in negotiating mitigation measures to protect Indian lands and gravesites and to obtain compensation for lands that would be flooded. Dealing with the Army Corps of Engineers was very different than dealing with the state of Washington. They seemed much more sensitive to the burdens they were imposing on the tribe. Perhaps their manner reflected the changing public opinion about big dams in the West. After extended negotiations, the corps agreed to mitigate impacts of the project by replacing wildlife habitat and taking measures to preserve archeological resources. Studies had shown that the area flooded by the dam had been inhabited by Native peoples for more than six thousand years, and the Army Corps was required to work with the tribe and archeologists to ensure that the area was given respectful and appropriate care. A compensation sum was also agreed on.

One issue was not resolved to the tribe's satisfaction. The corps had acquired tribal lands for its project, but had then leased 748 acres of these lands to Washington for a state park, which in turn leased some of the land to a local golf club for a golf course. The tribe was incensed that tribal land ended up as state lands under state jurisdiction, some of which would now be a private golf course. The Army Corps was unyielding, and the transaction stood. The only consolation for the tribe was that it had the right to require fishing permits from park users fishing in the reservoir. The Colvilles may also have taken perverse satisfaction that park users were warned of the danger of rattlesnakes.

At about the same time, in the early 1980s, the Bureau of Reclamation was completing the activation of a third powerhouse at Grand Coulee, which would impose new burdens on the Colville Tribe. Again I worked with tribal officials to negotiate mitigation measures. The tribe also had a claim pending against the United States for a share of the revenues generated by Grand Coulee Dam based on the tribe's claim of ownership of the Columbia River bed on which the dam was built. That claim was being pursued by a Washington, D.C., law firm that specialized in Indian claims against the United States. The tribe ultimately won a very large settlement consisting of a lump sum and a continuing share of power revenues. This no doubt brought some satisfaction, but the Colvilles never forgot that part of their heritage was destroyed by the Grand Coulee Dam, nor did they forget the paltry amounts they were paid for their lands—which they could not remedy through the courts because such recourse was limited by Congress.[7] These two cases not only give some idea of the work of a tribal attorney. They show how Indian lands and waters are still usurped for projects that benefit the non-Indian economy.

Our firm's work with the Colvilles required that we become knowledgeable about a body of law highly important in the western states: water rights. Water rights are an extremely sensitive issue for the tribes of the arid lands of the West. The Colvilles feel strongly about their water and they became embroiled in a lengthy water rights dispute with a non-Indian landowner on the reservation named Boyd Walton. The case involved the question of whether a non-Indian who buys land from an Indian on a reservation also gets an Indian water right as part of the land ownership. And if he does, how does the law apportion the quantity of water he is entitled to? For several years, I worked on this case with a government attorney, a noted specialist in Indian water rights, Bill Veeder.

Indian water rights are derived from a 1908 U.S. Supreme Court case, *U.S. v. Winters*.[8] In that case, the court ruled that a tribe whose lands abut a watercourse is entitled to priority in present or future use of that water over downstream non-Indians. The rationale was that in setting aside lands for the Indians, the right to use water was part of the reservation's reserved rights, otherwise the Indians could not farm or ranch arid reservation lands—which would defeat the government's purpose in establishing the reservation. The quantity of water reserved to Indians is the amount that a tribe can use to irrigate its practically irrigable land. The decision also held the date of the tribe's priority to be the date when the reservation was established. Since most farms, ranches, and cities came after the reservations were established, that rule of priority gives tribes superior rights to water. These "*Winters* rights" loom like a cloud over downstream non-Indian water users in the West, since their water can be cut off whenever a tribe decides to use its water. Because the tribes' rights do not lapse with nonuse or the passage of time, *Winters* rights are very valuable. Are they transferable to a non-Indian?

Boyd Walton owned and operated a dairy farm on the Colville reservation. He had purchased the land from an Indian allottee and had constructed a dam on a small stream to create a pond for his cattle. He claimed that he had acquired *Winters* rights that belonged to the Indian who sold him the land. The conflict arose because the tribe had planted Lahontan trout in the lake that the stream fed. The unrestricted flow of this small creek, claimed the tribe, was needed to sustain the fish. The tribe rejected Walton's water rights claim that he had acquired *Winters* rights when he purchased his land.

The Colvilles asked that Bill Veeder, a Justice Department water rights attorney, be assigned to the case. Veeder was no ordinary mortal. He had established himself nationally as a ferocious advocate of Indian water rights and had become revered by the tribes. Indeed, his mastery of water rights law and litigation was awesome. Veeder filed suit against Walton in federal court in the name of the Colville Tribe, basically alleging that Indian water rights could not be acquired through land purchase. I was co-counsel. I learned a good deal about water law and hydrology from Veeder, but early on I saw he would brook no dissent concerning how the case should be handled, and that did not bode well for our working relationship.

We finally had a head-on conflict over a simple procedural issue. The tribe had been served with interrogatories by Walton's attorney, written questions to be answered under oath. Veeder was adamant; we would not answer these questions, since it might reveal our strategy. There are ways to object that are permissible under court rules, and there are ways to couch your answers so as to avoid disclosing legal strategies. But Veeder wanted to go further and stonewall all factual inquiries. When my remonstrances met with complete rejection, I concluded that it was not wise for me to continue as co-counsel. I withdrew from the case and Veeder then ran the case as he saw fit.

The litigation, which began in 1977, went on until 1989, when the Ninth Circuit Court of Appeals ruled that Walton did indeed acquire Indian water rights, but remanded the case for additional factual inquiries.[9] One lasting result of this litigation is that in Indian water law, the water rights of a non-Indian who purchases land from an Indian are now known as *Walton* rights.

Throughout my work with the Colvilles there were two members of the tribe whom I came to know well, Mel Tonasket and Lucy Covington. Mel was a young man when I first met him, but he was already showing the signs of leadership that would make him a valuable asset to the Colvilles and to Indians nationally. He is soft-spoken, but can deliver an oratorical wallop when the occasion demands it. Mel has a first-rate mind and an instinctive grasp of politics, tribal and national. He eventually was elected chairman of the Colville Business Council and, later, president of the National Congress of American Indians. He was one of the national Indian figures the Colvilles produced. The other was, of course, Lucy Covington.

I have already described Lucy's role in stopping the termination of the Colville Tribe, but I want to add a few personal notes. Lucy was a very dignified and formal woman, and it was not easy to establish a personal relationship with her. She was in her sixties when we first met, and her appearance was striking. She was a large woman who wore her hair in a long braid. Whenever I saw Lucy, she was bedecked with Indian jewelry—heavy silver and turquoise necklaces and bracelets. As I spent many hours with her during my work with the tribe, the formality with which we treated each other gradually dropped away and we became comfortable in each other's company.

Once I offered to fly her from Seattle to Spokane, and I was pleased when she accepted. I drove her to the field where my rental airplane was kept, and we walked out to the plane. There was only one entry, a large door on the right side. To get in, you had to step up onto the wing and then lower yourself into the seat. Since there was only the single door, the pilot had to enter and seat himself before the passenger did. I was a little concerned about Lucy's ability to get up on the wing. But she had gumption; all she asked for was a hand up. At one point, she clearly needed some help, and it was a measure of our comfort with one another that, without a word, I reached over to help her and she let me. Flying from Seattle to Spokane meant flying across the Cascade Mountains and then over the fields and hills of eastern Washington. I had a chart on my knee and was studying the landmarks, but I needn't have bothered. Lucy knew the terrain like the back of her hand and told me exactly where we were.

In 1980, her health began to deteriorate with a lung disease. At her request, I went to her home and drew up her will. Then I sadly attended her funeral in 1982. There was a traditional ceremony and an Indian burial. It was fitting. She had almost single-handedly brought the Colville Tribe back from the brink of extinction. Lucy Covington should take her place in the pantheon of Indian heroes.

SEVENTEEN

The Northern Cheyennes
Fight Strip-Mining

IN 1973, I RECEIVED A PHONE CALL FROM A YOUNG INDIAN NAMED George Crossland. George was an Osage from Oklahoma whom I had met in 1971 when he was a student at the University of Chicago Law School. I had been in Chicago for a class reunion, and I stopped at the school to watch a moot court argument. George was one of the student lawyers and he was impressive. Afterward, I introduced myself and we talked. I wound up inviting him to contact our firm if he ever was interested in practicing Indian law. He didn't call, and I lost track of him until he called two years later.

George told me he had been on the Northern Cheyenne Indian Reservation in Montana and they were facing serious legal problems. He thought our firm could help. Would we be interested? When I said yes, he told me he would have the tribal president, Allan Rowland, call me, and the next night I was talking to Rowland. Rowland explained that the tribe had signed coal exploration permits and mining leases with several companies, only learning later how destructive a mining operation would be on their reservation. The tribe wanted to find a way to cancel the leases and put an end to the threat. They had a local attorney, but he had supported the leasing. The tribe wanted new legal counsel. "George tells me your firm is the best Indian law firm in the country," Rowland said, "and we need the best." I was flattered by George's endorsement and arranged to meet with the tribal council.

The Northern Cheyenne reservation is about a hundred miles east of Billings, in eastern Montana. It's not large as western reservations go, about 440,000 acres consisting of low rolling hills, mainly used for cattle grazing. There are three towns on the reservation: the principal town and home of the tribal government offices is Lame Deer; the others are Busby and Ashland, on the reservation's eastern border. When I visited the reservation, the population was more than 90 percent Indian, mainly Northern Cheyenne. The tribe had about three thousand members—living in poverty, but proud.

The Northern Cheyennes were a warrior people; they and the Sioux defeated Custer at the Battle of Little Big Horn in 1876. The Custer battlefield site lies only twenty miles west of Busby. After Custer was defeated, the U.S. government banished the Northern Cheyennes to Indian Territory (which would become Oklahoma). Alone among all the other tribes banished to Indian Territory, the Northern Cheyennes fought their way back to their historic home in Montana. The Cheyennes have never forgotten their past and they remain a tough people, capable of withstanding great hardship and never yielding to an opponent.

In the 1960s, the Northern Cheyenne reservation became the focus of intense corporate interest. Just beneath the rolling hills lay immense coal deposits—billions of tons of high-quality, low-sulfur coal. That these deposits were close to the surface made them even more valuable. They could be strip-mined, removing just the top layer of earth to expose the coal beneath for removal by giant shovels. The U.S. Geological Survey had described these deposits in the 1920s, and they were well-known to the coal-mining industry. But for forty years this coal had been too distant from the power plants of the Midwest to make mining it worthwhile. By the 1960s, however, environmental legislation forcing power plants to install expensive sulfur-removing scrubbers improved the economic equation. Montana coal began to look increasingly attractive.

The coal industry approached the Bureau of Indian Affairs and proposed that the reservation be opened to bidding for coal leases. BIA officials were excited. Here was an opportunity for an impoverished tribe to acquire wealth. So BIA officers came to the Northern Cheyenne Tribal Council and told them of this wonderful opportunity. The tribe gave its consent for the process to go ahead. Only later did the tribe begin to realize the grave consequences of this action. That is when we were called in.

When I agreed to go to the reservation to discuss the coal-leasing problem, I decided to take Steve Chestnut with me, the newest member of the firm. Though he had no background in Indian law, he had a master's degree in civil engineering as well being a lawyer, and I thought his engineering background would be useful. We traveled to Lame Deer and entered the council chambers, where we met the fifteen members of the council, all of whom had been eagerly awaiting the meeting.

When we walked into the room, the tension was almost palpable. The council members were seated around a table, and Allan Rowland, the tribal president, greeted us. He was a tall man who walked with a cane, and it was clear that he commanded respect. His words were clipped and to the point, and he wasted little time on niceties as he introduced us to the council, which included John Woodenlegs, Ted Rising Sun, Turkey Shoulderblades, Kenneth Beartusk, Dennis Limberhand, and Burt Medicine Bull.

Only Allan Rowland spoke; the others remained silent. Allan told us that the reservation was threatened by massive strip mining and that the council wanted us to stop it. He then turned to one of the councilmen and said, "Ed Dahle will explain it." With that, Edwin Dahle rose and launched into our first introduction to the complex background of coal leasing on the Northern Cheyenne Reservation. The BIA had persuaded the council to approve coal-exploration permits with attached mining lease options, covering vast acreage on the reservation. The council had not fully appreciated that these exploration permits were convertible to leases. Once the permit was signed, the permit holder held an irrevocable right to a lease and to begin mining. The permits had been acquired by what was supposed to be public bidding. Those bidders offering the highest fee for the right to explore, called a "bonus payment," won the permits. The BIA had conducted these coal sales in 1966, 1969, and 1971. They resulted in exploration permits covering 324,000 acres, about 73 percent of the reservation, all binding the tribe to subsequent mining leases.

The bidder with rights to the largest area of Cheyenne land was the Peabody Coal Company, one of the largest coal companies in the world. Peabody invited the tribal council to visit their headquarters in

St. Louis, where they showed films of lands that had been strip-mined in Kentucky and had been "reclaimed." The company's plan backfired. Seeing these films drove home the profound devastation that strip-mining would bring to the tribe's homeland, and the Cheyennes returned to Montana deeply upset. George Crossland met with them and pointed out that these coal permits covered more than half of the reservation. The mining operations would destroy Cheyenne life as they knew it. The council decided to act.

At the conclusion of Ed Dahle's presentation, I was invited to respond. I told the council of our firm's background, our commitment to defending tribal sovereignty, and our policy of never representing a client who wanted to do business with a tribe—a policy intended to avoid the firm being in conflict with an Indian tribe. I told them of our commitment to seeking justice for the Indian people. The coal leases at Northern Cheyenne must be set aside, I said, and we would work tirelessly to accomplish that. I introduced Steve, and he spoke briefly. At that point, he had only been with our firm a few months and had never been on an Indian reservation. He was trying to grasp the overwhelming and unusual legal work that we would be taking on. I had no worries about him. Something about him conveyed the intelligence and the enormous concentration he would bring to the case.

We were asked to step out of the room while the council took a vote. After a few minutes the chamber door opened and we were ushered back in. Allan Rowland told us the council had voted to retain us. His parting words were, "We sure need your help."

Ed Dahle offered to put us up at his house and we gratefully accepted. Ed and his wife, Donna, lived in a cozy ranch house near Busby, some fifteen miles from Lame Deer. Ed was a cowboy and ran cattle on his ranch. Over the years, we came to know the entire Dahle family and stayed with them many times. While Ed did not appear Indian at all, he was in fact part Northern Cheyenne and an enrolled member of the tribe, meeting the one-quarter blood requirement. Although Ed had only a high-school education, he had high intelligence. This, coupled with a curious and analytical mind, made him the ideal tribal person to lead the fight against the coal leases.

We asked the tribal council to direct the BIA to release to us all the documents pertaining to the coal transactions, and a week or so later several boxes of documents arrived at our Seattle office. Steve Chestnut soon became the master of the documentary history. What we learned was shocking.

One of the first exploration permits had been issued to Peabody Coal Company in 1966, during the first sale. It authorized them to explore and then mine on 94,000 acres of the reservation. Attached to the permit was the lease. It stipulated that the company would pay the tribe a royalty of 17.5 cents a ton, or 15 cents a ton if the coal was processed on the reservation. At the same time, we learned, U.S. government coal leases on federal lands provided for a royalty of 12.5 percent of the value of the coal removed, a return far higher than 17.5 cents a ton. Not only was this disturbing, but we found that the state of Montana imposed a "severance tax" of 30 percent of the value of the coal, or $1.80 a ton. The Cheyennes who owned the coal would receive far less than the state. On its face, the return to the Northern Cheyennes appeared grossly unjust.

A second coal sale followed in 1969. In that sale, Peabody acquired a permit for an additional 55,000 acres, giving them the right to mine a total of 149,000 acres of the reservation, all on the terms of the first permit. Some of the other permit holders had already exercised their options to convert to leases, and there was nothing stopping them from promptly commencing mining operations. The amounts paid by the permit holders for their sweeping right to mine were paltry compared to the rights they were acquiring.

The entire process of granting mining rights on Indian reservations is governed by federal regulations. As we plunged deeper into the documentary record, it became apparent that all of the permits had been issued in flagrant violation of those regulations. We compiled a list of twenty-two major violations, later expanded to thirty-six. I went to Washington, D.C., and met with attorneys of the U.S. Interior Department, telling them that, in the face of these illegalities, the tribe intended to ask the Interior secretary to void the permits and leases. Associate Solicitor for Indian Affairs Reid Chambers and his boss, Kent Frizzell, looked grave. The interests of powerful companies and hundreds of millions of dollars were at stake, and this dispute also had national implications. Coal was essential for power generation in the Midwest and the eastern United States, and the Northern Cheyenne coal deposits figured prominently in plans for the future. Chambers asked that we submit our petition for corrective action as soon as possible, because the Interior Department was under pressure from the permit holders to resolve this crisis swiftly.

When I got back to the office in Seattle, I met with my partners and outlined the problem. I had promised a quick turnaround, and we needed to immediately begin our legal attack on the leases and permits. Steve Chestnut, Barry Ernstoff, Mason Morisset, and myself set to work on the petition. After a preliminary analysis of the issues, we parceled out the topics, which included regulatory violations, breach of trust responsibility, violation of the corporate charter limitations on duration of leases, and statutory violations. Steve took on the huge task of document analysis and identifying the violations of federal regulations. One by one we finished our assigned sections of the petition, except for Steve. He would not be hurried as he prepared what would become one of the most damning documents of Indian administrative malfeasance ever compiled. When it was finished, the petition and the supporting documentary evidence were presented in two volumes totaling 630 pages.

The tribe had repeatedly asked whether we intended to take this to court. After intense internal discussion, we reached a decision that we would not. Such a lawsuit would enable the coal companies to intervene and litigate their rights against the tribe. By bringing a lawsuit, the tribe would likely lose its sovereign immunity and could become subject to a court judgment. Instead, we adopted the position that this matter was strictly between the tribe and its trustee, the secretary of the Interior. We were confident that once our petition was reviewed by the government's attorneys, there was no way they could defend the legitimacy of these transactions. They would have no alternative but to declare them void. Perhaps this was an act of chutzpah, throwing our accusations in the face of the department and expecting them to acknowledge their wrongdoing—but that is precisely what we planned to do. We were so confident because the naked illegalities we had unearthed were blatant. Some of the more serious ones follow.

Federal regulations barred leases of Indian lands larger than 2,560 acres, unless the permit holder needed larger acreage to establish a thermal electric power plant or other industrial facility and the project was shown to be in the best interests of the tribe. No permit holders had met this requirement, and this language had been illegally deleted from the permits and ignored by the Bureau of Indian Affairs.

Federal regulations required that mining companies post bonds sufficient for environmental remediation. But the bond amounts set by the BIA for the Northern Cheyenne permits bore no relation to real-world land reclamation costs: $1.87 an acre for lands under lease, and from 5¢ to 83¢ an acre for lands under exploration permit. Actual reclamation costs could run into thousands of dollars per acre.

The tribe's corporate charter limited all leases on the reservation to five years. The coal leases had no time limits.

Federal regulations required that bidders at federal coal sales be bona fide mining companies. Speculators were prohibited from bidding. Yet at the third coal sale in 1971, four of the eight successful bidders were in fact speculators. One paid $75,000 for his permit and promptly sold it to the Chevron Company for $1.2 million, retaining an overriding royalty of 9¢ a ton on the coal mined. The speculator's royalty was more than half the amount the tribe would receive (17.5¢ per ton). The gross inequity of the tribe's royalty compared to those of the permit holders and even to Montana's severance tax was, we claimed, a fundamental failure of federal trust responsibility to the tribe.

In 1969 the secretary of Interior had promulgated regulations to ensure that no surface mining on Indian reservations could take place until *after* federal studies had established control standards that would attach to the permits and leases. These studies were designated "technical examinations," and they were supposed to investigate a broad range of physical, geologic, and hydrologic factors, as well as identifying cultural, recreational, scenic, and historic values that might be affected— something like environmental impact statements. It turned out that the BIA had taken no steps whatever to implement this regulation; the requirement was simply ignored. No technical examinations were performed prior to the issuance of the Northern Cheyenne permits.

This violation was exposed when, in 1972, a year prior to our petition, the General Accounting Office had issued a report highlighting the bureau's failure to perform the required technical examination. To put a gloss of legality on the illegal permits, the BIA papered its files with a document that it titled "Technical Assessment." The technical assessment had been prepared by the new BIA superintendent at the Lame Deer office, Dr. Alonzo Spang. Spang, a highly intelligent and conscientious officer, reported that the consequences of the proposed strip-mining on the Northern Cheyenne reservation would include "destruction of Cheyenne culture," "the Cheyenne becoming a minority in their own homeland," and "pollution of all sorts, human, cultural, air, sound, noise, etc." Despite this devastating report, the BIA nevertheless recommended that the permits and leases should go forward.

All in all, the thirty-six serious violations we found amounted to a massive breach of trust by the Interior Department. What we submitted would be far more than a petition; it was a detailed investigation into the conduct of BIA officials and some of America's largest corporations. During the months we were preparing the petition, the pressure on us mounted. Our client was impatient to see the results of our work, and the coal companies and permit holders were clamoring for the Interior Department to end the cloud of uncertainty that hung over these transactions. The companies and permit holders knew only that the Northern Cheyennes had disavowed the transactions and were preparing a petition to the Interior secretary, but they knew nothing of the specifics and were demanding to know exactly what the tribe would say.

When we completed the petition and printed hundreds of copies in late December of 1973, we told Allan Rowland we were ready to deliver the long-awaited document to the tribal council. We arrived at Lame Deer with a copy for each council member, but we had decided to keep the contents out of the public eye. We handed the documents around, telling the council that the information was to be held in strictest confidence, not to be circulated—we warned that the coal companies would love to get their hands on this petition. We also wrote to the Interior Department's solicitor's office, telling them the petition was ready but that we insisted on confidentiality—the petition was not to be shared with the coal companies. This matter was strictly between the tribe and the Interior secretary. Reid Chambers accepted this condition and assured us that he would not release copies to the permit holders. He did tell us, though, that he thought it necessary to inform the permit holders that the department was investigating complaints of irregularities. The confidentiality wall held firm. Council members accepted their responsibility gravely, and the government kept its word not to release the petition to outsiders.

That Reid Chambers was the principal government lawyer on the case was a stroke of good fortune for the Cheyennes. Chambers had a law degree from Harvard Law School, where his academic achievement earned him a place on the law review. He had then gone on to receive a degree in economics at Oxford, still later joining the faculty at the UCLA School of Law. While there he became attracted to Indian causes and worked on cases for the Native American Rights Fund, a nonprofit Indian advocacy organization. He had just become associate solicitor for Indian affairs, the government's top lawyer on Indian issues, in 1973. Because of his background with NARF, Chambers had no difficulty in grasping the legal implications of the government's trust responsibility to tribes.

After we sent our two-volume petition to Washington, D.C., we waited for the Interior Department's response. It came in the form of a call from Kent Frizzell, the chief legal advisor to the department. The petition had been read, and he invited us to Washington for a meeting with him, Chambers, and Secretary of the Interior Rogers C. B. Morton. Representatives of the coal companies had been insisting on a meeting with the Northern Cheyenne attorneys and the Interior Department, he told us, and they would be there too.

Steve Chestnut and I made the trip. I was not going to be intimidated by the coming confrontation with power. As Steve and I got off the elevator at the sixth floor, we were met by Frizzell himself. He greeted us and walked us down the corridor. We were ushered into outer offices and then made our way into the Interior secretary's office. It was almost breathtaking: a huge room, with Native American art and artifacts among the many decorations. There was an arrangement of plush armchairs facing each other across an elegant coffee table. Rogers C. B. Morton, a very tall and impressive looking man, came over and greeted us affably. Morton was from a wealthy Kentucky family, had served several terms as a congressman from Maryland, and had been chairman of the Republican National Committee. President Nixon had tapped him to be secretary of the Interior in 1971. Now we were sitting in his office along with Kent Frizzell and Reid Chambers for a showdown over the Northern Cheyenne petition. The secretary cut to the chase.

"Is there any way we can settle this?" It seemed that Morton hoped the Cheyenne grievance could be cured with money.

I told him bluntly, "Mr. Secretary, the Cheyennes have made their decision and it is final. They totally reject any strip-mining on their reservation. So the issue is not one of money. The Cheyennes are not willing to allow any mining, no matter what the coal companies might offer. They do not want the deal to go forward on any terms. No, as we made clear in our petition, Mr. Secretary, we want you to cancel all the permits and leases on the grounds that they were the product of illegal actions taken in violation of federal regulations. We are confident you have the legal authority to do that, and we have cited the applicable court decisions in the petition. We have no authority from our client to take any other position."

Morton sighed heavily and Frizzell made one last pitch, pointing out the potential wealth that would come to the Northern Cheyenne Tribe. I again said we had no authority from the tribe other than to seek the cancellation of the permits. Frizzell gave up and said, "Gentlemen, I think you better tell that to the people who are waiting for us down the hall."

With that we bade farewell to Secretary Morton and walked with Frizzell and Chambers to a large meeting room where there were fifteen or twenty people assembled to hear us. They included not only the lawyers and executives of the coal companies, but also staff members of the House and Senate Indian Affairs committees. After Frizzell introduced us, he told the assemblage that they would probably be disappointed by what we had to say, and then he turned the meeting over to us. Addressing what seemed a hostile audience, I spelled out in clear and emphatic terms what we had found in our examination of the permit transactions and what the tribe had decided—to cancel the leases.

One by one, industry people asked us in various ways whether it was simply a matter of the Indians wanting a better deal. The company spokesmen told us they had acted in good faith, relying on the Bureau of Indian Affairs, which had led them to believe this was what the Cheyennes wanted. The practices they followed were standard in the industry. In other words, this was the way they always did coal business. After about a half hour of this, I said if they thought this was simply a negotiating ploy by the Cheyennes, they were wrong. There would be no negotiation, the deal was dead. The meeting ended.

Then we waited for the Interior secretary to reach a decision on the tribe's petition. It took five months and finally came on June 4, 1974. In a lengthy written ruling, Secretary Morton said he recognized his responsibility to preserve the environment and cultural interests of the tribe and would not subvert those interests to anyone's desire to strip-mine the reservation. Therefore, he said, he would not permit any strip-mining unless it was approved and supported by the tribe. But he stopped short of declaring an outright cancellation of the permits and leases, perhaps because that would have exposed the government to legal liability. The transactions were thus frozen, unable to go forward—in limbo.

Soon after, the coal companies began to call us. They wanted to explore the possibility of a deal. The prize was too rich to surrender easily, and each company hoped they might put together such an attractive proposition that the tribe could not afford to refuse them. Clearly, they didn't believe us when we said the tribe was willing to walk away from riches that would make every man, woman, and child in the tribe wealthy forever. The companies clung to the belief, fostered no doubt by their own values and business experience, that every man has his price—that the tribe was simply maneuvering to get the highest royalty deal in the industry.

The first contact came from the largest coal company in the world and the holder of the largest acreage on the reservation, Peabody Coal Company. Ed Phelps, the company president, wanted to meet with us and the tribal council. The council agreed and sent a delegation to Seattle. When we met with the Cheyennes the day before Phelps arrived, they made it clear that they had no intention of changing their position—they just wanted to hear what Peabody had to say. Actually, I believe the Cheyennes wanted to humble their enemy and see him grovel.

When the Peabody delegation arrived in our office, the atmosphere was strained. We sat around the conference table and introduced the Cheyenne council members: Allan Rowland, Ed Dahle, Dennis Limberhand, and Kenneth Beartusk. Ed Phelps, the Peabody president, had an international reputation in the coal industry and exuded confidence and friendliness. But this did not entirely conceal his uneasiness and uncertainty, discomfort I had seen many times when non-Indian businessmen talked business with Indians; the non-Indians weren't sure how to act because they were dealing with an unknown and, in this case, an openly hostile group. But Phelps went forward and tried to make the case that Peabody was the industry expert in reclamation of lands. Apparently, he had decided that this was the point on which the Cheyennes were likely to be the most receptive. It didn't work. The Cheyennes said almost nothing. The meeting ended awkwardly, without the usual formulaic phrases, and the two parties went their separate ways.

The other coal companies called, and all but one dropped their efforts to reach an accommodation. But Northern States Power Company, a Minnesota operation that had acquired a permit through a firm of Billings, Montana, coal speculators, said they wanted a meeting. Representatives of the tribal council again came to Seattle, this time to hear from Northern States Power.

The meeting turned out to be volatile because of one Northern Cheyenne councilman, Ray Spang. Ray was the youngest member of the council and had by far the most education. He had been to Harvard and Berkeley, though he never got a degree from either school. Ray was an angry young Indian and had been associated with the militant American Indian Movement, or AIM. He carried himself with a certain air of belligerence. I was actually surprised when he was elected to the council. He had been a draft resister during the Vietnam War, and the Northern Cheyennes are very patriotic and hold military service in high esteem. When I asked some older Cheyennes how the people felt about Ray's refusal to serve, the answer was enlightening. Ray didn't refuse to serve because of fear, they said, just the opposite. He had the courage of his beliefs and stood up for them. The Cheyennes admired that. But Ray had a serious drinking problem and everyone knew it. I had seen him show up for meetings drunk and I felt badly for him. When I heard he was coming to Seattle for the meeting with Northern States Power, I was worried.

On the day of the meeting, the Cheyenne delegation assembled in our office to wait for the company representatives. Ray didn't show up, and no one seemed to know where he was or whether he would come. The Northern States group arrived: three men, including the principal vice president in charge of mining and the company's attorney, Bruce Ennis. Ray was still not there, so the meeting began.

The atmosphere was similar to the meeting with Peabody: chilly. It was particularly tense because Ennis spoke for the company. The Cheyennes regarded him with particular hostility because he had been one of the bidders at the coal sale, ostensibly as a mining company, while actually acting as the agent for Northern States Power. Ennis was in the middle of his presentation when the door to the office opened and in walked Ray Spang, drunk. The coal company people greeted him cordially, but he didn't respond. He took his seat at the conference table and glared at them sullenly, his eyes red-rimmed.

Ennis was going on about how sensitive Northern States Power was to the cultural values of the Cheyenne Tribe, when I noticed that Ray had stretched a rubber band between his thumb and forefinger. Then he took a paper clip, bent it, and placed it against the rubber band to make a slingshot. Ennis also noticed, but tried to ignore Ray and kept talking. Then Ray pulled the paper clip back, stretching the rubber band, and raised his hand to take aim at Ennis. Ennis began to blink and twitch in anticipation of the impact. But Ray didn't release the paper clip. He just kept brandishing his weapon while Ennis grew more and more flustered. Finally, one of the Cheyenne councilmen told Ray to put the slingshot down, and he did. But Ray wasn't through. He leered at Ennis and said, "You know where you belong? You belong in prison."

The meeting didn't last long after that, and the coal companies gave up trying to get the Northern Cheyennes to make a deal. But Ray Spang's invective should have told any listener how angry the tribe was. After the Cheyennes had read our report on the machinations of the coal companies and the Bureau of Indian Affairs, they recognized the disdain others had for them and they were insulted that white men had tried to exploit them so blatantly. I had tried to convey this in my conversations with the companies. When we met with Ed Phelps, the president of Peabody, I said to him, "Ed, if I were your attorney and you asked me what to do, I would tell you, 'Go to the tribe and tell them you're sorry,' and tear up the permits. And then say, 'We want nothing to do with that transaction.' The tribe would respect that and maybe someday, if they wanted to mine, they might want to make a deal with Peabody."

Phelps looked at me as if I were some kind of fool and told me the company couldn't do that. The permits were an extremely valuable corporate asset and no company officer could simply tear them up. They just didn't get it. The Indians and the companies lived in different worlds.

EIGHTEEN

The Northern Cheyennes
and the Hollowbreast Case

WHILE THE NORTHERN CHEYENNE TRIBE NO LONGER HAD TO FEAR coal mining resulting from the discredited exploration permits, a new threat appeared with the 1974 Ninth Circuit Court of Appeals decision in *Hollowbreast v. Northern Cheyenne Tribe.*[1] The case involved a strange combination of circumstances that could only happen in Indian country. The lands of the Northern Cheyenne reservation had remained in undivided tribal ownership until 1926, when Congress had allotted tribal lands to members in 160-acre parcels. But this Northern Cheyenne Allotment Act separated ownership of surface rights from the mineral rights belowground. The holders of the allotments, called allottees, were given only surface rights; the mineral rights were reserved for the tribe, *but for only fifty years.* After fifty years, or in 1976, the mineral rights would pass to the allottees.

The years passed, and there was no coal mining on the reservation. But the tribe was fully aware of the potential for mining. They wanted control of any mining to remain with the tribe, instead of being divided among several thousand allottees, at least a third of whom lived off-reservation and so had less interest in land preservation. Since the coal underground would become the property of the allottees in 1976, the tribe asked Congress to amend the 1926 act to make the tribe owner of all subsurface rights in perpetuity.

In 1969, Congress passed the amendment, but the Interior Department attorneys who wrote the legislation were uncertain of its constitutionality. If the 1926 act gave the allottees a vested ownership interest in the coal under their lands, then it was unconstitutional for Congress to take away that interest and give it to the tribe. The Interior lawyers came up with an unorthodox solution. Since no one could say with certainty whether the rights of the allottees under the 1926 law were vested and could not be taken from them, the 1969 amendment provided that the tribe would get perpetual ownership of the coal only if a court ruled that it was constitutional for Congress to give it to them. The amendment required that the tribe go to court and get a declaratory judgment on the constitutionality of the law. I doubt this had any precedent in American history, that is, Congress taking legislative action, but conditioning its effectiveness on whether a court would later declare they had the right to take the action.

The Northern Cheyennes directed their local attorney to file suit, but also retained a Billings, Montana, law firm to represent them. The allottees also had attorneys: a private attorney, a federally funded Legal Services attorney, and Justice Department attorneys. This litigation had begun long before our firm was retained by the tribe and was going on at the same time we were working to set aside the permits. In the allottees' case, called *Hollowbreast v. Northern Cheyenne Tribe*, the federal District Court ruled in favor of the tribe, but the allottees appealed to the Ninth Circuit. In 1974, the Ninth Circuit overturned the District Court and ruled that Congress could not constitutionally extend the period of the tribe's ownership. The coal belonged to the individual allottees.

The *Hollowbreast* decision was a serious threat. If it stood, it would substantially undermine the victory the tribe had achieved in its petition to the secretary of the Interior. The extent of the coal beneath the allotted lands amounted to about 40 percent of the coal on the reservation. Coal companies, promoters, and speculators began approaching the Cheyennes who had allotments with attractive offers to buy the mining rights. In order for mining to be feasible, large tracts had to be assembled, and so a meeting of the allottees was called to organize for a sale of rights on large parcels of land. A sufficient number were persuaded, and an organization calling itself the Rosebud Society was formed. The Rosebud Society could negotiate a sale of all the coal lying beneath allotted lands, which would wreak havoc on the reservation. It was at this point that the tribe turned to us for help.

Coming into a case after a final decision has been made by a federal court of appeals is a bad time for any lawyer. What steps can you take? You can petition the court of appeals to grant a rehearing *en banc*, with the full membership of the court reviewing the decision made by three of its members. If that fails, the only hope is to try to get the U.S. Supreme Court to hear the case—a very difficult and usually futile undertaking. Still, we hadn't come this far in protecting Cheyenne lands to give up now.

We began the first step of asking the Ninth Circuit to grant a rehearing. This had to be a powerful presentation, since appellate courts rarely agree to review a decision by one of their own panels. Steve Chestnut, who had proved his mettle in the massive task of preparing our successful petition to the Interior Department, was given full responsibility for the litigation of *Hollowbreast*—a long shot. But there were few lawyers who could bring the intensity and stamina to case preparation that Chestnut did. He went to work with the full support of the firm. He thought it might be helpful if we could find out how the original 1926 allotment act came to be introduced. Barry Ernstoff was dispatched to Washington, D.C., to search the papers of Senator Thomas Walsh, the Montana senator who had written and sponsored the legislation, to see what he could find.

Ernstoff went through Walsh's extensive files at the Library of Congress, methodically searching dusty boxes crammed with old papers. He stumbled across the nugget that answered our prayers. He found the original petition of the Northern Cheyenne Tribe sent to Washington, D.C., in 1924, asking that tribal lands be allotted among the tribe's members. But the petition asked only that the surface lands to be allotted, with the subsurface coal remaining the *permanent* property of the tribe. Somehow, in the bill-drafting process, this condition was deleted. The original petition contained pages and pages of tribal members' signatures, most a sign or an X. This gave evidence of the allottees' original intention for the tribe to retain permanent ownership of subsurface rights. Steve Chestnut attached the original petition to our submission to the Ninth Circuit, and it became part of the record that we would later submit to the U.S. Supreme Court.

Our petition to the Ninth Circuit was prepared with all the legal research and skill Steve could muster, but we were denied. We turned to our last hope, the Supreme Court. Persuading the Court to interpret an act of Congress affecting only a single tribe called for more than just persuasive briefs. We needed the United States to join with us in asking the Court to take the case. But the Justice Department had represented the allottees in the lower court proceedings. So Steve's first task was to convince the solicitor general, the government's lawyer in Supreme Court proceedings, to at least stay neutral on the issue of whether the Court should hear the case. Steve somehow managed to do just that.

Then Steve had to persuade the solicitor's office of the Interior Department that the department should file a brief supporting our request for Supreme Court review. Fortunately, our dealings with the Interior secretary concerning the Northern Cheyenne coal leases and his decision on the petition had given the case unique status with the Interior Department. Still, Steve had to convince Kent Frizzell that the *Hollowbreast* case had far-reaching implications, affecting not only the private rights of the parties, but also important questions of law and public policy. Once again Chestnut was successful—Frizzell fully appreciated the importance of the issues involved, and the Interior Department filed a brief supporting our petition. Ultimate success for this phase came when the Court granted the tribe's petition. *Hollowbreast* would be decided by the Supreme Court of the United States.

Steve redoubled his intensive research into the legislative history of the 1926 act and the applicable case law. He was aided by a talented young summer law clerk from the University of Chicago Law School, Peter Birge. Steve labored tirelessly to write the most persuasive brief he could. Then we received the brief from the allottees' attorneys, and a response had to be written—all to the highest standards. Finally, there was oral argument before the Supreme Court. Steve was ready—nervous, but ready. Unfortunately, the Cheyennes didn't have the money to send a delegation to hear the argument, so Steve was alone when he went before the Court.

The case was argued March 29, 1976, and the Court made a ruling with uncharacteristic speed. Only five weeks later, on May 19, 1976, the decision came down: a unanimous nine-justice opinion upholding the tribe's case and ruling that the 1968 act giving the tribe permanent title to all subsurface minerals was constitutional.[2]

Steve Chestnut had accomplished the near impossible: taking a case that had been lost by other attorneys in the court of appeals, persuading the Supreme Court to hear the case, and then winning it. The consequences were huge. It was estimated that over two billion tons of coal would have been strip-mined if the case were lost—a devastating impact on the reservation. Now that threat was gone, and the Rosebud Society quietly disappeared.

Steve had come into our firm only three years earlier, and his achievements marked him as the leader on Northern Cheyenne cases. While the threat of mining under the original permits and leases had ended, the leases were not actually voided; they were only in a state of suspension. Something had to be done to free the reservation from the legal encumbrances these permits created.

Steve began discussions with the coal companies to explore ways to get the leases and permits cancelled. The companies were finally reconciled to having no hope of future mining on the reservation. But they believed they had legal rights, since the permits and leases had never been voided. At worst, the companies could make a claim for damages against the United States. But businessmen abhor litigation. They far prefer deals. And the companies had their eyes on other coal deposits under federal lands off the reservation. Maybe in exchange for canceling their rights on the reservation and releasing their claims against the government for damages, the companies could get coal leases on lands outside the reservation. Such an exchange would require an act of Congress. Further, Steve Chestnut and Ed Dahle told the companies that any arrangement would have to compensate the tribe for damages. There had been holes drilled and roads cut through tribal lands, and the tribe had incurred legal fees and expenses in challenging the permits and leases.

Again, Steve went to work. He helped draft the Northern Cheyenne Lease Cancellation Act and made sure it included a provision requiring the consent of the Northern Cheyenne Tribe and payment of all damages sustained by the tribe. Because getting access to federal coal was a valuable prize, the coal companies supported the bill. It was passed by Congress in 1980.[3] The legislation provided that if the companies and tribe did not reach agreements by the end of 1981, all company rights to funds deposited in escrow would terminate and the companies would have to bring any claims against the United States in the Court of Claims. Now the companies had to come to the tribe to negotiate.

They found the Cheyennes in an ungenerous mood. Deals were finally struck with three of the companies for financial compensation. One of the companies, Consolidation Coal Company, in lieu of a cash payment agreed to transfer title of a ranch it had on the reservation. The ranch consisted of seven thousand acres valued at $5 million. Another group of permit holders, the Norsworthy and Reger firm of Billings, Montana, and their principal, the Northern States Power Company—the group who had faced the wrath of Ray Spang—offered a settlement of approximately $300,000 and a share in some of their royalties. This was an unattractive offer on its face, but the Cheyennes were particularly incensed at this group because they had obtained leases for speculation, using straw men to do their bidding. So the tribe refused to deal with them, and they were left to sue the United States. The group sued for millions and lost, receiving only a nominal award of $400,000. The chief government witness against them, testifying that the tribe would never have given them any right to mine, was Steve Chestnut.

More than thirty years have passed since the Northern Cheyennes rejected coal mining on their reservation, and to this day there has been no mining there. This has meant foregoing millions of dollars in royalties and wages. The Cheyennes remain dirt poor, but they are proud. Their lands are undisturbed and their culture is intact. The wisdom of the tribe's decision can be seen in the unfortunate example of Peabody Coal's Black Mesa Mine on the Navajo and Hopi reservations.

In 2005, environmental groups successfully sued the power company that was burning the mine's coal, citing air pollution caused by the plant's sulfur dioxide emissions. When the power company elected to shut down its operations rather than install expensive scrubbers, Peabody closed down its mine. This left hundreds of Indians suddenly unemployed. The mine had been operating for thirty-five years, and the Navajo and Hopi tribes and their members had come to rely on the income—the royalties and the wages. Yet from the outset, the mine had been a source of controversy within the tribes. Many had opposed it. Now these Indians were pleased that the mining had come to an end.

But the operation had depleted and polluted underground aquifers and had irrevocably changed the land. A former Hopi tribal chairman said that the agreements made with Peabody had been unfair, and the mining destructive and wasteful. Rather than enriching the lives of all tribal members and contributing to a sustainable way of life, the coal had been used to light the casinos of Las Vegas and heat the hot tubs of Los Angeles. The benefits, he said, were not much and not worth the price.[4] The Northern Cheyennes, by choosing to forego the benefits of strip-mining, had kept their land and water undefiled—at the cost of continuing poverty.

NINETEEN

The Oliphant Case:
A Setback for Tribal
Government

OUR FIRM'S RECORD OF SUCCESS IN THE U.S. SUPREME COURT WAS extraordinary—victory after victory, with only one partial loss. But litigating Indian rights in the Supreme Court was a high-risk undertaking, often asking the Court to rule against local citizens or state governments on issues at the cutting edge of the law. The case of *Mark David Oliphant v. Suquamish Tribe* proved to be a turning point.

The Suquamish Indian Reservation lies just across Puget Sound from Seattle and is formally called the Port Madison Reservation. It was established under the treaties made with the United States in the mid-nineteenth century by Territorial Governor Isaac Stevens. The reservation is small, only about 7,300 acres, 63 percent of it owned by non-Indians—they comprise the overwhelming majority of the local population. When we got involved with the tribe, only fifty Suquamish members lived on the reservation, though other members lived in the area. But the tiny Suquamish Tribe had pride. Chief Seattle, the namesake for the city across the Sound, was a Suquamish, and he is buried on the reservation.

The white residents were scornful and irritated when the tribe began to exercise its governmental authority. In some cases they became openly hostile. It was another example of the Charlie Peterson principle: they want our names, but they have no use for us.

The tribe retained our firm to represent them, and Barry Ernstoff took responsibility for being their advisor. The tribe, though small, had tribal police officers and police cars. There was a tribal Law and Order Code and a tribal court. The Indian Civil Rights Act, a federal law enacted in 1968, applied to tribal court proceedings.[1] The law required Indian tribes to afford all persons the rights guaranteed under the Bill of Rights, including due process of law. Juries, however, were limited to six persons, and there was no requirement that nonmembers be allowed to sit on these juries. The maximum penalty allowed under the act was a fine of $500 or six months in jail (amended in 1986 to a fine of $5,000 or one year in jail, or both). Aggrieved parties had access to the federal courts by writ of habeas corpus. The Suquamish had experienced rowdy behavior and reckless driving on the reservation and had posted signs declaring that entry onto the reservation subjected all persons to the jurisdiction of the Suquamish tribal court. Arrested persons would be confined in the local county jail under a contract between the tribe and the county.

In August of 1973 the tribe was holding its annual Chief Seattle Days. It was a weekend celebration held on tribal land, with Indian drumming and songs, salmon barbecue, and handicraft sales. A number of Indian people had camped overnight on the tribal grounds. The tribe had asked the Kitsap County Sheriff's Department for assistance with policing the event, but the sheriff's office had refused. At about four o'clock in the morning, a fight broke out involving a local non-Indian youth, Mark David Oliphant. When tribal police tried to break up the fight, Oliphant fought with them. Tribal police arrested Oliphant and charged him with resisting arrest and assaulting a police officer.

The next morning, the tribal chairman called Barry Ernstoff at our firm to inform him what had happened and ask for his advice. Barry was perplexed. Tribal criminal jurisdiction over non-Indians was a completely uncharted area of Indian law. In principle, there was no reason why a tribe should not have that authority, but the politics were volatile and Barry knew it. He advised the tribe to release Oliphant on his own recognizance and file the charges in tribal court. He would have to sort out the legal issues later.

Before any proceedings could begin, the entire matter escalated into a conflagration. The white residents were outraged that the tribe would have the audacity to arrest a white man, no matter how drunk or disorderly he might have been. Oliphant's case quickly became a focal point for anti-Indian hostility. A wealthy local realtor retained an attorney for the defendant. Real-estate interests were concerned that tribal jurisdiction over non-Indians could affect their ability to sell properties on the reservation. And Oliphant soon found another important ally: the Washington State attorney general, Slade Gorton, that indefatigable opponent of tribal government, joined in his defense.

Oliphant's attorneys immediately filed a writ of habeas corpus in the federal District Court in Seattle. The Suquamish Tribe had two choices: defend the legality of the arrest, or dismiss the charges and concede that it had no jurisdiction over non-Indians. After intense and soul-searching discussions with Barry, the tribe decided to defend its authority. If it could not preserve law and order on its reservation, its fundamental governmental responsibility was threatened.

While the habeas corpus case was pending, another non-Indian criminal case arose on the reservation. This time a pickup truck driven by a non-Indian, Daniel Belgarde, was speeding through the town of Suquamish on the reservation around midnight. The tribal police officer tried to pull him over, but Belgarde took off and a chase ensued. When the police car finally cornered Belgarde, he tried to ram the officer's car. He had a passenger in his truck—Mark Oliphant. The two were arrested, and Belgarde's case was joined with Oliphant's.

Barry Ernstoff had a tough legal battle facing him. There was no direct legal authority supporting tribal criminal jurisdiction over nonmembers on the reservation. But there was abundant legal authority for the principle that an Indian tribe enjoys all the powers of a sovereign government unless the U.S. Congress has explicitly divested it of that power. There had been no such divestment. Indeed, U.S. laws supported the full exercise of tribal government authority, though none mentioned criminal jurisdiction. The Indian Civil Rights Act of 1968 did imply that tribes had such criminal jurisdiction over non-Indians because it specifically imposed on tribes the duty to afford constitutional rights to *all* persons. The *Oliphant* case was going to break new ground.

Barry wrote his usual strong brief and made an effective presentation in the hearing on the writ of habeas corpus. The District Court upheld the tribe's authority. Oliphant's attorneys then appealed to the Ninth Circuit Court of Appeals. An even more thorough brief was presented, and Barry made a highly persuasive argument. Barry won again;

the Ninth Circuit also upheld the tribe. Oliphant's attorneys then petitioned the U.S. Supreme Court. State Attorney General Slade Gorton did not hesitate to take the side of the non-Indian against tribal jurisdiction. The state of Washington joined in his petition as amicus curiae. We were very concerned. This could make law for every tribe in the United States, and the facts on our side were weak for such an important issue.

The Supreme Court accepted the appeal. That the Court agreed to review the case was ominous. Justice William Rehnquist had already shown himself to be hostile to tribal sovereignty and was a strong states' rights advocate. Barry was worried. The politics of the case were bad: fifty Indians living on a reservation two-thirds owned by non-Indians, with the tribe imposing its jurisdiction on Indians and non-Indians alike. This was a very difficult setting in which to assert tribal criminal jurisdiction over non-Indians based on abstract principles of Indian law.

Barry contacted other tribal attorneys around the country. Theoretically, he thought, it might be possible to dismiss the charges against Oliphant and Belgarde and make the whole case moot. The Indians could wait for the issue to arise on a reservation where the demographics were more favorable. At a meeting of the National Congress of American Indians, Barry and the National Tribal Attorney's Association made an exhaustive analysis of the pros and cons. In the end, the fact that two lower federal courts had found in favor of tribal jurisdiction was decisive. The attorney group recommended that Barry go forward and not dismiss the charges.

The case drew amicus briefs from both sides of the tribal sovereignty issue. Opposing the tribe was, of course, Slade Gorton and the state of Washington. We heard that the attorney general's office even arranged for the state to underwrite the cost of printing the Oliphant briefs. Other amicus briefs for the Oliphant side came from the states of South Dakota, Montana, Nebraska, Nevada, New Mexico, North Dakota, Oregon, and Wyoming. Supporting the tribe's authority were the Colvilles, the Utes, the Colorado tribes, the Lummis, and all the national Indian organizations—the National Congress of American Indians, the National Tribal Chairmen's Association, and the American Association on Indian Affairs. There was one surprise among the tribe's supporters: Kitsap County, the county where the Suquamish reservation was located. Since the county sheriff had declined to provide police protection to the Suquamish, we concluded that the county simply wanted the tribe to be responsible for its own law and order.

The argument before the Supreme Court did not go well. Rehnquist was down Barry Ernstoff's throat from the beginning. The other justices peppered Barry with hostile questions so steadily that he was unable to make a coherent argument. The only justice that was supportive was Thurgood Marshall, who had consistently supported tribal sovereignty. The outcome was a foregone conclusion. *Oliphant* was a 6–2 decision overturning the lower court decisions and holding that Indian tribes had no criminal jurisdiction over non-Indians.[2]

The majority opinion was written by Rehnquist, and it was a sorry example of naked judicial policy making. It ignored the well-established principles laid down by the Court in all its prior decisions defining the powers of an Indian tribe, and it gutted the principle of inherent sovereign authority. Rehnquist seized on a phrase in the Ninth Circuit's opinion to undercut the tribe's legal authority. The lower court had said that tribes retain all governmental power unless it has been expressly terminated by Congress—or unless it is "inconsistent with their status."

This phrase was a gloss on the seminal Supreme Court decisions in *Cherokee v. Georgia* and *Worcester v. Georgia*.[3] The Ninth Circuit, in the *Oliphant* appeal, had been trying to point out that the Supreme Court in those cases had found nothing in the principle of inherent tribal sovereignty that was inconsistent with the tribe's status. The Ninth Circuit therefore had ruled that the tribe retained its inherent authority to assert criminal jurisdiction over all persons on the reservation and upheld the Suquamish assertion of jurisdiction over Oliphant and Belgarde. But Rehnquist lifted the phrase used by the Ninth Circuit to *support* tribal jurisdiction and constructed a strained argument. Instead, Rehnquist reasoned, tribes had never been regarded as having criminal jurisdiction over non-Indians and thus to assert such jurisdiction now was "inconsistent with their status." To support his position, Rehnquist cited an obscure 1880 opinion of a federal District Court judge in Arkansas. District Court opinions normally have no standing as binding precedent, and that particular case was never regarded as an authority for any principle of Indian law until Justice Rehnquist dredged it up.

Contrary to Rehnquist's assertion, there was nothing inconsistent with a tribe's status in seeking to uphold law and order on its reservation. It was not only consistent, it was essential to tribal government. I felt the Supreme Court ruling was contemptible in its disregard of the law and entirely lacking in integrity. I could not avoid feeling that the decision had been motivated by racism; the idea that Indians could arrest, try, and imprison a non-Indian was simply too much for the justices to stomach. Perhaps it is better to call the decision political, one that assumed the country was not ready to accept the idea of Indian jurisdiction over non-Indians.

Oliphant was a severe blow to tribal authority and an invitation to assault long-established principles of Indian law. The "inconsistent with their status" standard opened up the possibility for political judgments to dismantle the protections that tribes had been afforded under American law for 150 years. *Oliphant* also marked a turning point in the course of Supreme Court decisions. The Court grew increasingly hostile to claims of Indian rights. It became even more difficult and more dangerous to subject Indian rights to the judgment of the Court after Rehnquist became chief justice in 1986 and Thurgood Marshall retired in 1991.

TWENTY

Writing about the
Indian Civil Rights Act

FOR YEARS THE AMERICAN CIVIL LIBERTIES UNION STRUGGLED with what its policy should be regarding Indians. On the one hand, the ACLU recognized American Indians as an ethnic minority with a long history of oppression and exploitation. On the other, since the organization's purpose was to defend individual rights guaranteed by the Bill of Rights, the group had a hard time seeing where Indian rights fit into the constitutional framework. The ACLU saw the Indian issue as a claim for group rights, which the organization has never advocated.

The ACLU board was almost entirely urban, and largely eastern, so there was little familiarity with tribal values and general ignorance of Indian treaty rights, especially applied to hunting and fishing. With the onset of the Pacific Northwest fishing disputes in the 1960s, the national organization was called on to develop a position on Indian rights. As other Indian issues continued to arise throughout the West, the ACLU formed an Indian Rights Committee, tasked with formulating policies to serve the national organization. The committee was based in Denver and consisted of about a dozen people knowledgeable about Indian issues, including a number of Indians. I was appointed to the committee when it was established in 1973, and we almost immediately began grappling with the 1968 Indian Civil Rights Act.[1]

The Indian Civil Rights Act was passed in response to congressional concerns that Indian tribes were not constrained by the Bill of Rights, which applied only to the federal and state governments. There had been incidents on reservations where tribal governments had denied due process, or had punished free expression, or had subjected members to criminal penalties without affording them the rights that non-Indians had under the U.S. Constitution. After conducting hearings around the country, the Constitutional Rights Subcommittee of the Senate Judiciary Committee drafted legislation that, for the first time, would require Indian tribal governments to protect individual rights.

The Senate Judiciary Committee concluded that Congress should not impose the same obligations on tribes as those required of federal and state governments. Adjustments were made to tailor the act to fit the circumstances of tribes and to avoid wholesale imposition of the American constitutional system. For example, the act protected the right of a criminal defendant to the assistance of counsel, but said this would be at the expense of the accused. This provision was inserted because of Congress's reluctance to saddle impoverished tribes with the cost of providing attorneys in criminal cases. The act did require tribal governments to respect the right to free speech and the free exercise of religion, to protect against unreasonable search and seizure and self-incrimination, and to afford criminal due process, equal protection, and the right to a jury trial. But the Indian Civil Rights Act provided only a single remedy to an aggrieved person: habeas corpus, the ancient writ that requires a governmental officer to come before a court and justify holding anyone against their will.

Almost immediately after the act went into effect, lawsuits were filed against tribes. These were not just habeas corpus actions, but civil rights suits seeking every conceivable remedy; declarations that a tribal action was illegal, money damages, and injunctions to prohibit or force a tribal government to act or to desist from acting. The ACLU began regularly receiving requests for legal representation from tribal members who wanted to sue their tribe. It was with this in mind that our Indian Rights Committee tried to draft principles to guide the organization.

The committee discussions soon revealed a profound schism among the committee members. Ardent civil liberties advocates argued for a sweeping enforcement of the act against tribes. The most articulate of these was a recent Harvard Law School graduate named Joseph De Raismes, who was legal counsel to the mountain states office of the ACLU. But those of us who were tribal advocates insisted on a more measured approach. The discussions were long and heated, but they were also productive. Gradually, we hammered out a policy that was eventually adopted by the national organization. The policy called for the ACLU to support the right of the Indian people to their land base and its natural resources, to self-government, to retention of cultural and religious heritage, and to protection of treaty rights. Our policy mandated that in determining a position on an Indian Civil Rights Act case, the ACLU had to respect tribal values and seek solutions within the framework of tribal government.

The committee discussions led the *South Dakota Law Review* to invite Joe De Raismes and me to write articles about our respective positions on the Indian Civil Rights Act. I agreed with some trepidation. Law reviews symbolized for me the lofty world of the best and brightest legal minds. I had always felt myself to be outside this circle of the legally gifted. But once I accepted the invitation, I was determined to work fiercely to produce a respectable piece of scholarship. I took on the formidable task of writing an article that would match the arguments that I knew De Raismes was capable of crafting. For me it was a duel—between an advocate for tribal sovereignty and those who would sacrifice that sovereignty to the majority view that individual rights trump tribal rights. We would write, in other words, dueling law review articles.

At the outset, I had no clear idea of what I was going to say. The Indian Civil Rights Act had been in force for more than five years and had been litigated in many federal courts. All of the courts followed the reasoning of one of the first cases, *Dodge v. Nakai*, decided in 1968.[2] The litigation arose out of a dramatic confrontation in the tribal council chambers of the Navajo Tribe and posed civil liberties questions in a highly charged setting. The director of the Navajo Legal Services Program (a federally funded program providing legal services), a non-Indian named Mr. Mitchell, had become embroiled in a dispute with the tribal council over Legal Services challenges to some council decisions. The matter came to a head over the operation of the tribal school system.

The council tried to find a way to remove Mitchell from his Legal Services position on the reservation, but were advised by their tribal attorney that they had no power to do this. Their lawyer said the council's only recourse was to exclude Mitchell from the reservation. The council then met with an attorney from the Interior Department to discuss how the Indian Civil Rights Act, or ICRA, might apply in this situation. When Annie Wauneka, a council member and one of the leaders of the tribe, asked if the ICRA would prevent the tribe from excluding someone from the reservation, the Interior lawyer asked if she had anyone particular in mind. This provoked laughter, and Mitchell, who was sitting in the council chambers, apparently laughed louder than the rest. Mrs. Wauneka rebuked him for laughing at the council, and the meeting was adjourned. The next day, the council reconvened and Mrs. Wauneka, seeing Mitchell sitting in the council room, got up and went over to him. She asked whether he intended to laugh again, and when he tried to explain she struck him several times and ordered him to leave the council chambers. After he left, the council voted to exclude him from the reservation and Mitchell then sued the tribe, alleging violation of rights under ICRA.

The federal District Court ruled that although ICRA provided only for habeas corpus, other remedies must be implied; otherwise, the court said, the act was unenforceable and meaningless. In *Dodge v. Nakai* the court struck down the tribe's exclusion order and enjoined all tribal officials from enforcing it. *Dodge* was followed by other federal court decisions, and ICRA was held to justify all judicial remedies against tribal governments to enforce its provisions. This was the state of affairs when I began to write my article.

The federal courts, it seemed to me, had trampled on the doctrine of tribal sovereign immunity and assumed they had the authority to impose legal remedies on tribes not provided for in ICRA. So I plunged into ICRA's legislative history to find out why Congress had not authorized any remedy but habeas corpus. Gradually, I found clear answers. The subcommittee that had drafted the bill, chaired by Senator Sam Ervin, had deliberately chosen to limit federal court jurisdiction in cases against Indian tribes. The decision to limit the remedy for violation of civil rights to habeas corpus review was a product of weighing the federal policy of respecting tribal sovereignty and recognizing the distinctions between tribal and non-Indian governments. The subcommittee was sensitive to the history of white America imposing its values on Indians. ICRA therefore sought a balanced approach to protecting individual rights against tribal governments.

My article, titled "In Defense of Tribal Sovereignty: An Analysis of Judicial Error in Construction of the Indian Civil Rights Act," was published in the winter of 1975 issue of the *South Dakota Law Review*.[3] It aimed to demonstrate that for seven years the federal courts had gotten it wrong; all those court decisions, many of them affirmed by appellate courts, were simply in error. De Raismes's article, "The Indian Civil Rights Act of 1968 and the Pursuit of Responsible Self-Government," was published in the same issue. It represented the thought of civil rights advocates who were willing to subordinate tribal values to mainstream values. My article was a lone voice. It was indeed presumptuous for me to declare that the courts were uniformly wrong, but it was my honest and firm conviction, based on the legislative history, that the courts had overridden the intentions of Congress.

I tried to point out the unconscious ethnocentrism underlying this judicial line of thought. The District Court had rejected the tribe's justification for asking Mitchell to leave the council chambers as unreasonable. But the court's decision came from applying Anglo-Saxon standards to the tribal milieu. Indians felt strongly that their reservations were their country, and when a white man who had pitted himself against tribal government laughed scornfully at that government, it was deeply offensive. How deeply may be gauged by the expression of Annie Wauneka's anger. Getting up and walking over to this man, striking him, and ordering him to leave the room was, I felt, powerful evidence of the depth of emotion generated by Mitchell's conduct. The action of the council in ordering him expelled from the reservation left little doubt that her anger was shared by the entire Navajo Tribal Council. While Mrs. Wauneka's conduct and the action of the council were offensive in non-Indian eyes, the right to make such judgments belonged to the tribe. Congress clearly had such factors in mind when it confined the federal courts to reviewing the incarceration of prisoners by tribal government.

My article attracted some attention, mainly from specialists in Indian law, and was cited in a few court decisions. But it remained a lonely voice until 1978, three years later, when the U.S. Supreme Court decided *Martinez v. Santa Clara Pueblo*.[4] This case had been brought against the Santa Clara Pueblo by a woman member of the Pueblo whose children were denied membership because their father, though an Indian, was not a member of the Santa Clara Pueblo. The Pueblo's law declared that the offspring of a woman who intermarried outside the Pueblo could not become members. But the Pueblo's law allowed the offspring of a *man* who intermarried outside the Pueblo to become members. The Pueblo argued that their law was based on cultural grounds. Evidence showed that the Santa Clara Pueblo had a deep traditional belief that tribal identity was passed through the patrilineal line. The woman and her daughter argued that, regardless of the reason, the action of the Pueblo's governing body violated the Indian Civil Rights Act by denying them equal protection.

The *Martinez* case posed a dilemma for the ACLU. It immediately tested the policy we had hammered out: that in determining a position on an Indian civil rights case, the ACLU had to respect tribal values and seek solutions within the framework of tribal government. To me, the ACLU position should have been clear: if the organization chose to file an amicus brief in the case, it had to do so on the side of the Pueblo. But my position was fiercely opposed. The national board was strongly inclined to support the claim of the plaintiff.

The board delegated the national executive committee to determine the ACLU's position and designated one of the committee's members, Ruth Bader Ginsberg, to debate the issue with me, since I was the outspoken advocate of tribal rights. In a telephone conversation that lasted about twenty minutes, I wrestled with Ginsberg over the question. I had never met her, though I had heard of her. She was a leading spokesperson for equality for women, and for her the equal protection issue clearly trumped any tribal interest. She was unyielding. Though there was no rancor in our discussion—it was clearly a lawyerly debate—I found her attitude culturally closed, showing little understanding or sympathy for tribal values. Our discussion long predated her ascension to the Supreme Court, and I hesitate to predict how she might rule in an Indian case not involving the Indian Civil Rights Act (she did later join with the majority in supporting the position of the Mille Lacs Band of Chippewas in their suit against the state of Minnesota). However, I think there is little doubt that she would support any person raising a clear civil rights claim against a tribe, especially if it involved an equal protection claim by a woman.

In the end, my arguments were overridden—Ruth Bader Ginsberg's position was adopted, and the ACLU filed an amicus brief against the Santa Clara Pueblo. The brief was written by Steven Pevar, legal director of the ACLU's mountain states regional office. I wrote an amicus brief in support of the Pueblo on behalf of one of our clients, the Confederated Tribes of the Colville Reservation. I argued that the Indian Civil Rights Act did not authorize federal courts to invalidate the laws of a tribe and override tribal sovereign immunity; the ICRA itself and its legislative history mandated deference to tribal classifications.

To the surprise, even shock, of most Indian law scholars and lawyers, the Supreme Court rejected the plaintiff's claim and upheld the position I had taken in the *South Dakota Law Review* article. The decision overturned ten years of lower court decision making and ruled that federal courts could not hear any cases against tribal governments alleging violations of the Indian Civil Rights Act except for habeas corpus proceedings. The Court did not discuss the equal protection issue, because ICRA did not give the courts jurisdiction to hear such claims against tribes.

The decision in *Martinez v. Santa Clara Pueblo* had far-reaching implications. It upheld tribal sovereignty, and particularly sovereign immunity from suit. It came as a sharp rebuke to courts that had assumed extensive remedial authority over tribes when such authority was not authorized by Congress; when such authority in fact ran counter to well-established doctrines of tribal sovereign immunity. The larger meaning of *Martinez* was that the tribes had to work out the solutions to these kinds of issues internally, in keeping with their traditions and in their own due course. In a later chapter, I describe how the Northern Arapaho Tribe resolved an identical issue through its internal democratic process, without the heavy-handed intervention of a non-Indian judge in a court hundreds of miles from the reservation.

Overnight, I had become a respected authority. I had tried to demonstrate that these court decisions were wrong in my law review article, but it had seemed a quixotic effort given the long line of federal court decisions to the contrary. Now, after *Martinez*, my name became increasingly well-known to lawyers and professors in the field of Indian law. Soon after the *Martinez* decision, I received a call from one of the student editors at the *UC Davis Law Review*, asking if I would write an article about the implications of the decision. Although the first article had involved long and arduous work, the results were so gratifying that I felt encouraged to say yes.

In March of 1979, the *UC Davis Law Review* published my second article, "After *Martinez*: Indian Civil Rights under Tribal Government."[5] In it I explored the question of how civil rights could be protected where the only recourse was tribal government—not the federal courts. This meant going into the structure of tribal government and the nature of tribal courts.

The American doctrine of judicial review of legislative or executive action could not be expected to work in the tribal system as it did in the American legal system. The biggest obstacle was that few tribes have adopted a separation of powers principle, in which courts are a co-equal branch of government. Instead tribal courts were created by tribal councils, and the judges were hired by the council. There was no tradition of a tribal judge overruling a council. Historically, tribal judges dealt with minor crimes and only recently had begun receiving training in civil matters. Since few tribal judges had any formal legal training, it was no surprise that council members would not grant to a tribal court the authority to overturn their decisions. This was a matter that would have to be pursued with great delicacy and care. In time, tribal courts would grow in expertise and prestige, but in the 1970s that day lay off in the future.

I also took on another issue: indications that the Bureau of Indian Affairs was considering assuming the authority of reviewing the constitutionality of tribal action. This, I said, would be contrary to law because Congress had twice considered the BIA's request for such power and twice rejected it. I wrote: "The Secretary of the Interior must bear in mind that *Martinez* was a mandate for tribal self-government, not for the substitution of administrative review for judicial review." I think this article influenced the policy of the Interior Department, since not long after it appeared the BIA proposal was quietly dropped.

My two articles have frequently been cited by the courts, and a substantial part of the text of the UC Davis article has been reproduced in a casebook for students of Indian law—all very heady for someone who was at the bottom of his law school class.

TWENTY-ONE

Leaving Law for Academia

WRITING THE LAW REVIEW ARTICLES HAD TAKEN ME INTO THE world of scholarship. In 1972, a friend at the University of Washington asked if I would be willing to teach a course in Indian law in the Indian Studies Department. The idea was attractive and I agreed. I taught only one quarter, but three years later the department asked if I would teach the class again. Starting in 1975, I taught the course every year for five years.

Many of my students were Indians, highly motivated to study Indian law. There were some difficulties. This was not a course for law students, yet it involved reading cases and understanding the language of the law. Some of the students were excellent, but lacked language skills. My philosophy was to work with everyone, treat every student with respect, and to try to present the important principles of law that affected Indian people.

Preparing for teaching took a lot of time. There was then no textbook, and I had to prepare copies of case and historical materials for my students. In the process, I had to master the cases myself and organize the materials so I could present an understandable history of U.S. policy toward the Indian people. I enjoyed teaching and felt I did a good job of it. I had been assigned a tiny office in one of the university buildings and it was fun playing at being an academic. I was away from the stress of a law office, without the pressures of cases and deadlines and without an adversary. It seemed worry-free. I began to toy with the idea of doing this permanently.

By 1979, I was looking for a respite from law practice. I had been practicing for twenty-five years, law was stressful, and my relationships within the firm had become strained. The calm of academia seemed very attractive. Gradually, an idea took shape: maybe I could find an academic post. I began to explore the possibility, calling some friends who were academics. In the spring of 1979 I attended an Indian law conference in Phoenix and ran into Bob Clinton, who was then a professor at the University of Iowa Law School. He told me there would be an opening at Iowa for a visiting professor in the spring semester of 1981. Though the position was for only one semester, there was a possibility that another appointment might open up in the fall. I was definitely interested, but I had to discuss this major change with my wife and my partners. My idea was to take a sabbatical, at my own expense—a leave of absence from the firm. I decided that I wanted a full year away from law practice, even if there was no certainty about my employment the second half of the year. I was hopeful that I could find a position somewhere.

Lennie knew that I was restless in my law practice, but she was deeply uneasy about this new enterprise. What if I found a new career that would take us away from Seattle permanently? Our children were here and she loved the city. What was more, it came at a bad time for her. She had earned an M.A. in museum administration and had an NEH grant for a museum project. Leaving would mean abandoning the project. I was asking a huge sacrifice of her. But because she was always devoted to my happiness and she knew how much I wanted to get away from the practice, she agreed.

I was somewhat surprised that there was no serious difficulty with my partners. I asked only that they allow me to leave for a year. Since I didn't propose to receive any compensation and was obviously determined to go, they agreed. I would leave in December of 1980 for Iowa City for a one-year absence. We called it a sabbatical, though it was not in the usual sense because I received no income from the firm.

Now came the hard part. I would be teaching a five-hour writing course in constitutional law to a relatively small class. Over thirty years had passed since I'd had any contact with constitutional law, apart from the narrow areas of civil liberties and treaty rights. What was more, I would not be teaching the exciting legal issues of the Bill of Rights, but the more mundane and technical topics like judicial review, the Commerce Clause as a limitation on the power of Congress, the political question doctrine—all topics familiar to students and teachers of constitutional law, but that I had largely forgotten. To prepare myself I actually took a night course in constitutional law at the University of Puget Sound.

Because we expected to be gone a year, Lennie and I decided to rent our house and put our furnishings in storage. Our youngest son, Ron, was fourteen and a student in junior high school. We planned to take him to Iowa City and enroll him in school there. He grumbled, but finally got into the spirit of the great adventure. The law school arranged housing for us in Iowa City, in the home of a faculty member who was away. When we arrived in Iowa and walked outdoors, we were shocked—we weren't at all prepared for the cold. The temperature was probably fifteen or twenty degrees above zero. To Iowans, this was bearable, but being used to the moderate weather of Seattle we felt actual pain in our cheeks and noses.

Iowa City turned out to be a delight. It was a little gem—neat, comfortable-looking houses, glistening in the sharp winter air. The frozen Iowa River wound through the city with university buildings on both sides. The building styles varied from Greek columned structures to American 1950s-modern brick. The law school was a hodgepodge, a new wing melded onto a converted dormitory. (The old school has since been replaced with an imposing new structure.)

Our house was a comfortable ranch-style home, well insulated against the Iowa winters and nicely furnished. We settled in quickly and easily and prepared to begin a new life. At the law school I met my new colleagues. The dean, Bill Hines, was a plainspoken and unpretentious academic who welcomed me and did everything he could to make my sojourn pleasant. As I got to know the faculty and their work, I was impressed by the quality of the scholars. For instance, David Baldus did a groundbreaking study of how the death penalty is administered in Georgia, to show disparate treatment by race. My friend Bob Clinton co-authored one of the principal casebooks in Indian law. Many of the faculty were away visiting at other schools, such as the owner of the house we lived in, Allen Vestal, an expert on civil procedure, and Burns

Weston, whose office I was using, an expert in international law.

I would be teaching both constitutional law and a seminar in tribal government and American Federalism. It was the constitutional law course that worried me. I was teaching a small class and I would give my class writing assignments that would have to be graded. Another constitutional law course covering the same subject matter was being taught at the same time. Since both courses used the same casebook, I was able to confer with my fellow instructor and determine which chapters to cover.

I had about a week to prepare for my first class. I plunged in, reading the cases in the first assigned section intensively. The course would open with the subject of judicial review and the famous 1803 Supreme Court decision by Justice John Marshall in *Marbury v. Madison*. I read a number of law review articles dealing with the case and the entire subject of judicial review. When the first day of class arrived, there was little about the case and its implications that I hadn't mastered. Still, I was tense when the appointed hour arrived to go into the classroom and meet my class. There were some twenty students, many of them very bright. Ironically, I found myself presenting the subject matter in the same way my law school professors had—using the Socratic method. All the students worked hard, and soon I felt that trying to stay ahead of my class was like running down a railroad track with the train just behind me.

I found myself working harder than I had ever worked in private practice. I had to prepare for three classes a week, including writing assignments, and I often met with the students individually to discuss their assignments. I found grading difficult and confusing, because I had to take into account the law school curve, a mathematical formula that my colleagues were familiar with, but that I struggled to figure out. I was not prepared for the occasional student challenges over the grades I gave. These grievance sessions often became intense confrontations— something I strongly disliked.

Meanwhile, Lennie and our son Ron were doing very well. Lennie was hired as the public relations director of the Johnson County Arts Council. She became immersed in planning art shows and writing publicity. She even had a radio show to promote the arts. Lennie was as surprised as I was to experience all this public prominence, because in

Seattle she had been a diffident, even shy woman. But she told me that in Iowa City she felt she could shed her old persona and simply slip into the part of a confident and scintillating person. Ron was enrolled in an Iowa City middle school and soon made friends. His teachers took a strong personal interest in each student and were extremely kind. He flourished.

As winter turned to spring and we became more attuned to the university town, we came to embrace its virtues. Iowa City was small and everything was convenient: no parking problems, no lines, an easy existence. When we wanted to go to a concert or a play at Hancher Hall, we could leave home ten minutes before curtain. The people of Iowa seemed extremely solicitous of children, not only their own, but all children. We felt very secure with Ron riding his bike all over town visiting his friends. There was an almost palpable atmosphere of tolerance and good will in Iowa City. Everywhere, it seemed, we met good-hearted, sincere people. Even the university community was a soft, friendly place, quite different than what I had experienced at the University of Chicago.

There was one aspect of life in Iowa City that was difficult to adjust to: living in a small island of urbanity bounded by a sea of corn, literally. Corn grew in all the fields of the surrounding countryside and even in small plots in town. The weather was also a change for us. While the winters seemed brutally cold, the spring brought monster thunderstorms. We had never heard such explosions of sound nor seen such cloudbursts. Sometimes the street in front of our house temporarily turned into a river. But Iowans were prepared. For winter, they had plenty of snowplows and the streets and roads were always cleared, and their storm sewer systems handled the runoff from rainstorms quickly.

We had some wonderful moments in Iowa City. While I had not found the peace and relaxation I thought would come with academic life, I was happy. My colleagues assured me that everyone experienced high stress when teaching new material and that with time teaching would become much easier. Lennie learned that two articles she had written would be published in historical journals, and we were all elated. Ron was becoming a teenager, beginning to look like a young adult. And we went to parties surrounded by new friends. At one, a visiting professor—a justice of the New Zealand High Court—played the piano and sang American pop songs of the 1930s and 1940s as everyone joined in. At another, we sat in the cool evening air outside the law school librarian's farmhouse, surrounded by fields and farm buildings—an exquisite experience.

As the spring semester drew to a close, I was offered a post teaching at the law school for the summer, and I agreed to teach a course in client representation. With that settled, I had employment through the end of August, but I had no idea what I would be doing after that. Then I received an offer from the law school at Washington University in St. Louis. While I was pondering this possibility, Dean Bill Hines came into my office and asked, "Would you be interested in going to Durham University in England and teaching there for a term?"

Wow! I could barely contain myself. Iowa had an exchange arrangement with Durham, but the Iowa professor who was supposed to go declined and so, to fulfill its obligation, the law school had to find someone to go in his place. Going to England! We had never been abroad and the idea of teaching at an English university was overwhelming. My first concern was over what I would be teaching. I was totally unfamiliar with English law and my knowledge of the English common law principles embedded in American law was hardly sufficient to instruct English law students. But Dean Hines laid my fears to rest. I would teach a small class in human rights and a tutorial session of torts. I naively assumed I was equipped to teach both. After all, I had been on the board of the American Civil Liberties Union and I certainly knew something about torts. Hadn't I done negligence cases, even trials? I was in for a big surprise.

Going to England was a dramatic development. In all of my sabbatical thinking I had never dreamed of going to Europe. Lennie was very excited. Of course, we assumed that our fourteen-year-old son would come with us and would also be excited by the prospect. But when we told Ron we were surprised and disappointed by his reaction. He wanted to start high school in the fall with his friends and had no enthusiasm for going to England. Eventually, we worked out an arrangement for him to stay with families of friends back home while we were gone.

In the meantime, there was the summer term to deal with. I taught the course in client relations, a subject that came easily to me. My main task that summer was preparing to teach human rights at Durham in the fall. When I obtained a casebook on the subject, I was stunned to find that I had completely misunderstood the content of this subject. Human rights, it turned out, was a branch of international law based on international human rights treaties and the decisions of the European Court of Human Rights in Strasbourg, France. The court applied the provisions of the European Convention on Human Rights, to which Great Britain was a party. The court was unique because it had jurisdiction over national governments and was empowered to hear complaints of citizens brought against their own country. Its decisions were published, and I would need to study those cases to teach the subject.

But that wasn't all. There were other international conventions on human rights, which could be applied to non-European countries. For example, the United States had signed the International Convention on Human Rights, but since it had never been ratified by our Congress, it was not law in America. The Geneva Convention remains one of the rare international human rights conventions that Congress has ratified. But there were others that had been signed and ratified by other countries. Once again I had to struggle to master new material, material I would have to teach to a class of law students.

The summer semester was not entirely pleasant. Summer in Iowa can be stifling hot. We were as little accustomed to this as to Iowa winters. The other problem was more serious. I gradually became aware of an ache in my right leg when I stood in front of my class. It got worse. I gave up jogging. Soon I couldn't walk more than a few hundred yards. Finally, I went to the university medical clinic. After a series of tests, they told me I had a spinal stenosis: a narrowing of the opening where the sciatic nerve emerges from the spinal column, putting pressure on the nerve and causing pain. The orthopedic surgeon told me the problem could worsen, prescribed some back exercises, and advised me to avoid all lifting. He even cautioned against driving from Iowa City to Seattle. We had to return to Seattle to get Ron settled. But Ron had turned fifteen and knew how to drive. Under Iowa law he was eligible for a license and got one. I told him he would have the responsibility of driving my car across the country. He took the news with suppressed glee, but with the appropriate outward sobriety. The spinal stenosis was to be a lifelong problem.

We left Iowa enriched by our experience. We got Ron settled in

Seattle, did some traveling in Europe, and arrived in Durham about a week before the term started. I was teaching during Michaelmas term, from mid-October to mid-December. Durham is a charming town on the River Wear in northeast England, about 225 miles north of London, close to Newcastle and the Scottish border. When we were there it had a population of about twenty-five thousand. The center of the city looks much the same as it did in the eighteenth century—narrow cobblestone streets going off at crazy angles, with sidewalks barely wide enough for two people to pass. The town is dominated by its cathedral, a huge Norman structure commenced in 1092 and completed in 1200. The cathedral stands on a bluff overlooking the river and is part of a medieval defensive complex that included a castle surrounded by walls. The castle and the walls are still there, as is the cathedral. But now the entire complex comprises Durham University. The cathedral remains a place of worship, but it also doubles as a hall for concerts and university functions.

Durham University is the third-oldest university in England, after Oxford and Cambridge, and was established in the relatively recent year of 1832. Like Oxford and Cambridge, it is organized around residential colleges, and every faculty member is required to be member of a college. In practice, this only meant joining a college's dining club for monthly dinners. There were fewer than 5,000 students when I was there, of whom only 180 were enrolled in the Law Department. The university is highly selective and considered quite prestigious. The Law Department accepted only 60 students a·year from about 1,500 applicants.

There is a great difference between the law schools in England and in the United States. In England, law is an undergraduate program, not a professional program. The students receive a bachelor's degree after three years. The law program is intended as an academic discipline, and though many of the students go on to become barristers and solicitors, not all do. Those who wish to go into practice must take an eighteen-month course offered by the Barristers or Solicitors Society and then clerk for a solicitor or take pupilage, that is, a clerkship in a barrister's chamber. Since the students in the Law Department are undergraduates, they are young, around eighteen or nineteen years old. Though I found them very bright and well-read, they lacked the sophistication and educational background of older American law students.

Lennie and I first had to settle into our housing. I was exchanging places with a Durham law professor, Colin Warbrick, and we would be living in his house. The Warbrick house was an attached two-story solid brick house, with "High Cliff" painted in gold letters above the entry. We had been told the house had central heating—which turned out to be primitive by American standards. There was a tiny coke-fueled furnace enclosed by a white enameled cabinet in the kitchen. We carried coke in from a large bin in the backyard and loaded the furnace. Then we started the fire by inserting a wand connected to the gas line of the house, turning on the gas, lighting the wand, and holding it in the coke until a steady fire got established. The fire heated water in pipes, which ran to radiators in different rooms, providing a barely noticeable amount of heat. At night, the fire had to be banked. I was not very good at this, and most mornings we awoke to a frigid house. I had to trudge outside in the cold to bring in a scupper loaded with coke and start the fire again. The house was otherwise quite comfortable, and I even had the use of Professor Warbrick's English car.

The law school was housed in a nineteenth-century building, which once functioned as the county courthouse. It was a rabbit warren of sloping connecting corridors between the original building and its additions. I met three times a week with my class of eleven students, nine young men and two young women, in a tutorial room where we sat around an oval table. I told them we would be dealing with United Nations human rights procedures, the European Convention on Human Rights, and the human rights of indigenous people, including American Indian law. At first they were uncomfortable with my dialectic style of teaching, being accustomed to the English lecture system. But they soon adjusted to the give and take. They were all very bright, though they didn't work as hard as American law students. Because of their youth, they didn't have the experiential base that American law students bring to their studies. Still, they responded well to the issues of human rights law, and they were particularly interested in the session I devoted to American Indian law. My impression was that only a few of them intended to go into practice.

My tutorial in torts was very different than an American law school course in torts. The assigned cases usually involved convoluted and complex facts that called for logical dissection. Social policy was not a factor, as it is in American law. Precedent ruled with an iron hand.

Most surprising to me was civil liberties under English law. It appeared to me that the courts refused to hold government accountable for infringement of individual liberties. Despite what many Americans believe, the English seemed to accept government authority docilely. Police could hold prisoners incommunicado, deny them access to counsel, and fail to advise citizens of their rights while subjecting them to lengthy interrogation. Absent a Bill of Rights, there was no concept of a core of inviolable civil liberties. Indeed, in one decision, the British High Court ruled that a police wiretap was lawful without judicial or other warrant on the principle that everything was permissible unless expressly forbidden. I hasten to add that this was the state of affairs when we were there in 1981 and things have changed substantially since then. In fact, there was intense debate at the time over the proper balance between individual rights and public welfare. There was even talk of the need to adopt a Bill of Rights, and legislation to protect individual rights was enacted in 1998.[1]

Our Durham experience was beyond anything I had ever imagined. One example will illustrate. Going to the mandatory dinner at my college was an experience out of the nineteenth century. The faculty gathered before dinner in a small, elegant paneled room off the main dining hall for sherry. All stood around and chattered away for about twenty minutes, and then the master of the college gave a signal and we paraded single file through a large wooden door into the dining hall. The hall was huge, with high ceilings and exposed supporting beams. There was a fireplace of medieval proportions. As we entered, all the students, about 150 of them, stood and remained standing until we were seated. We walked to a table on a raised level, called, descriptively, "the high table." Then waitresses wearing traditional black uniforms with white lace cuffs and collars bustled around us taking orders. I discovered that the British academics were great wine connoisseurs, and each college took pride in its wine cellar. So the choice of dinner wines was a serious matter. A few students were sprinkled among the faculty at the table, presumably to give them the experience of rubbing elbows with the luminaries of the academic world.

I wanted to get a better understanding of the English legal system, so when I was in London I arranged to visit some barristers' offices (called "chambers"). The barristers are the trial lawyers, and the solicitors are the office lawyers. Solicitors handle all legal matters not requiring a court proceeding, such as contracts, deeds, business and corporate work, and the like. They also serve as conduits to a barrister if a case involves courtroom appearances. The barristers I met were courteous and open, and a typical practice did not remotely resemble an American law office. Usually, the number of barristers in a single chamber was not more than three or four. Their chief clerk, though not trained in law, was a powerful figure. He determined what cases went to which barrister through his connections with the solicitors who called on the firm to represent their clients.

No visit to England would be complete for an American lawyer without a visit to London's Law Courts. I attended a full-day trial of a rape case and listened with fascination to the high formality of a British court. The barristers were impressive for their incisive questions. But I was dumbfounded by their practices. A barrister was not permitted to meet with a witness before the trial and had to rely on his staff to prepare him for examination in court. There was very little argument before the judge about the law; it seemed almost as though it would insult the judge's intelligence to suggest that he needed lecturing on what the law was. The trial was a spectacle for me, but the system seemed to satisfy everyone.

By the time my sabbatical year drew to a close, I had resolved my doubts about the future. I wanted to return to my law firm and resume the practice of law. Many of my illusions about academic life had been dashed. There was no leisure to do independent research, to write articles, or to think big thoughts. What was more important, I felt impotent as a professor. What could I do to influence events in the real world? As a lawyer I could pick up the phone or the microphone of a dictating machine and start things happening with a telephone call or a letter. You can certainly get things rolling by filing a lawsuit. The academic can't do any of those things. I missed the ringing of my phone. The solitude of my faculty office became a pall. It had been a wonderful year and I had learned a good deal about the law, my country, and other countries. Now I was ready to go back and pick up where I had left off. I would return to the quest for justice for Indians, an undertaking that gave moral dimension to my professional life.

TWENTY-TWO

A Firm of Tribal Attorneys

I WAS A TRIBAL ATTORNEY FOR THIRTY YEARS, ALL SPENT IN THE environment of a law firm. A law firm can be a group of lawyers bound together only by economic ties, or it can be an entity with a group character, bound together by shared values. That is who we were, a firm of lawyers bound together by the unique identity and underdog position of our clients—Indian tribes—and by a commitment to fight their battles. We had esprit de corps, a spirit that rejoiced in every victory, no matter which lawyer led the case. Each of us was proud to identify himself as a tribal attorney.

I started this firm in 1963 with two other lawyers and we remained a three-man firm for five years before we hired our first associate. Over the years, the composition of the firm changed; one of the original partners left and an associate was invited to be a partner. We maintained the original principle of income sharing—share and share alike among the partners. As the firm became known, the practice grew and the firm grew with it. New associates were hired and some became partners. We were regularly inundated by résumés from law school graduates and even practicing lawyers who wanted to work in Indian law. I was very selective and looked for candidates with extraordinary abilities: keen legal intellect, special background in relevant areas, or personal qualities that indicated an unusually capable person.

We tried to keep our fees modest because of the clients we served. As the quality of our work became known in Indian country, other tribes retained us. Starting with the Makahs, we came to represent the Lummi, Suquamish, and Colville tribes in Washington State. We were retained by the Ukpeagvik Inupiat Corporation (UIC), an Eskimo Native corporation in the village of Barrow, Alaska. In 1973, we were hired by the Northern Cheyenne Tribe in Montana and a few years later by the Mille Lacs Band of Chippewas in Minnesota. In the 1980s, we were hired by the Hoopa Tribe of California, the Metlakatla Indian community of Alaska, and the Kake Tribal Corporation in Alaska. We were retained by the Standing Rock Sioux Tribe of South Dakota to litigate an appeal of a lower federal court ruling. We filed an amicus curiae brief in the U.S. Supreme Court case involving the Santa Clara Pueblo of New Mexico. In the 1990s we were retained by the Northern Arapaho Tribe of Wyoming and then by the Fallon Paiute-Shoshone and the Moapa Paiutes in Nevada.

From our beginning as a three-lawyer partnership, we grew to fourteen—nine partners and five associates. Even with fourteen lawyers, we were tiny—a boutique firm. But we had a national practice and a national reputation. We became known and respected in the national community of Indian lawyers and Indian leaders. Our work brought us to the attention of government officials, especially many in the Bureau of Indian Affairs. I came to see their respect for our ability and our integrity. Many in the BIA knew how much lawyers charged their tribal clients and saw that our fees were far lower—a policy that gave us high credibility with the bureau, many of whose employees were Indian themselves. One mark of the firm's work was the number of cases we brought before the U.S. Supreme Court: seven. For a small Seattle law firm, that was exceptional.

We established a branch office on the Makah reservation and we associated with attorneys in Washington, D.C., and Anchorage, Alaska. For more than ten years we maintained a strong spirit of unity. We never disputed who would do the work on a particular case. The attorney who had the closest relationship with the tribal client would do the work or would call on another to take over or assist. Usually we had a good idea of the strengths and talents of everyone in the firm and would approach another lawyer in the firm with, "Are you busy?" Anyone was invited to offer suggestions or theories that might help the work of another lawyer. In some cases, two or more of us would form a team to work on a case.

The work was exciting, and the firm included some striking personalities. We had a pool of talent that I felt was second to none in the United States.

From the inception of our Indian practice, I emphasized the critical importance of tribal sovereignty—a legal concept and a political goal. Ideally, it meant total government authority over the tribe's territory and the people on it, whether residents or transients, Indians or non-Indians—the same scope of authority exercised by any government. While the principle was affirmed in the abstract by many court decisions, in practice full sovereignty was extremely difficult to establish. Every effort to exercise that authority was met by determined resistance from state governments and non-Indians claiming immunity from tribal authority. Nevertheless, this remained our pole star, and I lectured and addressed tribal officials around the country with that message. We became widely known as aggressive advocates for tribal sovereignty in all of our work. The courts were frequently reluctant to accept the principle, the *Oliphant v. Suquamish Tribe* decision being a prime example. Today, the phrase *tribal sovereignty* is accepted throughout Indian country as a keystone of Indian policy. Another principle that formed the basis of much of our work was the protection of treaty rights. The U.S. Constitution declared that the treaties of the United States were the supreme law of the land, binding on all states and superseding all state laws. The treaties were regarded by the tribes as sacred—to be protected at all costs.

Every lawyer in our firm was committed to these principles. Despite our low hourly rates, we never took a share of any money we recovered for our tribal clients, nor did we take any of their cases on a contingent fee. We would not accept legal work from any company that wanted to do business with a tribe. The principle was simple: undivided loyalty to the tribes. All of this meant that the lawyers in the firm had to accept lower incomes than their counterparts in general law practice. In time, this led to strains within the firm, as some of our partners grew increasingly discontented with their personal incomes.

Our Indian law practice rested on an insecure foundation—the ability of tribes to pay a private law firm for legal services. Some managed, but others found it more practical to replace us with lawyers from the Legal Services program—federally funded lawyers available to tribes. That was to be expected. Besides being free, Legal Services presented another challenge to our Indian law practice—the on-reservation attorney. Early on, we recognized that having to depend on lawyers to travel to a reservation periodically was not satisfactory to many of our tribal clients. Problems arose daily on any particular reservation calling for legal guidance. The ideal solution would be to have an in-house or on-reservation attorney. It was a topic we often addressed internally. But our practice model was a traditional law firm based in Seattle. None of the members of the firm were willing to move onto a reservation with their families, though it was an idea we frequently explored. The Legal Services attorneys, on the other hand, were not only willing, but wanted to live on the reservations. The result was inevitable. Over time, some of our tribal clients chose the free Legal Services and parted company with our firm. I came to know many of the Legal Services lawyers, and they were a highly competent and dedicated group of lawyers, young and idealistic. The tribes got excellent representation from them. We did finally hire an attorney to live on the Makah reservation and this proved highly successful. We probably should have done that much sooner.

But the advent of publicly funded lawyers was not the only problem facing the firm. Strains within the organization grew more serious. As the firm grew, we recognized the need to have a managing partner. The post fell naturally to one of the partners who was the most management minded. He gradually inaugurated a structure and a discipline that, at first, was easily accepted. First came the time sheets—a log of each attorney's day with every fifteen-minute block of time recorded and coded so each client could be billed for the time. Soon, fines were imposed for turning in time sheets late. Then came the computerization of the practice. Our managing partner was enamored of computers, not merely for secretarial tasks, but for billing, financial analysis, and evaluation of attorney performance.

Eventually, the collegial atmosphere eroded. The first principle to go was my simplistic philosophy of equal sharing of income among the partners. Under pressure, this was scrapped in favor of a formula that credited hours worked and clients produced. The managing partner and his supporters became a bloc that steadily pressed us to adopt the methods of the big money-making law firms. I went along reluctantly as did several other partners. Underlying all of this was the strong feeling among the management bloc that the firm's income had to be increased. I realized that the character of the firm was changing. While I was still treated with respect by my partners, it was clear that the reins were in the hands of the management group, whom we began to refer to as "the bottom-liners."

The change in the firm's character was driven home to me when my son Martin wanted to work for us as a summer clerk. Martin was bright and hard-working. He had gotten his undergraduate degree from the University of Chicago and his law degree from Northwestern University, where he had done very well. As the summer of 1979 approached, he expressed an interest in working as a summer clerk for the firm. I told him I wanted to discuss it with my partners before he made a formal application. I thought it was possible that someone might have reservations, but I was confident that if I made a personal presentation to the partners Martin would be given at least a shot at a job with us. But to my surprise, several of the bottom-liners raised objections. Their stated reasons were lofty. They said they would not be able to objectively evaluate his performance or be critical of his work because of his relationship with me. They raised concerns about nepotism and the problem of bad precedent. But it all came to the same thing. I had no choice but to yield, and I was bitter. I realized that this was no longer "my firm"; something fundamental had changed.

As I look back, it's clear that this changed relationship with the firm played an important part in my decision to leave on a sabbatical. I had become alienated from the firm. Had I found academic life to my liking and secured an attractive position, I likely would have left the firm and the private practice of law altogether.

When I returned to Seattle after my year in the academic world, though I initially embraced life in the law firm, I soon found the atmosphere even further deteriorated. Our managing partner decided that we needed a program of new client development. We needed to diversify our practice, he said, and shed our identity as an Indian law firm. That identity was driving away business clients. One of his targets was the art prominently displayed throughout our office, which depicted Indian themes. In the reception area was a large beautiful print by the American artist Leonard Baskin, a portrait of an Indian titled *Yellow Magpie, Arapaho* (see print in background of frontispiece). Hanging in our conference room was an original symbolic painting titled *The Birth of a Whale*. In the corridors we had a number of valuable Edward Curtis photographs of Indians, including Makahs. I had purchased these for the firm and felt pride in the beauty and meaning they gave to our office. The managing partner wanted to take down this art because it identified us as an "Indian" law firm. As for the business clients that would supplant the tribes, we were given quotas and had to report how many hours each month we spent in new client development. The managing partner actually proposed that we call on businesses and try to get appointments with them to solicit their legal work. This went against my principles and those of some of the other partners as well. We were told that this was the new wave in the legal profession and that we were resisting progress if we opposed it. A core of three partners and I simply refused. We were also against removing our Indian art from the office.

The tension within the firm produced a fissure between the group that wanted to drive harder for more money and those of us opposed to treating lawyers as billing units. The fissure ultimately led to a complete split. One morning in 1986 I received a shocking telephone call from one of my partners. He had been approached by the management bloc to join with them and dissolve the partnership. They would remain, and those of us who disagreed with their philosophy would be ousted. Since the partnership agreement gave advantages to the partners in the surviving firm over those who withdrew, there began a period of intense maneuvering to obtain a majority of the partners in one group that could then be considered the surviving partnership. After a week, the choices had been made, and four of the partners and I elected to remain as a group, making us the surviving firm and the others the withdrawing partners. That week was a nightmare. It shook the world I had come to believe was rock solid.

It was a very painful time. Despite the tensions, I hated to see the entity that I had created fall apart. I had a last uncomfortable meeting with the partner heading up the split, our managing partner, and tried to persuade him not to do it. He was polite, but did not budge. His group left and formed a separate firm, taking some of the firm's clients with them. The most painful blow was that the managing partner, who had been doing the fisheries work for the Makah Tribe, took the Makahs with him. I felt deep sadness every time I thought about losing the Makahs, my first Indian clients and the foundation of the firm's Indian practice. But this changed to exultation two years later when the Makahs came back—they said they could no longer stay with the other firm because of what they felt was a conflict of interest.

It soon became apparent that the firm's split had been healthy. Those of us who had stuck together shared the same philosophy. As one of my partners described it, if the departing group were the bottom-liners, we were the flower children. We pulled together and determined not to let this trauma affect us. And we returned to the principle of equal sharing among partners. Gone were the days when partners were reading printouts of the billable hours of other partners. We relied on a sense of honor. We were aware of our mutual obligation to put in the hours of work necessary to achieve excellent results for our clients. It was old-fashioned professionalism.

The departing partners had initially taken with them the Hoopas and the Makahs, as well as a number of other clients. But we retained our relationship with the Mille Lacs, the Northern Cheyennes, and Metlakatla in Alaska. Our remaining firm consisted of six lawyers, one of whom left in the first year following the split, reducing us to five. We were anxious about our practice, which had shrunk substantially. But soon other clients appeared, and in time we again had a busy and healthy law practice. In the years following 1986, we resumed representing the Makahs and we were retained by the Northern Arapaho Tribe of Wyoming, the Fallon Paiute-Shoshone, and the Moapa Paiute Tribe in Nevada. We were also retained by an organization representing the fishermen of the Alaska Peninsula called the Peninsula Marketing Association, or PMA.

But we had lost something. Our most colorful partners were gone; one had left before the split to move to Israel with his family, and the other went with the managing partner's group. The esprit de corps was replaced with a sense of anger at those who had broken our unity. We never again replaced the élan we had all felt at being a firm of tribal attorneys. The golden age of the firm was over, and a chapter in my life was closed.

TWENTY-THREE

Representing Fishermen of the Alaska Peninsula

AFTER THE FIRM SPLIT, THOSE OF US REMAINING WERE CONSIDER-ably buoyed when a group of fishermen in Alaska called asking to meet with us. The group was the Peninsula Marketing Association, taking its name from their location on the Alaska Peninsula. They wanted to talk to us, they said, because of our expertise in representing the Makahs, a group of fishermen who like themselves faced complaints that their ocean fishery was intercepting runs of salmon returning to inland rivers and streams. We were pleased at the prospect of a new and interesting client and prepared to meet with their representatives.

The Alaska Peninsula juts into the Bering Sea like a long tail, point-ing to the Aleutian Islands. Near the southerly tip of the peninsula are several fishing villages—Sand Point, King Cove, Cold Bay, and Nelson Lagoon. The villages exist because of the great runs of salmon passing en route to Bristol Bay and the rivers of western Alaska. The communi-ties are predominantly, but not entirely, Aleut.

Our new clients told us that their livelihood was threatened by increasingly aggressive efforts to close or severely restrict their fishery. Native communities on western Alaska rivers complained that the Alaska Peninsula fishery harmed their river fisheries by intercepting the salmon runs. In rebuttal, the peninsula fishermen pointed to biological studies that showed no harm had been done to the river fisheries. This struggle had been going on for years, fought annually in the hearings of the Alaska Fish Board and in the state courts of Alaska. The Peninsula

Marketing Association, or PMA, asked us to come to Sand Point to meet their fishermen and get a better understanding of the problem.

Sand Point is an interesting community. The trip there from Seattle requires a flight to Anchorage and then a flight on a local air carrier to the village. Although the permanent population as of 2000 was 950, Sand Point is home to the largest fishing fleet in the Aleutian chain. During fishing season, the population explodes as fishermen and processors take up temporary residence. The village was founded in 1898 by a San Francisco fishing company as a cod fishing station and trading post. It was populated by Aleuts from neighboring villages as well as by Scandinavians. It retains some of its Aleut character, and the Aleut fishermen are members of the Aleut Native Corporation, one of the Native corporations created by the Alaska Native Claims Settlement Act of 1971.

My partner Marc Slonim and I met with a group of fishermen in Sand Point and described our experience representing fishermen in mixed-stock fisheries, that is, where fish from different river systems move undifferentiated through an ocean area. The PMA fishermen felt they had been wrongly accused of intercepting salmon by demagogues who had whipped up emotions against them. They had already suffered losses from restrictions imposed by the Alaska Fish Board in response to those complaints. Marc and I went out in a boat with one of the fishermen to see a group of purse seiners setting their nets. It was a dramatic sight, the seiner holding position against a backdrop of steep cliffs, while one of its small tenders motored around with the net to close the purse. A lawyer is always better able to understand his client's case if he actually goes out on site. Seeing our clients in action, out here on the Pacific Ocean, gave us a feel for who they were and what they did.

Over the next several days, I met with PMA fishermen in other communities (Marc had to return to Seattle). Paul Gronholt, who like many of the fishermen was part Aleut, flew me to neighboring villages in his Cessna 180. It had oversize tires for landing on rough terrain, but was otherwise standard. Paul was an experienced Alaskan and obviously knew the country. Our first stop, King Cove, was 125 miles away, over land and water. As we flew, Paul was on the radio talking to people at King Cove alerting them to our expected time of arrival. Even though I was a licensed pilot myself and had flown over rugged terrain in a light plane, I had to suppress my fears as I looked out at the desolate landscape and the sea beneath us. There was no sign of civilization—no roads, no buildings, nothing. The thought of a forced landing here made me shudder.

As we crossed over the shore to land, Paul took the plane down to show me some of the wildlife of Alaska. We descended till we were flying two hundred feet above the terrain. Now I could appreciate the beauty of this land. Suddenly a herd of animals appeared below. They were caribou and they were running hard to escape the airplane. We flashed over them at a hundred miles an hour and they disappeared behind us. In a few minutes, we dropped lower over a flat area alongside a river. Paul banked into a turn and pointed out a female brown bear and her cubs below us. The mother looked at us over her shoulder, then sat down and turned her head directly up to watch as we circled. Paul leveled the wings and we flew on.

After about twenty minutes, we flew over a body of water toward a landmass and began to descend. At first I wondered where he planned to land, and then I saw a wide grassy field. There was nothing and no one there. But as we came down I saw four or five pickup trucks and one or two cars approaching. By the time we landed, they were parked and waiting for us. A group of men ambled over to our plane and Paul introduced me. I was astonished at the sudden appearance of all these vehicles in what had been an empty field minutes before. I had much to learn of life in the Alaska bush, where airplanes and radio are as commonplace as cars and telephones in the Lower 48.

We got into one of the trucks and were driven into King Cove. Everyone, it seems, knew we were coming, and a meeting had been called for later that afternoon. In the meantime, we waited in a nearby bar. It was busy and noisy. As I sat drinking my beer, I looked around at the faces of the men there. They were mostly young, but some were middle-aged; there were Aleuts, African Americans, Asians, Indians, Filipinos, and whites, all dressed in the rough clothes of working fishermen. At the meeting, I listened as the fishermen spoke—earnestly, plainly, and intensely. They felt threatened, and they looked to our firm to protect them. I outlined the plan of action Marc and I had discussed: building a strong case based on scientific fish-run data and making a forceful presentation to the Alaska Fish Board, with witness testimony and a warning of litigation in the courts if our evidence was ignored. The fishermen seemed to be satisfied.

The next morning we headed for Nelson Lagoon, a tiny Aleut community, population eighty-three. We took off in the Cessna, climbing over desolate terrain, and flew for about an hour. Ahead I saw a shoreline, the Bering Sea, Paul said. We had flown over the Alaska Peninsula from one side to the other. Paul circled over a cluster of houses on a spit of land, and we saw several men getting into their pickups. But here there was no wide expanse of land, just a narrow spit with only a short space to touch down and stop. Paul brought our little craft in slowly and it seemed we came to a stop only a hundred yards after touching down. I could appreciate the big tires on the plane; the surface was rough and the wheels rode over it with ease.

A small group of people, men and women, were on hand to meet us. They joked and laughed as we went over to their trucks. Paul handed me off to the man who, he said, was the mayor and told me I was invited to lunch at his house. The mayor was Aleut, and his strong facial features reflected his ethnicity. His house was less than half a mile away. As we approached, I saw fishing boats drawn up on the beach and men working on them. The mayor's house was a substantial one, resting on posts elevating it above the terrain. Under the house were heaps of fishing nets and gear.

The mayor told me his wife had prepared a special lunch for me and was looking forward to my visit. We mounted a flight of stairs to enter the house. There was an outer mudroom for stowing wet and muddy boots, and then we passed into his kitchen. As I walked through the kitchen and glimpsed the interior of the living room, I stared in disbelief. Hanging on the walls were abstract modern paintings and artwork. He then introduced his wife, a non-Indian woman, a gracious hostess, who invited me to sit down. She smiled as she saw me looking at the art. "I suppose you didn't expect to find this in Nelson Lagoon, did you?" I told her I was flabbergasted and asked how the art, which was obviously not Native, came to be there. She explained that she had lived most of her life in Seattle and loved art. She was the collector of all these lovely pieces, but she said her husband had grown to like them too.

I will never forget my experience in Nelson Lagoon. It taught me a few things. People cannot be stereotyped safely; there will always be surprises. And I saw a story of a people making a home in what seemed one of the most remote places imaginable.

Our firm's work for PMA involved us in protracted proceedings and meetings with fish biologists, reviews of statistical studies, and eventually, litigation. Marc carried the responsibility for most of this work and to this day continues to represent the fishermen of the Alaska Peninsula. For me, the experience was yet another example of how rich my life has been as an attorney working with Native groups and their natural environment. I would have missed so much had I remained in Chicago. I savored all that I saw and the people whose lives I observed, ever conscious of my identity and the privileged role I played as a tribal attorney.

TWENTY-FOUR

The Mille Lacs
Band of Chippewas

I HAD NO AWARENESS, AND CERTAINLY NO KNOWLEDGE, OF THE Mille Lacs Band of Chippewas before they contacted us in 1983. But this very interesting band became our clients, and in the years that followed we immersed ourselves in their legal problems. Their home is at Mille Lacs Lake, which lies 100 miles north of Minneapolis. It is a huge, beautiful lake, covering 207 square miles. It is one of Minnesota's most popular fishing lakes, containing large populations of walleye and bass. Around the shore are fishing resorts that do a booming business in the summer. In winter, thousands come to the lake for ice fishing, using little huts that are hauled onto the frozen lake surface.

Unfortunately for the Mille Lacs Band of Chippewas, or Ojibwe, as they call themselves, their reservation is in the midst of an intense concentration of fishing resorts and sports businesses, and their treaty rights and even their reservation have been threatened by their neighbors and by the state of Minnesota. The band has about 2,300 members and their reservation encompasses 61,000 acres. But it has been "checkerboarded" into small parcels of Indian land, scattered over a large area and surrounded by non-Indian land except for a few contiguous parcels.[1] Still, the Mille Lacs people have managed to retain much of their cultural integrity as an Indian people, gathering wild rice on Mille Lacs Lake and other nearby lakes, fishing and hunting, conducting traditional ceremonies and dances, and retaining their Ojibwe language.

I first went out to the reservation in the winter of 1983 to meet with their governing body, the band council. The Mille Lacs seemed different than other tribal people I had worked with. When I first met them they seemed tense and beleaguered. The band had struggled to overcome poverty and the problems of alcohol and poor health. They seemed determined to build their tribal government, but they also seemed bruised by the intolerance of the non-Indian community and tensions with the state government. They felt frustrated at every turn, and their existence as a tribe seemed to hang by a thread. Yet they retained their Ojibwe culture and language. As an outsider, one doesn't see this immediately, except for a few phrases of Ojibwe casually exchanged around the band offices. But at the annual meeting of the band, Art Gahbow, the band's chairman, delivered his address entirely in Ojibwe as his audience listened intently. Art Gahbow was a heavyset middle-aged man with a hearty laugh, and he wielded power with the self-assurance of an old-fashioned political boss.

Over time I came to know many band members. On one of my trips I was invited to attend a Mille Lacs dance held in a low one-story building that served as a community hall. One of my Mille Lacs friends told me that, if I attended the dance, I would certainly be called on to join in the dancing, so I should learn the basic dance step. He showed me and I tried it. At first I was clumsy and couldn't do it, though it was actually a simple rhythmic movement, but after a little practice I got it.

That evening when I entered the hall with my friend, the drumming and chanting was already in progress as I took my seat along the wall. Groups of Mille Lacs women danced arm in arm followed by groups of Mille Lacs men. The air was incredibly thick with smoke. At first I thought it was all from cigarettes, but then I saw an Indian pipe with a clay bowl and a long wooden stem being passed around. It came to me and I put the mouthpiece to my lips and drew gingerly on it. The taste of tobacco was rough on my tongue. I carefully blew the smoke out of my mouth and passed the pipe on to the man sitting next to me. Then I noticed that the women seated against the opposite wall were eying me, and my Mille Lacs friend chuckled. "They're going to ask you to dance," he said. Almost immediately two women came over and held out their hands. "Come on, you dance with us." I stood up, went out on the floor, and awkwardly joined in the group's dancing. This was greeted with amusement and approving smiles on the faces of the women in the hall. After resuming my seat, I noticed a pile of quilts in the corner of the room. These were being given as gifts, and to my surprise a woman brought one over and presented it to me. Before the evening was over, I was given three of these hand-sewn patterned quilts. I was deeply touched.

As I came to know the Mille Lacs government, I was surprised and impressed. They were the only tribe in the United States that had adopted a separation of powers form of government modeled on the American system. Their band code established clearly separate and independent legislative, executive, and judicial branches. The code was written in its entirety by an unusual person. His name was Jay Kanassetega, and his status was somewhat anomalous. Jay was not an enrolled member of the band, although he had been adopted by an Ojibwe family as an adult, spoke Ojibwe, knew and practiced the Ojibwe religion, had a Mille Lacs wife, and was conversant with all the traditional practices of the tribe. Jay, who had jet-black hair, had been adopted and raised by a non-Indian family in Boston. As a child, he began to think he might be of Indian ancestry when his adoptive parents showed him a letter they had received about him from someone claiming to be a relative. The name of the writer was Kanassetega. As a young man, Jay adopted the name.

He came to the reservation by a circuitous route. Jay had gone to a small Connecticut college and then to Purdue University, where he earned a master's degree in education. He was going to be a teacher. His teaching career began in the Minneapolis public schools, where he taught special education, working primarily with Indian children. There he developed a close relationship with the parents of one of his students; they were Ojibwe and members of the Mille Lacs Band. Over time Jay came to be considered a member of their family. As he met other relatives, he gradually immersed himself in the culture of the Ojibwe. The family adopted him in accordance with Ojibwe culture, and Jay felt himself to be Ojibwe. Ultimately, he moved north to the reservation at Mille Lacs and began teaching there. His roots in the band deepened. The band government then hired him.

Jay began discussions with the members of the government and Chairman Art Gahbow about their desire to reconstruct the band government and to establish a structure separate and apart from the

Chippewa Tribe, a federal construct of the seven Chippewa bands in Minnesota. Those discussions led Jay to seriously consider establishing a separation of powers band government. When the council gave him their approval, Jay set about drafting a complete band code of laws. This was an extraordinarily ambitious undertaking for someone with no training in law. When he was finished, the Mille Lacs Code comprised a structure for band government, a complete civil code, and a criminal code. Much of it was taken from the Minnesota statutes, but a good deal of it was designed to preserve the Ojibwe tradition and to fit the functional structure of the band. His acquired knowledge of the law, especially since he had personally drafted the code, led to his being appointed solicitor general, the band's chief legal officer.

Jay was, not surprisingly, deeply interested in the band's new attorneys, and we began working closely together on many tribal issues. He was particularly concerned over the quality of the band judges and the court system. The band asked me to conduct training sessions for the judges, so I prepared a syllabus with hypothetical cases and we had all-day training sessions. I tried to explain the method of analyzing a legal problem, the distinction between factual issues and legal issues. Due process was heavily emphasized and discussed. I asked the judges to try their hand at writing opinions and orders, and we discussed the results. It was an enriching experience to try to convert laypeople into judges with some understanding of the role of a court and of due process, all the while preserving tribal values.

As I worked closely with Jay on the band's legal system, I came to appreciate his extraordinary mastery of legal ideas. It became clear to me that though he was then thirty-seven years old, he should get trained as a lawyer.

"Jay, have you thought about going to law school?" I asked him one day.

He smiled in a self-deprecating manner. "Who, me? Naaw. I have thought about it, but I don't think I could get in. I don't have the grades. Besides, I'm too old."

"Jay, you're not too old. And as for the grades, they're not nearly as important to a law school as your real-world accomplishments. Why don't you apply?"

Jay found the suggestion intriguing, even exciting, especially since it came from me. Then I added, "Jay, if you apply to law school, let me know and I'll write you such a strong letter of recommendation that I guarantee you'll get in."

From that point on, Jay set his course for law school. He applied to several schools, including the University of Minnesota and, to my surprise, the University of Washington. When I asked him why he applied to Washington, he smiled and said, "Because you're there." I wrote the University of Washington admissions committee the strongest endorsement I could for Jay, describing his extraordinary achievement, how he wrote a complete civil and criminal code for the Mille Lacs Band and established the first separation of powers tribal government in America. Jay was accepted at the University of Washington Law School, graduated, and eventually became a partner in a large, prestigious Minneapolis law firm. But that was much later.

Meanwhile, the central issue for the band was its right to fish and hunt under their treaty. The more the band attempted to assert its rights, the more antagonism it aroused in the non-Indian community. The resort owners felt Indian fishing rights threatened their sportfishing livelihood, even though the Mille Lacs fished only for personal consumption and the size of their catch was minuscule compared to the sportsmen's catch. In my conversations with non-Indians that lived around the reservation, I saw their contempt for the Mille Lacs people. The non-Indians seemed, for the most part, to regard the Mille Lacs as a shiftless bunch of drunks. Their attitude was racist. And the Mille Lacs people felt this every time they had to deal with the local businesses. These attitudes and the hostility of sportsmen to Indian rights would ultimately come to a head in the courts. But that didn't occur till seven years later.

There had long been friction between the people of Mille Lacs and their non-Indian neighbors. Everything from the existence of the reservation to Indian fishing, hunting, and gathering wild rice had been a source of conflict. Some of the tension derived from simple racism, some from resentment that Indians claimed to be exempt from laws that applied to non-Indian sportsmen. That the reservation was located on Minnesota's largest and most popular lake increased the tensions. Like the tribes of the Pacific Northwest, the Minnesota, Michigan, and Wisconsin tribes insisted they had rights under treaties made with the

United States in the nineteenth century. The three states resisted those claims, just as the states of Oregon and Washington had, and the consequences for the Indians were the same: jail and confiscation of their catch and fishing gear.

In the 1970s, the midwestern tribes began to challenge the states in the courts. In 1983, the Seventh Circuit Court of Appeals handed down a decision in *Lac Courte Oreilles Band of Chippewas v. Voigt*, holding that the treaty of 1837 with the tribes of the Upper Mississippi preserved hunting and fishing rights and superseded state fishing and hunting laws.[2] The *Voigt* decision encouraged the Wisconsin tribes to spear-fish in the lakes where they had treaty rights. What followed was ugly. Non-Indian fishermen confronted Indians in massive demonstrations, rocks were thrown, ball bearings were shot from slingshots, Indians were threatened with physical violence, and had it not been for the presence of large numbers of police, there would have been riots.

The Minnesota tribes thought the *Voigt* decision upheld their rights, since they were among the parties to the 1837 treaty. The Mille Lacs and the other Minnesota Chippewas were claiming that they had rights under the 1837 treaty, as well as under an 1842 treaty. The state of Minnesota did not agree. The state attorney general and the Department of Natural Resources, or DNR, took the position that the *Voigt* decision was not binding on them, since they were in a different circuit. And besides, they felt the Minnesota tribes' rights under the treaty had been extinguished by an 1850 executive order of President Zachary Taylor. Still, the Minnesota DNR wanted to avoid the kind of violence that had plagued Wisconsin. They began negotiations with the tribes to settle the long-running conflict. Agreements were reached with some of the Minnesota Chippewa bands, but the Mille Lacs situation was more complex. The lake involved was huge, and the stakes were higher.

The Mille Lacs Band had its own director of natural resources, a young man named Don Wedll. Wedll was educated, intelligent, and dedicated to the protection of the band. Though he was not an Indian by blood, he became a band member culturally. His wife was a band member and he learned to speak Ojibwe. He learned the customs and the traditions. He was able to build a birch-bark canoe, something no one else in the band could do. But his great value to the band was his knowledge of the lake's fishery and his ability to come to reasoned and reasonable positions. Through Don Wedll's efforts and with the assistance of Marc Slonim of our firm, an agreement was reached between the band and the Minnesota DNR to resolve the conflict by limiting the catch of the Mille Lacs fisheries. But the white sportsmen vehemently opposed the settlement and caused the state to abandon it. The band, under the leadership of its chairman, Margie Anderson, decided it would fight. Litigation presented our law firm with a dilemma: the band had no money to pay for the suit, which would be expensive. We decided to go forward anyway and finance the case. Maybe attorneys' fees might be awarded if we won—a distant prospect—or perhaps the band would find some means to pay in the future.

The case of *Mille Lacs v. Minnesota* was filed in 1990, charging that the state of Minnesota had interfered with the band's right to hunt and fish in the ceded territory protected under the 1837 treaty. The lawsuit put the state in a difficult position. If the *Voigt* decision was held to apply to Minnesota, the argument was over: treaty rights would trump state law. Within a month, officials of the state DNR approached the band. They wanted to negotiate. Over the next two years the band and the state carried on negotiations. Don Wedll and Marc Slonim worked hard to achieve a settlement. The negotiations were difficult; there was much at stake. Every step had to be approved by the Minnesota state government. By January of 1993, the parties came to a tentative agreement. The main provisions included the transfer of 7,500 acres of state land to Mille Lacs ownership, the establishment of a 6,000-acre treaty fishing zone on the 132,000-acre Mille Lacs Lake, and a $10 million payment to the band spread over five years. In exchange, the Mille Lacs Band would limit its harvest of walleye to 24,000 pounds a year.

Again, the agreement met with opposition from non-Indian sportfishing and resort interests and even from some band members. Ultimately, the band decided to submit the agreement to a vote of its members, and 60 percent voted for the settlement. But the sportfishing interests were another story. They would not be placated. The state concluded that any agreement would have to be approved by the Minnesota legislature, so in 1993 a bill was introduced and hearings began. The sports interests mobilized their supporters around the state, including the well-known former coach of the Minnesota Vikings football team, Bud Grant. The hearings were contentious. In the end, the legislature bowed to public pressure and rejected the settlement. The die was cast, and Minnesota would have to run the risk of a lawsuit.

The legal challenge facing Marc Slonim and his co-counsel, John Arum, another member of our firm, was to demonstrate that the 1850 executive order of President Taylor—which explicitly terminated Indian hunting and fishing rights under the 1837 treaty—was invalid. The treaty language read: "The privilege of hunting and fishing, and gathering the wild rice upon the lands, the rivers and the lakes ceded, is guaranteed to the Indians, during the pleasure of the President of the United States." In 1850, President Taylor ordered the Indians removed and revoked their hunting and fishing rights. To show why this did not conclusively terminate the rights of Mille Lacs and the other bands under the treaty would require extensive historical research into the background of the executive order.

The costs of the litigation were mounting, but a fortunate development eliminated the financial worry. In 1991 the Mille Lacs Band opened a casino. Soon, the casino was booming, and it expanded to accommodate the growing number of customers. The band now had the funds to support the heavy costs of litigation. But their opponents were even better funded. An anti–treaty rights organization raised more than $1.25 million to oppose the Mille Lacs. The opposition broadened when, after the Band filed its case against the state, nine Minnesota counties intervened to join with the state. The counties and a group of local landowners were represented by Jim Johnson, the same Jim Johnson who as an assistant attorney general in *U.S. v. Washington* had assured the commercial fishermen that the Boldt decision would be overturned on appeal.

The case went to trial in the court of District Judge Diana Murphy in 1994. The Mille Lacs evidence developed by its anthropologists and historians showed that President Taylor's executive order was issued to assuage Minnesota interests. Those interests had actually wanted the tribes removed from Wisconsin *to* Minnesota to bring Indian trade and federal money to the state. But despite Machiavellian deceptions, the tribes ultimately returned to their Wisconsin homes. The executive order became a dead letter and was abandoned. The federal government never implemented the order and dealt with the tribes as though the order no longer existed. After a three-week trial, Judge Murphy issued her decision upholding the Mille Lacs position and ruling that they had rights under the 1837 treaty, unaffected by the executive order. The state and its interveners appealed to the Eighth Circuit Court of Appeals. In 1997, the Eighth Circuit affirmed Judge Murphy's decision in a unanimous three-judge opinion.[3]

The state of Minnesota then sought review by the U.S. Supreme Court, and in the spring of 1998 the Court granted certiorari. This was ominous. The court rarely grants certiorari unless it is concerned about the lower court decision. It was particularly worrisome because the Rehnquist Supreme Court had been notoriously hostile to Indian causes. The attitude of tribes and tribal attorneys was that no one wanted this Court to pass judgment on important Indian rights. Indian hunting and fishing rights in Minnesota, Michigan, and Wisconsin were at risk. The case could overturn the *Voigt* decision because it would deal with the rights of all tribes and bands under the 1837 treaty. It was reported that at a fund-raising banquet, Jim Johnson addressed the audience and, citing recent rulings against tribal claims, predicted victory in the Supreme Court. He had said much the same thing thirty-four years earlier when *U.S. v. Washington* was under appellate review. He was wrong then, and our clients and all the Indians of the upper Midwest prayed he would be wrong again.

A year was consumed in intense preparation of legal briefs by all the parties. The Mille Lacs case was in the hands of Marc Slonim and John Arum. The Ojibwes of Michigan, Wisconsin, and Minnesota conducted ceremonies to bless the actions of the attorneys. They decided to take their spirituality directly to the Supreme Court. They organized a thousand-mile run to carry a ceremonial treaty staff all the way to the Court in Washington, D.C. The run, called the Waabanong, began at the Lac Du Flambeau reservation in northern Wisconsin and continued in relays until the last group arrived at the steps of the Supreme Court. By the courtesy of the Court clerk, the ceremonial treaty staff was allowed into an office adjacent to the Court's chamber. The courtroom itself was packed to capacity. Every Indian who could get to the Court sat in the courtroom or in an adjacent room, where the proceedings were piped in.[4]

Marc Slonim stepped to the podium to persuade a skeptical court that a presidential executive order was a nullity. His argument, according to those who heard it, was a masterful presentation of the tangled history demonstrating that the executive order had been abandoned and never implemented. He also had to show that President Taylor's unilateral order for the removal of the Indian people was unauthorized by the Constitution and federal law. As he expected, he was hammered by Chief Justice William Rehnquist. Most of the tribal attorneys sitting in the courtroom predicted a 9–0 ruling against the Mille Lacs. The Indians in the courtroom, however, predicted that Marc would win. The Indians were right.

In March 1999, the Supreme Court upheld the Eighth Circuit in a 5–4 opinion. Writing for the majority, Justice Sandra Day O'Connor said the president's power to issue a removal order must stem from either Congress or the Constitution itself. The state of Minnesota had failed to show that any such authority existed. The order itself, she said, was a dead letter, never implemented or enforced, and effectively abandoned. The Indians' prayers had been answered and they rejoiced in the outcome. This decision was a great victory, but by a razor-thin majority of the court.[5]

The magnitude of the legal achievement can hardly be overstated. Marc and John had put before a Supreme Court that was highly deferential to presidential power and unsympathetic to Indian rights the question of whether a president had the authority to diminish Indian treaty rights—and they had won. Prudence cautions against reading too much into the decision. It was based on a precise reading of history, a history that was carefully exhumed and presented forcefully. The victory was a triumph of lawyers' skills partnered with scholars' research. The political consequences were great. The tribes of Minnesota, Wisconsin, and Michigan could breathe more easily. Their treaty rights were no longer hanging in the balance. It was another building block in the reconstruction of an Indian nation, back from near destruction.

I have described the attitude of the Mille Lacs Band's non-Indian neighbors as disparaging and racist. That may not be true of all their neighbors, but I believe it is a fair description of many, perhaps most of them. I have recounted their determined effort to suppress Mille Lacs treaty hunting and fishing; they were instrumental in preventing the state of Minnesota from reaching a reasonable settlement with the band, and they forced the band into litigation and persuaded the Minnesota legislature to reject settlement and risk everything in a contest in the courts. Their hard-core antagonism to treaty rights ultimately led to a defeat in the U.S. Supreme Court. But unlike the public's acceptance of Indian treaty rights in the Pacific Northwest after the Boldt decision was affirmed, the Supreme Court's disposition of the Mille Lacs case did not lead to non-Indian acceptance of Mille Lacs rights. Instead, non-Indians challenged the very existence of the reservation.

The reservation is located in Mille Lacs County, and most of the members of the band live in a tiny town called Vineland. Onamia is an adjacent town, larger than Vineland and predominantly non-Indian. The band and its members have dealt with local businesses, stores, banks, and services for more than fifty years. Reports of bias and discrimination against the members of the band are commonplace. Their neighbors have made no secret of their low opinion of the Mille Lacs Indians.

In 1991, the band opened a small casino at Onamia. Its patronage grew rapidly and the band soon enlarged it. Eventually the band built an adjoining hotel with 494 rooms that also enjoyed a flourishing business. The band built a second casino on the reservation at Hinckley, Minnesota. This too flourished, and hotel of 281 rooms was built to accommodate guests at this casino. The revenues generated by the two casinos made them the largest businesses in Mille Lacs and Pine counties. They employed almost three thousand people, 90 percent non-Indian. Before the casinos were opened, the Mille Lacs Band was one of the poorest tribes in the nation, with an 81 percent poverty rate. After the casinos were developed, the poverty rate dropped to less than 17 percent.[6]

The casinos have brought great benefits to the non-Indian neighbors of the Mille Lacs. They are the largest employers in each of their counties. New local businesses have been established, the local hospital has expanded, mainly because the casinos provide health benefits not previously enjoyed by the residents. The casinos pay almost $1 million in taxes each year to the two counties, as well as state and local taxes collected on the employees and on sales and services generated by the casinos. The casinos have given millions in charitable donations to state, local, and private institutions. You might think this would earn the Mille Lacs Band the respect and appreciation of its neighbors. Sadly, this has not been the case.

In 2003, the non-Indian citizens of the counties in which the Mille Lacs reservation is located joined with local business interests to bring suit against the band in federal court. What were they seeking? Nothing less than a declaration that the reservation had no legal existence. The attackers had gathered contributions to support the suit totaling almost a million dollars. The case against the band was brought by Mille Lacs County, and it was joined by the First National Bank of Milaca. They were supported by non-Indian property owners and resort owners. Now the Mille Lacs Band had to defend its very right to exist. Again, Marc Slonim huddled with anthropologists and historians to defend the reservation.

The case was assigned to Judge James Rosenbaum, the same judge who had presided over the Wanda Boswell case fourteen years earlier, which I describe in the next chapter. Pretrial proceedings involved extensive depositions in which all the experts were closely interrogated by both sides. Marc was ready to go to trial, confident that the Mille Lacs would win. But before subjecting the reservation to the vagaries of protracted litigation, and perhaps an antagonistic Supreme Court, he felt bound to take a legal step based on what he perceived to be a fatal flaw in the plaintiffs' case—lack of standing to sue. Marc filed a motion to dismiss the case on the grounds that the plaintiffs could not demonstrate that the reservation caused them any damage. Absent any damage, they had no standing to bring a suit.

The county was represented by Tom Tobin, a South Dakota attorney who has made a career attacking the existence of Indian reservations. The case was argued before Judge Rosenbaum, with Marc and the county's attorney squaring off against each other. Rosenbaum was blunt. He asked the plaintiffs' attorneys: "What's your problem?" When they tried to spin out some fanciful harms that their clients might suffer from the existence of the reservation, Rosenbaum repeated his ominous question: "What's the problem, counsel?" He made it clear that he hadn't heard anything that constituted actual harm. And with that, he threw the case out of court. The good citizens of Mille Lacs County had spent $1.3 million in a losing effort to destroy the reservation.

For the sake of the Mille Lacs people, I hope that their neighbors begin to recognize that the Indian people living in their midst are not a foreign body, to be extirpated. They are the area's original inhabitants whose presence enriches the state and the nation. It is shameful that in the twenty-first century any group of Americans should be so hostile to the indigenous people of this nation and to the treaties made with them by the nation. But as of this writing, the legal existence of the reservation has been challenged by the state of Minnesota, and that issue is still not resolved.

TWENTY-FIVE

The Wanda Boswell Case

IN 1984, I BROUGHT A LAWSUIT ON BEHALF OF A YOUNG WOMAN who lived on the Mille Lacs reservation, Wanda Boswell. It is a case I have never forgotten. It began with a call from Jay Kanassetega from the reservation. "Niji," he said, when I picked up the phone, and I knew it was Jay. He always called me Niji, Ojibwe for "friend."

"Niji, we wonder if you might be interested in taking some legal action for a young woman here. Her name is Wanda Boswell. She's married to a band member, Billy Joe Boyd. About seven or eight months ago, she was in the Elk River jail and she lost her baby. It sounds to me like they didn't treat her right. A lot of people here are upset with the way she was treated. Since you're coming out here next week, would you be willing to talk to her and see if she has a case? If you do take her case, it would be a private case because the band is not asking you to handle it as a band case."

The following week I met Wanda to discuss whether or not she had a case. She was a handsome young woman in her late twenties. She carried herself with dignity, but was ill at ease when she began to tell me of her time in the jail at Elk River. I had never met Wanda Boswell before, but perhaps because I was the band's attorney she spoke frankly, reciting the events slowly and deliberately.

"I had drove down to the Twin Cities to visit my sisters on a Saturday. We were all at Marie's house till about eight o'clock and Joanna said, 'Let's go out and have a few beers.' [These are not the real names of Wanda's sisters.] So we went to this place she knew and the three of us sat around and had some beers. We had a nice time. I don't see them so often and we talked a lot. Around ten thirty, eleven o'clock, I said I better get started driving home, 'cause it takes about two hours to get to Onamia. I was just getting to Elk River when this state patrol pulls me over. He asked me how much I had to drink and I told him some beers. Then he checks on warrants and finds two old ones that I had forgot about and says he's sorry but because of them he has to take me to jail.

"When I got into the jail there was this lady jailer at the booking desk and she was filling out forms. There was a health questionnaire and she asked me if I had any medical condition and I told her I was six and a half months pregnant. She asked if I had any problem with it and I told her that I had a bloody discharge from my vagina about a week ago and I had fainted three days ago. She didn't say nothin' about it. Then she asked if I had a doctor, and I told her my doctor's name and I gave her his phone number and she wrote it all down on the medical form. This lady said they couldn't release me till I made bail on the two warrants and the DUI, and she told me I would have to post three hundred and fifty dollars. She let me use the phone and I called Billy Joe and told him where I was and that we needed to raise three hundred and fifty dollars to bail out. Billy said he didn't have that kind of money and his mother didn't either, but he was going to go around the next day and see if he could borrow the money, and if he couldn't raise enough he was going to pawn his rifle. I told this to the jailer and she said I would be locked up till someone from my family came with the bail money."

Wanda was looking down at the table and seemed to have difficulty continuing. "Tell me what happened next," I encouraged. Wanda gathered herself and went on.

"She [the jailer] gave me a jail uniform and took me to the women's bathroom to shower and change. She stood there and watched me the whole time I was taking the shower. In the shower I saw that I was bleeding again from my vagina. I told her about it. She didn't say nothin' and just handed me a sanitary napkin and took me back to the cell.

"They had a separate women's section and it was closed off by a steel door with a little window in it. Inside there was a kind of day room, and then there were two or three cells in there. The cells weren't locked— you could go in and out to the day room. But the day room had a steel door that was locked. She put me in one of the cells. There was a bunk and a toilet and a sink in the cell. So I laid down and went to sleep. I woke up real early the next morning with bad cramps. They got worse and worse and I was afraid my labor was starting. So I got out of my bunk and went to the dayroom door to call the jailer. I yelled, 'I need a doctor, get me a doctor.' But nobody came. So I began pounding on the door with my fist. Finally a woman jailer came and unlocked the door and came in and asked me why I was yelling. I told her I was cramping and bleeding and I needed a doctor right away. I thought my labor had started. This jailer said I would have to bail out."

"What did she say about getting a doctor?" I asked.

"She didn't say nothin' about getting a doctor," Wanda answered.

"So what happened then?"

"I went back to my cell and laid down. But the pain got worse and I began crying and yelling for help. I thought maybe that if I used the toilet it would ease the pain, but when I was on the toilet I felt something pass and looked in the toilet and there was a bloody piece of tissue in it. I thought if I showed this to the jailer maybe she would believe me that I needed a doctor. So, I got a little plastic baggie and scooped it out of the toilet and put it in the baggie. I went to the door and banged on it again with my fists and screamed for the jailer. Finally, after a long while she came. I showed her the bloody tissue in the baggie. She said my family would have to post bail before I could be released, but she said she would take me to make another call to find out if they were coming with the bail money. So she led me to the phone and I called home. My mother in law, Shirley Boyd answered. Shirley told me Billy was running around the village trying to raise the money but he didn't have it yet. Shirley said to have this jailer call her if she didn't believe I needed to go to a hospital right away. So I told the jailer I needed to get to a hospital right away. She said I would have to get the bail. I told her to call Shirley Boyd and she did. Shirley told me later that she had told this jailer that I needed to get to the hospital immediately, because I had a history of fast deliveries with my first two kids. But the only thing the jailer did was tell Shirley that she needed three hundred and fifty dollars to let me out. She didn't say nothin' about getting a doctor or getting me to the hospital."

There was a long pause before Wanda continued. "I went back to my cell and the pains started coming quicker and harder, and I was screaming for help. There was a one-way speakerphone in my cell and the jailer came on and asked me what was going on and I told her. She just said to lay down and put my feet up because nothing can be done till your family gets here with the bail money. I tried to ask her how soon they would be there, but there was no answer. The speakerphone was turned off.

"I was laying in my bunk, crying and screaming in pain for about two hours and nobody came. Finally the jailer came back with a cop and he seemed to know what he was doing. He came in and looked at me and heard me yelling from pain, looked at the bleeding and told the jailer to get an ambulance right away. In the ambulance on the way to the hospital, I felt the baby coming out and the ambulance attendant looked and said to the driver, 'Radio the hospital and tell them she's delivering now and it looks like a breech birth.'

"When we got to the hospital in Elk River, the doctor and some nurses were waiting and they got the baby out, but I knew there was something wrong because they were working on him. I was crying and saying, 'Oh, God, let him live!' But after about a half-hour, the doctor came over and said, 'I'm sorry, but we couldn't save him.'

"They took me to a room and put me to bed. I told them I wanted my son's body because I wanted to take him back to Onamia and give him an Indian burial. A little while later, Billy and Shirley came in. They had gone to the jail with the bail money and the jailers told them I was in the hospital. They didn't tell them our son was dead. So Billy and Shirley came to the hospital. We asked the nurse to bring us the body. She did, and we named him Joseph and wrapped him in an Indian blanket to take back to Onamia. I held him in my arms on the drive back and we had an Indian burial the next day."

With this, Wanda finished. She had maintained her composure until she reached the scene in the hospital where Joseph's body was turned over to her, and then she broke down sobbing.

Listening to Wanda, I was angry. I understood why the Mille Lacs people were upset. How could the jailers be so callous? Their behavior was inexcusable. I told Wanda I was convinced the county authorities had violated her rights and I felt she had grounds to sue them. I asked her if that's what she wanted to do and she said yes.

We filed a lawsuit in federal District Court in Minneapolis against the Sherburne County Sheriff, the jail, and the jailers for violation of Wanda's constitutional rights. I needed a Minneapolis attorney to join me in the case, and I was fortunate to find a smart, experienced young attorney. Mark Kosieradzki was a battle-hardened plaintiff's attorney who proved invaluable. We began the process of pretrial discovery. This meant interrogating the sheriff and each of the jailers and examining all of the jail's records surrounding Wanda's incarceration. What we found explained why the jailers had refused to call an ambulance. We learned that the jailer, instead of getting trained medical help, had called the chief jailer for instructions. This official was operating under the sheriff's policy of denying prisoners medical treatment and especially hospitalization, in order to save money. Jailers had been instructed to use their own judgment about the seriousness of a prisoner's medical needs rather than consulting trained medical personnel. The jailers had no training in medical care. The sheriff's policy had paid off—the jail's medical expenditures had fallen in each of the three preceding years.

In Wanda's case, the chief jailer instructed the woman jailer on duty to try to get Wanda released on bail rather than summon medical help. We discovered a telex message that the Sherburne County jailer had sent to the Crow Wing County Jail, which held outstanding warrants on Wanda: "We have in custody Wanda Charlene Boswell on DWI. She has a warrant for your co. $50.00 bail. She also has a warrant in Becker Co. She has the bail for $150 for this one. She is 6 mo. pregnant and is starting to bleed. What would you like done about your bail. We want her out of our facility as soon as possible. Any suggestions?" Crow Wing County responded, "If she has the bail take it—if she doesn't release her from our charges, we'll try for her later. We don't want the medical bills either."

But Becker County refused to release their warrant and, contrary to the telex, Wanda did not have the $150 for that bail. So the Sherburne County Jail authorities persisted in trying to get Wanda's family to come up with the bail money so they could rid themselves of her. The jailer called Billy Joe several times and urged him to get the money. When Billy Joe and his mother told the jailer they had better get Wanda to a hospital quickly because of her history of fast deliveries, the only response was, "Get the bail money."

Billy Joe ran around the community frantically trying to borrow money and raised only part of the bail. Then he tried to pawn his rifle, but the pawnshop didn't open till nine o'clock. When it opened, he got his money and drove to Elk River. But it was too late. They told him to go to the hospital, where he found a grieving Wanda. All they could do was wrap the baby in an Indian blanket and drive back to the reservation to bury him.

This was the case we intended to present to a federal jury in Minneapolis. The attorney for the jailers and the county sheriff fought us every inch of the way. After we completed our pretrial discovery, the defendants moved to have the case thrown out without a trial, claiming "qualified immunity." They argued that government officials performing a discretionary function were shielded from liability so long as they did not violate clearly established constitutional rights that a reasonable official would have known about. The District Court judge denied the motion. To our surprise, the defendants appealed the ruling to the Eighth Circuit Court of Appeals. This meant a substantial delay, which turned out to be almost a year. My partner, Marc Slonim, wrote the brief and argued the case before the appeals court. The decision came down in June of 1988, upholding the District Court's refusal to dismiss the case.[1] We could finally go forward with the trial.

The defendants' strategy of bringing an appeal proved unwise. The Eighth Circuit was so emphatic that Wanda's constitutional rights had been violated if what we alleged was true, and the court's indignation at her treatment was so blunt, that the appeals court ruling removed any uncertainty about her rights in the mind of the subsequent trial judge. The appeal was also an expensive misstep for the defendants. The delay ultimately increased our award for attorneys' fees and interest for the time Wanda's case had been pending.

We went to trial in the courtroom of the Honorable James Rosenbaum, a tough, practical, no-nonsense judge. Our jury was made up of equal numbers of men and women. One of the men had been a farmer. The other jury members represented a general cross-section of Minneapolis. In my opening statement, I pointed to the United States seal that hung on the wall: "Ladies and gentlemen, that is the great seal of the United States and we are here in a United States federal court because Wanda Boswell's rights under our constitution were violated by these defendants." Then I recited the painful details of what happened in the

Sherburne County Jail. When I was finished and looked at the jury, I was confident that we would win.

The trial consumed three and a half weeks and turned into a battle of medical experts. We put into evidence the jailer's communications with the other counties, which demonstrated that all counties wanted to avoid medical expenses. We showed that neither of the women jailers on duty during Wanda's incarceration made any effort to contact her doctor or any other trained medical person. There was not much the defense could do to refute the facts—the refusal to provide medical care was indisputable. Instead, the defense concentrated on different issues: They tried to pin the blame on Wanda for drinking in the first place. And they said it wouldn't have made any difference if she had been taken to a hospital earlier; Joseph would not have survived anyway. They retained a pathologist who had examined slides of Wanda's placental tissue, and the doctor claimed she found evidence of a condition that would have resulted in a miscarriage. Here, Mark Kosieradzki's extensive contacts in the Minneapolis medical community proved invaluable. He found a perinatologist and a neonatologist, as well as a placental pathologist, all of whom testified that if Wanda had been taken to the hospital even forty-five minutes sooner, there was an 87 percent probability that Joseph would have survived.

We called as one of our witnesses the Elk River police officer who had seen Wanda after her night in jail and had finally ordered that she be taken to the hospital. He had just stopped in to have a cup of coffee at the jail, when the jailer asked if he knew anything about pregnancy and miscarriages. The officer was a trained emergency medical technician and did have some basic knowledge, had done some deliveries. The jailer asked him if he could take a look at one of the women being held. That was at about ten o'clock in the morning. Wanda had been calling for help since seven. The police officer testified that as he walked down the corridor toward the women's cell block, he could hear Wanda's cries several hundred feet away, through a steel door. They were "quite loud," he said. He found her bleeding and in severe pain. After a brief examination, he told the jailer to get an ambulance immediately. Our best witness was, of course, Wanda Boswell. She was well-dressed and carried herself with dignity. She took the stand and told her story straightforwardly. But she was unable to maintain her self-control throughout her testimony. At several points, she had to stop as she wept.

There was little the defense could do to mitigate the power of our evidence. Before the trial was over, the attorney representing the Sherburne County Sheriff's insurance company offered a $175,000 settlement for the sheriff's office to be released from the case. Our case against the sheriff would have been difficult to sustain—our main case was against the jail and the jailers. So we felt the offer was a good one, and with Wanda's approval we accepted it. That left the main defendants.

At the conclusion of the trial, Judge Rosenbaum declared a recess and indicated he wanted to see all the attorneys in his chambers before closing arguments. Mark Kosieradzki and I had no idea what he was going to say and were a little surprised. The judge was emphatic: "I think the defendants ought to settle this case." When the defendants' attorney began to remonstrate, citing the strength of their medical defense, the judge cut him off: "Mr. X [the defense counsel], I have been a judge for many years and I have heard all of the evidence. If you think this jury is going to return a verdict for the defendants, you're barking up the wrong tree. The plaintiff is going to get a verdict in her favor and the only question is how much. Now I'm going to recess until this afternoon. That gives you about two hours to reach a settlement. If you don't, then we'll move right into closing argument and the case will go to the jury."

We walked into the courtroom, and the defendants' attorney went to telephone the insurance company that would have to pay the award. He came back with a figure: $250,000, take it or leave it. We thought we would do better than that. We had spent a lot retaining expert medical witnesses as well as on other expenses of the litigation. Paying those costs and deducting attorney fees would leave Wanda with an amount we considered inadequate in view of her suffering and the loss of her son. We laid out the risks for Wanda. Did she want to accept the settlement or gamble on the jury? Wanda's answer was thoughtful and measured: "I didn't have no money before you guys took my case, and if I don't have no money after this is over, I'll still feel it was worth it to make those people face me in court. No amount of money is going to bring Joseph back anyway, so let's go ahead and see what that jury decides."

Mark and I shared the closing argument. I dealt with the inhuman treatment Wanda had received, and Mark did a masterful job explaining the complex medical testimony. Our opponent blustered through his closing argument. When he sat down, I was confident we had carried the day. The jury deliberated for about six hours. When they returned to the courtroom, many of them were smiling, a good sign. They awarded $680,000. After the verdict was announced and the jury polled, Judge Rosenbaum thanked them for their service and adjourned the proceedings. As we stood up, a number of the jurors came over to Wanda and shook her hand. Several of the women jurors embraced her. There were smiles and tears. Then Wanda came back to Mark and me and hugged us. It was one of those moments that a lawyer treasures. We had vindicated Wanda's rights and in the process had the sweet satisfaction of righting a wrong.

There was more. Because the case was brought as a violation of Wanda's constitutional rights, the law awarded the victim her attorney fees in addition to the damage award. We had a hearing before the judge on that issue, which was hotly contested. The judge's written decision came out a few days later and we were awarded $275,000 in fees; Wanda was awarded $155,000 in interest. Wanda and Billy Joe and all their relatives who had traveled to Minneapolis for the trial were jubilant. To celebrate our win, my co-counsel Mark Kosieradzki hosted an elegant dinner in a hotel for Wanda and Billy Joe and everyone who had worked on the case. Lennie even flew out from Seattle to join us. This case was one of the high points of my career as a lawyer.

We wanted Wanda and her children to enjoy the benefits of her award, so after consulting with her we set aside a sum of money to enable her to buy a house on the White Earth reservation, about 150 miles northeast of the Mille Lacs reservation, where she was enrolled and had family. The remainder was put into a trust fund for her and her children. The balance would be distributed to her in regular installments over the next twenty years, until 2009.

After our success in Minneapolis, I learned that the victory was greeted with quiet satisfaction on the Mille Lacs reservation. Many felt that Wanda had been mistreated by the white authorities in the same way Indians have often been mistreated by police and jailers. But few go to attorneys or are able to launch such a powerful response. Indeed, seven months had elapsed before our firm had been contacted. That wouldn't have happened if the Mille Lacs Band did not have Jay

Kanassetega, who had some knowledge of the legal system.

Several years ago, Wanda and her children came out to Seattle to visit us. She was very happy and affectionate with my wife and me. The ability to operate the legal machinery in order to get justice for a victimized individual is deeply satisfying. Perhaps it also sends a message to people who would deny the humanity of those over whom they have power.

TWENTY-SIX

The Northern Arapaho Tribe

IN JANUARY OF 1992 OUR FIRM RECEIVED AN UNUSUAL COMMU-
nication in the mail: an invitation from the Northern Arapaho Tribe
of Wyoming seeking law firms to apply as the tribe's general counsel.
We had never seen anything like it. In our experience, this was not
the way tribes went about selecting a tribal attorney. Steve Chestnut
wrote a response indicating our interest and telling the tribe who we
were, which prompted a return phone call and some discussion. We
were invited to the reservation for a personal interview.

We did a little homework on the tribe before meeting them. The
Northern Arapahos lived on the Wind River Indian Reservation in
north-central Wyoming, but their occupancy was highly unusual; they
shared the reservation with another tribe, the Eastern Shoshones.
Though there was no formal boundary delineating territorial ownership of the reservation's 2.2 million acres, the Northern Arapahos
lived mainly on the eastern half and the Shoshones on the western
half. The Northern Arapahos outnumbered the Shoshones 7,500 to
4,200, according to the 1990 census, but the tribes shared ownership of all reservation resources equally. The two tribes had entirely
separate tribal governments and government centers—the Northern
Arapaho center was at Ethete on the east side, and the Shoshone's
was at Fort Washakie on the west side. Each tribe governed its own
members, but where matters affected both tribes, the two governments
met in joint session. This curious state of affairs had resulted when

the United States settled a destitute and landless band of Northern Arapahos "temporarily" on the Shoshone reservation for the winter of 1877–78—and there they remained. In 1938, the United States paid the Shoshones $4.5 million to compensate them for the land occupied by the Arapahos.[1] The two tribes have peacefully coexisted on the Wind River reservation.

What made the Northern Arapahos unique for us was their income from oil and gas. While we had some experience in this area, we were not specialists in oil and gas law. But the tribe's immediate legal problem was not related to those resources. They were involved in a major water rights case against the state of Wyoming and a large number of non-Indian ranchers and farmers. We did have some experience with *Winters* rights and *Walton* rights—the water rights that had been decided by *U.S. v. Winters* (1908) and *Colville Tribes v. Walton* (1989)—though we felt at a disadvantage compared to firms with more expertise in oil and gas law and water rights. On the other hand, there were not many law firms that had the experience as well as the commitment to Indian tribes that we did.

Steve Chestnut, Rich Berley (another partner in our firm), and I flew to Riverton, Wyoming, for our meeting with the Northern Arapaho Tribe. We met first with a selection committee in a motel in Riverton. It didn't go well. We learned that three firms were under consideration, the two others with considerable experience in oil and gas. We also learned that we would appear before the entire tribal membership the following morning at the tribal gym in Ethete, in what turned out to be something of a beauty contest. Representatives of each of the three firms would make presentations and answer questions. We would draw straws to determine the order of presentation. The membership would then vote on which firm they wanted.

At the gym the next morning, we met our competition. Although we exchanged cordial remarks, everyone felt awkward. Lawyers rarely experience such personal competition for a client. We drew the last position and waited in an outer room for the other two firms to finish. Since we couldn't hear what they were saying or what the audience response was, we were left to speculate about how the firms were received based on how much time had elapsed. Finally, we were called in. The gym was full, with about two hundred Arapahos in the audience. I spoke first:

Thank you very much for having us come out here. No matter how it turns out, it's been a good experience and we're proud to be one of the three firms you people thought were best suited to you...I'm the senior member of my firm. I began that firm twenty-eight years ago. There are six of us. We have been specializing in Indian tribal representation for the past twenty-seven years. I'm proud to say that we still represent the very first tribe that hired us twenty-seven years ago, the Makah Tribe. And we have represented other tribes like the Northern Cheyenne for nineteen years...and I think that means something about their satisfaction with us.

We do have a philosophy in our law firm and it's a very simple one. We decided a long time ago which side we were on. We decided we're on the Indian side. That means we will not represent anybody that is going to do business with a tribe simply because we are not willing to take a chance that they might have a conflict with the tribe. We would never take a case against a tribe.

A second policy we have is that we are committed to tribal sovereignty, and we have been since the first day we began working for tribes.

A third part of our philosophy is that we do the highest-quality work we can do: not just good, not just excellent, but superior. And, we have found that superior work gets superior results. We have been successful, I think, because we have taken new looks at old problems, and we have figured out new ways to solve those problems.

So I don't think it is just a matter of finding a law firm that has experience...All these firms, including us, have experience. What is important is what kind of results did we get?

One category of our work has been in what I call rescues, where we've been called in when other lawyers have been doing the work on an Indian case and it's gone badly, and we have been called on to try to rescue it, to save it. I can think of two such cases. One of them was called *Hollowbreast v. Northern Cheyenne Tribe*.

Here I described *Hollowbreast*, in which a court ruling that the tribe did not own the subsurface coal would have resulted in large areas of the reservation being strip-mined. I told of how, after the case had been lost in the court of appeals, Steve Chestnut took it to the U.S. Supreme Court and won. Then I talked about a case in which the Standing Rock Sioux Tribe had called us after its sister tribe, the Lower Brule Sioux, had lost a case involving hunting and fishing. We were able to get that decision reversed in the Eighth Circuit Court of Appeals. I went on to describe our work in water rights, including the *Walton* case, water settlements for our tribal clients in Nevada, and finally talked more about our work for the Northern Cheyennes in canceling the coal leases. This was a very important association for the Northern Arapahos. Historically, they were allies of the Northern Cheyennes, and I felt that being trusted by the Northern Cheyennes gave us credibility. After this, I turned to Steve Chestnut for his presentation.

Steve described his work with the Northern Cheyennes and then discussed the work he did in mineral development and preserving tribal interests, emphasizing the innovative ideas he developed for ensuring benefits for tribes. He told the Arapahos about the $43 million settlement he had won for the Fallon Shoshone-Paiutes in a water rights case. Steve said he thought there was a potential for using the strengths of the Arapahos' legal rights to their advantage in their water rights claims. Then Rich Berley spoke about his work on behalf of the Inupiat Eskimos to stop offshore oil development in Alaska, with the Pacific Northwest tribes concerning fishing rights, and with the Fallon Shoshone-Paiutes protecting water rights.

After several questions from tribal members, we were excused to wait in an adjoining room with the other firms' attorneys. In about twenty minutes, a councilman came into the room and announced the results: Ziontz, Chestnut, 147; the next firm, 84; and the third firm, 12. We had somehow reached the people with our presentation and now found ourselves with a major new client.

It turned out that the Arapahos' legal issues did not center on oil and gas. Though they had producing wells on the reservation that had been there for years, there was very little exploration going on; the existing wells were running out, and production was declining. The tribe did have an important claim based on oil and gas, but it was an accounting claim, arising from failure of the federal government to properly collect or account for royalties from oil and gas. The Arapahos' main legal issue was water rights.

The water rights issue for both tribes of the Wind River reservation centered primarily on the allocation of water in the Bighorn River. A case over this allocation had been in the courts since 1977, and it pitted the tribes against ranchers and farmers. One of the thorniest questions was how to determine the *Walton* rights of non-Indian landowners. *Walton* rights are rights claimed by non-Indians derived from purchasing land from an Indian. Fortunately, our water rights background centered precisely on these kinds of rights—indeed, fifteen years earlier I had represented the Colville Tribe in the litigation with Boyd Walton. The Arapahos and Shoshones also had other water rights issues, such as a controversy between the tribes and the Wyoming Water Engineer over the amount of water released from the Bull Lake Dam, which affected water levels in the Wind River. Another issue was the tribes' claim for a share of the electric power revenues generated by the Boysen Dam, downstream on the Wind River. In all of these water questions, the tribes had the benefit of expert advice from their consultant, a professional hydrologist.

I wish I could say that these conflicts were resolved while I worked with the Arapahos, but they were not. Water rights cases go on and on. One of my partners, Rich Berley, took up the cause and carried on after I retired. Rich also took on litigating the Arapahos' claim against the federal government for improperly accounting for the tribe's oil and gas revenues and turning over to the tribe payment for sand and gravel that had been removed from tribal lands. Rich was ultimately successful in obtaining multimillion dollar payments for money due to the Northern Arapahos.

During the three years that I worked with the Northern Arapaho people, I came to know them and to enjoy their company. I attended their pow-wows and dances and spent many hours talking with tribal members about the issues they faced. My relationships led to an invitation to take part in a sweat lodge, something I knew about, but had never experienced. It was November and there was snow on the ground at Wind River when the invitation was made. I thought briefly of politely declining—because of the unpleasant prospect of stripping down to my underwear outdoors in November. But the invitation was an honor I couldn't refuse. I followed my Arapaho friends to the home of a tribal member who was a spiritual man. There, in the yard behind his house, I saw the igloo-like structure. It seemed very small, especially when I saw the seven or eight people preparing to enter the lodge. In front of it, a fire burned, heating the rocks that would be used in the ceremony.

The lodge was covered with tarpaulins, one of which overhung the entry. A corner of the tarp was lifted away and held open to allow us to enter. Inside, it was dark, the only source of light being the entry opening. In the center of the lodge was a pit filled with hot rocks. I crawled in on my hands and knees and joined the Arapahos who had preceded me. I could make out their faces only dimly. There were two women and five men in addition to myself. One of my Arapaho friends who had taken it upon himself to watch out for me showed me where to sit. I was crammed in, body to body along with the others. Near the doorway sat the man who I'll call the lodge master. It was his responsibility to periodically dip a metal ladle into a pot of water and pour it over the red-hot stones, replacing them with new heated stones from the fire outside when they cooled. Pouring water over the stones produced clouds of steam that filled the enclosure and produced the high temperatures and dry air that enveloped us.

The flap over the door had been closed after the last of us entered, and the interior was pitch dark. In a few minutes I began to sweat. After twenty minutes or so, I was distinctly uncomfortable. Breathing was difficult and the heat verged on unbearable. Getting up and leaving was out of the question. For one thing, I would have to crawl along the edge of the pit where the red-hot stones were piled, and I wasn't sure I could find the edge. There was also the problem of squeezing between people and crawling over their legs. Just when I began to reach the limit of my endurance, there was a reprieve when the lodge master flung open the flap over the doorway to bring in more hot stones. When he opened the flap and went out, there was a delicious interval of cool air for about two minutes until he returned and closed the flap again.

Someone began a chant in Arapaho and I realized that this was, in fact, a religious ceremony. My Arapaho friend explained that the chanter was praying for the well-being of all of us in the lodge and then for the tribe. The chanting went on for a long, long time. When it ended, one by one, individuals spoke their own prayers in English—for the power to overcome their shortcomings, for help for family members and relatives who had problems or were ill. I knew that I was expected to participate in what was a communal airing of hopes and wishes. So I searched my own heart and spoke: "My dear friends, I know that each of us has problems in his life. Some we can solve by ourselves, some seem to be beyond our power. Some have problems with health, with sickness, with death. I pray with you that each and every one of you and your families will have health and peace in his life."

When the prayers and speeches stopped, the chanter resumed his Arapaho song. We had probably been in the lodge for close to an hour, and I wondered how long I could hold out. I was making an effort to endure the heat, and it was turning into a serious exercise of mind over matter. Soon I saw there was a pattern. We would go thirty to forty minutes, and then the lodge master would open the flap to get more hot stones. When he returned, there was another thirty or forty minutes until he repeated the operation. I began to eagerly anticipate when the flap would open, and to regret when it was closed—knowing that my suffering would continue.

As the time went on, I found myself entering into a meditative state. There was no alternative; I was seated in a pitch-black enclosure, surrounded by Indian people who were having a deep spiritual experience, listening to Indian chanting and singing. Gradually, my mind let go of its attachments and I felt the intensity of the group experience. Even my concerns for my stamina faded, and I adjusted my breathing and my attitude toward the heat so that I could continue. After about three hours, the ceremony ended. The flap was opened and one by one we all crawled out. My Arapaho friends shook my hand solemnly. It was clear that I had crossed a boundary and entered into an intimate relationship with them.

Working with the Arapahos was interesting and rewarding, but the experience always intensified when the tribe held a meeting of its general council—that is, the entire membership. With Rich Berley, I would drive to the gym at Ethete, and we would see from the cars and pickups in the parking lot how well attended the meeting might be. If there were very few, there was a chance that there would not be a quorum and the meeting would be postponed to the following month, making our trip futile. That had happened. More often, though, there were latecomers and the lot filled up, so that by ten thirty or eleven in the morning two or three hundred Arapahos were assembled.

In the gym entryway there was a registration table always attended by two young Arapaho women. They greeted us cordially as we signed the attendance register. Then we entered the gym, greeting and shaking hands with people we knew. Indians do not shake hands with the same enthusiasm as non-Indians. Usually it is a limp offering. I don't know why—perhaps because the hand shake is foreign to Indian culture. As we took our seats in the front row, agendas were handed out, sometimes multipage affairs, listing numerous items. I knew from past experience that we would never get to most of what was on the agenda.

Since these were general tribal meetings, the council did not preside. Indeed, the first order of business was to elect a chairperson. Usually, this was an older member of the tribe who was respected and had experience running these gatherings. The meetings usually lasted most of the day, but there was always a lunch break. The women of the tribe prepared a hearty meal, usually slices of beef, potatoes, Indian fry bread and butter, and dessert, all served from the kitchen in the gym. A long line would form, and Rich and I would wait until most of the tribal members had gone through before we stepped into line.

For me there was always an undercurrent of tension in these general membership meetings—anything could happen. Typically, disaffected members used an agenda item to launch an attack against some target. Our presence was mandatory; not only were we expected to give reports on subjects that were on the agenda, but we were frequently called on to render on-the-spot legal opinions. Often, when the proceedings descended into a parliamentary snarl, we were asked to clarify the procedure. One of these meetings, in 1993, turned out to have historic consequences for the tribe.

I went to the reservation with Rich Berley as usual. We heard there might be some highly contentious issues brought up, but had no advance knowledge of what these might be. The agenda was lengthy. One of the items listed was something called "membership," without any elaboration. When the item was reached and the chairperson called for speakers on the subject, a woman stepped up to the microphone and read out a motion. Although it was clumsily worded, the objective was clear: to change the basic law of the Northern Arapahos that governed tribal membership. Her motion was promptly seconded by another woman and the battle was on.

The Northern Arapahos' enrollment law was extremely restrictive. In addition to a blood quantum requirement, the applicant's father—not mother—had to be Arapaho. Women who married Indian men from other tribes or non-Indians found their children barred for life. Illegitimate children were altogether barred from becoming tribal members. And unless a child was enrolled within two years of birth, he or she could never become members—this often affected otherwise eligible children whose parents lived off-reservation, only to return too late to register their sons and daughters. It seemed these policies were a legacy from the heyday of oil and gas royalties: fewer tribal members meant larger per capita income distribution. The issue was a hot one among the women of the tribe, because they bore the brunt of the discriminatory gender-based policies.

When the motion was seconded, there was a barrage of objections, most having to do with whether there had been adequate notice that this issue would be taken up at the meeting. There were also claims that the language of the motion was confusing and ambiguous, and if it passed in the form proposed no one would be sure who was covered. It was obvious that the issue went to the heart of the tribe's identity. It was also obvious that it stirred up strong feelings. Many felt the law was well established and didn't want to see any change. Others thought it was time for the Arapahos to become a larger tribe in order to have more clout with federal and state governments. Individual per capita payments had been falling with lower oil prices, and many members were tired of constant requests for financial help from needy relatives who did not qualify for tribal membership.

I became directly involved when the chairperson asked for my opinion on whether the motion was in order at all because of the question of proper notice. After considering the common practice of the tribe in its agenda procedure, I gave my opinion that the motion was in order under the title "membership." Any other opinion would have imposed a technical requirement of specific wording, something that might have been required in a non-Indian setting, but that seemed inconsistent with the informal, nontechnical style I had seen at Arapaho meetings. Then the question of the motion's ambiguity arose, and the chairperson turned to me to redraft the motion on the spot. During a brief adjournment called to give me time, I sat on the edge of the gym's stage with the two women who were the principal proponents. We carefully rewrote the motion to provide a workable law of membership, and the meeting was reconvened.

As speaker after speaker rose to support or oppose the motion, it was clear that the membership question had been a sore spot for many years. Many of the women voiced anger at the injustice that had been done to them and their children. This was *Martinez v. Santa Clara Pueblo* transposed to Wyoming. *Martinez* was the 1978 case challenging a similar membership ordinance, in which I disputed the authority of the courts to hear such cases, and the Supreme Court ruled that courts had no such authority. But the solution here in Wyoming was being thrashed out by the Arapahos themselves—exactly what I believed should happen—not by a non-Indian judge in a federal court hundreds of miles away. Finally, a motion calling for the question was made and seconded, and a written vote was called for.

Despite the bitter debate, the motion to adopt new and more liberal enrollment standards passed 191–0. Many Arapahos came up to me and thanked me. It was a historic day. Though I disclaimed any personal credit and repeatedly pointed out that I had only tried to help with suitable wording, many at the meeting saw me as a key figure in passing this new policy. I have since learned that this has remained in Arapaho memory, and my name is still mentioned in connection with that day as a catalyst for the historic change. I take some pride in having helped the Arapahos, and the episode remains my favorite memory of work with that tribe.

TWENTY-SEVEN

Photographing the
Northern Cheyennes

AS MY SIXTY-FIFTH BIRTHDAY NEARED, I BEGAN TO THINK OF RET-
irement. I decided to retire at the end of 1994, when I would be sixty-six.
My partners accepted my announcement graciously, and a small celebration dinner was planned at a downtown restaurant. All the partners
and their families came, as well as our staff and my children and their
spouses. There were the usual embarrassing speeches and toasts. The
Makahs, the Northern Cheyennes, the Northern Arapahos, and the
Mille Lacs sent touching letters of appreciation. But the most unusual
and amusing tribute came from my former partner, Barry Ernstoff, then
living in Jerusalem:

> A philosopher, an artist, a doer
> Always an actor, not just a viewer
> For our firm he set the tone
> And the right path he's always shown
> For me the firm will remain
> As if Ziontz continues to reign.

I had no regrets. All of my cases had been concluded and there was
no unfinished work on my desk. I was happy to bring my legal career to a
close, and I knew exactly what I wanted to do with my life after leaving
law: I wanted to pursue fine art photography seriously.

As I child I'd won a scholarship to the Art Institute of Chicago, but my pursuit of drawing and painting stopped after my first year of high school. When I was thirteen I received a Kodak Brownie as a bar mitzvah gift and I became fascinated by snapshot photography. During the years of raising a family and building a law career, the only photography I had time for was travel mementos and family snapshots. My interest in art, however, never left me—we went to galleries, read art publications, and in the late 1960s I rediscovered the joys of drawing. My creative impulses finally found their outlet when in 1975 I purchased a high-quality camera. I took to the streets of Seattle and suddenly felt liberated. I could shoot anything that attracted my eye. Gradually, I enlarged my knowledge and explored more challenging and difficult projects. But I didn't know very much about the technical side of photography. I had never been in a darkroom and knew nothing of the developing and printing processes. I was eager to learn more. So in 1996 I enrolled at a fine-art photography school and took courses in a new and exciting world—so different from law.

My hunger to explore led me to do portraits and urban landscapes, to photograph theatrical performances, parades, and celebrations, to do architectural photography, to photograph children at a community center, to photograph members of a black motorcycle club with their bikes and on their rides. I even did fashion photography, shooting aspiring young models in a studio I equipped for the purpose, though eventually I became bored with this. Photographing people turned out to be my strength, and I built a portfolio of portraits and studies of people in ordinary life.

I photographed in Chicago, New York, Los Angeles, Mexico, Spain, Russia, India, the Czech Republic, and Paris. Some of my work was shown in galleries in New York, San Francisco, Portland, and other cities. I was no longer a lawyer—I was a photographer. Photography, like law, can be a gateway—an opening to other people, to other lives, to other places. The depth of the photographer's understanding of his subjects is a result of the empathy and knowledge he brings to the process.

I had spent forty years among the Indian people, but I had rarely photographed them. I did take my camera to pow-wows and tribal celebrations and made an occasional photograph. But I never used my visits to a reservation primarily for photography. It didn't seem right: I was on the reservation as a tribal attorney. To photograph Indian clients would be exploitative, using my status to get people to pose. I also thought it would distract from why I was on the reservation, blurring the lines. But with retirement, all that changed. Now if I wanted to do an in-depth photographic study of an Indian community on a reservation, my presence there would be unambiguous—I would be there as a photographer, not as a tribal attorney. I decided to arrange a trip to the Northern Cheyenne reservation in Montana.

On a cold, snowy Sunday in October of 1996, I pulled into the driveway of Joe and Charlene Alden's house on the reservation. Charlene was a member of the Northern Cheyenne Tribe and her husband was a member of the Crow Tribe, whose reservation adjoined the Northern Cheyenne's on the west. They had generously offered to be my hosts for two weeks. Charlene worked in the tribal accounting office; Joe worked seasonally as a carpenter and otherwise as a cowboy. The Aldens had four children: a recently married daughter named Shannon, who didn't live at home; two teenage girls, Leslie and Crystal; and a young son called JP who was about ten tears old. Their home was a comfortable four-bedroom rambler with an attached all-purpose room, used as a mudroom.

Everyone was home when I arrived, Charlene and her daughters in the kitchen, Joe in the dining room working on a leather quirt, and JP watching television. Charlene was talkative, while Joe seemed taciturn. It turned out Joe was silent mainly when Charlene was around, when she was usually the one doing the talking. Charlene is a very intelligent and articulate woman. She enjoyed talking and seemed to welcome my presence as an interested listener. While she worked around the kitchen, with Crystal and Leslie helping, her remarks ranged over the problems on the reservation, Crystal's plans, and gossip about friends and acquaintances. She spoke at length about sending her children to school at Colstrip, a nearby non-Indian community. Charlene herself, she told me, had gone to St. Labre, a Catholic school just off the reservation, and then to a Mormon family in Utah.

After lunch, we all went to her parent's house for the birthday party of her fifteen-year-old niece, Thelma White Man. I felt a little awkward as I was introduced to the many family members: Charlene's sisters, Jolene, Luanna, and Florene; their husbands, James Walks Last, Johnathan Walks Last, and James Walks Along. Five of James and Florene's six children were there, including their newborn son Jaidell, eleven days old. Charlene's oldest daughter, Shannon, came later with her husband, Henry Wilson. And at the center of it all was the birthday celebrant, Thelma, an attractive fifteen-year-old.

The house was full, everyone busy talking. Charlene's parents, Phillip and Florence, were a dignified couple in their seventies and lent an air of gravitas. Phillip kept his cowboy hat on throughout the evening, and although elderly and toothless, was trim and athletic looking. He didn't speak much, but was obviously enjoying the gathering of the entire family at his house. I learned later that he held the position of Keeper of the Sacred Drum, a priestly status in the Northern Cheyenne culture. Florence proudly showed me the certificates and plaques hanging on the walls, honoring the achievements of her grandchildren and particularly her son Phillip Jr., who was a world champion Indian bronco rider and grass dancer. I shot many family photographs and several asked for prints. Everyone made a fuss over Jaidell.

The following day I arose at eight and emerged from the bedroom to find only Joe at home. Charlene had already gone to work and the girls and JP were at school. Joe served coffee, a tasty brew, and we sat around the dining room table talking. The topic was horses, a subject on which Joe seemed to have a bottomless fund of knowledge. Joe was a good talker, intelligent and far more talkative than the previous day.

I left the Alden house midmorning for a meeting of the tribal council in Lame Deer. There was snow on the roads, but it was not deep and driving was not difficult. The surrounding hills were covered with snow-laden trees, which made for a beautiful winter panorama. When I entered the council chambers, the council was already in session and I took my seat quietly against the wall. But the chairman, Llevando "Cowboy" Fisher, looked up. "Well, I see that Al Ziontz is here. I understand you want to make some pictures while you're here. Want to say anything to the council?" His manner was cordial.

"I'm glad to be back at Lame Deer again," I told the council. "But I'm not out here as a tribal attorney now. As you know, I retired. I've been doing quite a bit of photography and, with your kind permission, I'd like to take some pictures of the people on the reservation. I'd like to start with a picture right here of the council in session. Would that be alright with you?" There was general approval and I thanked them. "Go right ahead with your business," I said, "don't pay any attention to me." They moved on with their discussion, and I snapped some pictures.

I went to see Dr. Alonzo Spang, a Northern Cheyenne who had once been superintendent of the Lame Deer Agency of the Bureau of Indian Affairs. He later became the first president of Dull Knife College, a community college named after a famous Northern Cheyenne chief, serving mainly tribal members on the reservation. I knew him well and always called him Alonzo. He was a kind and thoughtful man with a huge amount of experience in tribal and governmental affairs. During my time on the reservation, he was on leave from the college because of a health problem. It turned out that Alonzo had to reschedule our appointment, so I dropped by Charlene's office to chat and she suggested I visit the casino and the tribal court—both good ideas, though probably not for photography.

The Northern Cheyenne casino was housed in a small, unimpressive building. Inside the darkened room were slot machines lined up against both walls with a row down the center. There were only two or three players, all Indians. This was not surprising since Lame Deer is far from any Montana population centers. So any money the casino brought in was recycled Northern Cheyenne money. The casino was managed by a tribal member, Patsy Tallbull. We had a long talk in her office about her work ethic: working hard to achieve something in her life. After making a few shots of the casino interior, I thanked Patsy and left. Next stop was the Northern Cheyenne Tribal Court, where I met the two judges, Rudolph King and Doris Littlewolf. We had a friendly discussion and, knowing that I was a lawyer, they were anxious to have me visit the court when it was in session. I promised to return.

I got back in my car and drove around Lame Deer looking for possible photographic subjects. My attention was attracted by a group of lodge poles, long poles used to make tepees. They were leaning against the wall of an old house. I got out of the car and took a few frames. As I stood there an old Indian man appeared, slowly walking around the corner of the house toward me. His face was weather beaten and around his head was an old stained, red headband. I greeted him and decided instantly I wanted to make a portrait of him. Of course I asked his permission. He didn't respond audibly, but nodded and stood patiently while I took the photographs. I learned later that his name was James

Black Wolf and that he was in fact a mute. He was also a holy man: the Keeper of the Sacred Buffalo Hat, a central artifact in the Cheyenne culture.

I kept my promise and returned to the tribal court, where some kind of hearing was in progress. It seemed that a bank wanted to repossess a truck for nonpayment. The defendant, a Cheyenne man, was standing in front of Judge Rudolph King with his mother at his side. They were represented by a relative who served as a lay advocate, a common practice in Tribal Courts. I was surprised that the bank was represented by a Cheyenne woman of rather scraggly appearance, wearing gym shoes. The judge spoke at length in Cheyenne to all the parties. A Cheyenne woman sitting next to me translated: the judge was explaining the terms of a stipulation by which the defendant would make up all the delinquent payments by December, two months hence. The defendant and his mother nodded their heads in agreement, and the hearing was over. While not encumbered with the formalism of an American non-Indian court, it functioned perfectly as a dispenser of justice in the Cheyenne way.

When I returned to the Alden house, Joe told me Charlene was at a meeting and we were on our own. Joe grumbled because this meant he would have to prepare the evening meal. I didn't see how it turned out because just then the phone rang; it was Charlene's sister, Florene, inviting me to a meeting of the Boosters Club in the high school. She explained that the club raised money for the Lame Deer basketball teams, and she said something about me making some pictures for them. When I arrived at the high school, I found a small group, three men and three women, seated around a table in an otherwise empty lunchroom. They seemed pleased to see me, and we ate a dinner of meatloaf, mashed potatoes, fry bread, and Kool-Aid. The group talked about fund-raising ideas, one of them for me to photograph the girl's basketball team so they could sell pins with the photographs on them. I agreed.

Following dinner, Florene asked me to accompany her to a meeting of the Lame Deer school board. Her husband, James Walks Along, was the chairman. She was obviously proud of him and the board and wanted me to see the proceedings. When we entered the meeting room, the session was in progress. James was a thoughtful and highly involved chairman. As I listened, I was fascinated by the discussion. These people were deeply concerned over issues of quality of teaching, student discipline, and absenteeism. The discussion was intense, focused, and constructive. I came away impressed by the school board's dedication to the education of Cheyenne children.

The next morning when I got up, everyone was gone. Joe came in shortly, explaining that he had been in the pasture behind the house working his horses. We sat down at the table and talked—about rodeos, ranching, and his own background. Joe Alden was from Lodge Grass on the Crow reservation. He met Charlene, he said, at the All-American Indian Days celebration in Sheridan, Wyoming. Charlene's parents had come there because her dad was an Indian singer and used to go to pow-wows all over the West. Joe and Charlene settled on the Northern Cheyenne reservation because Charlene got a good job with the tribe, and they had raised their children here.

After breakfast, Joe went to help a friend, Francis Harris, move some horses on his ranch, and I went back to Lame Deer to take more photographs. I parked at Cady's, the grocery store and gas station at the intersection of the town's two main roads. Crystal, the Aldens' daughter, was working behind the counter. The gas pump was attended by the store's other employee, a young Cheyenne I knew only as Van. I watched as Cheyennes came in, bantered with Crystal, made their purchases, and left. I tried to photograph the scene, but without much success.

Later that afternoon, Crystal returned home, angry and disappointed because the tribe had refused to fund her for the coming semester at Dull Knife College. Trying to be sympathetic, I asked, "How come they did that, Crystal?"

"They funded me till last year. But then my grade point average dropped to a 2.0 and they canceled it. So I paid my own way the next semester and worked hard to get my grades up. I got all A's on my midterms, but they told me they had already made their decision for January and they wouldn't change it. So now I'm going to have to find the money to pay again." Crystal was upset and refused to see any justice in the tribe's position. In a little while, Leslie and JP came home and all of us sat around waiting for Charlene. Finally at six o'clock, Joe said to me, "Let's go for a ride."

We drove to the site of the next day's cattle drive—I think to allow Joe to scout the terrain. Then we drove to the house of the rancher who had hired Joe to help with the drive, a man named Earl. Earl was in the backyard with another man, a young fellow, and they were engaged in target practice with pistols. Earl was a huge, 250-pound middle-aged man who worked doing maintenance for the Indian Health Service. The younger man was an Indian Health Service doctor. Earl was not Indian, but was married to a Cheyenne. He was from South Dakota and operated a good-sized ranch here on the reservation. I listened to them talk about the next day's cattle drive, puzzled to hear about a cow "on a fight." When I asked Joe about it later, he explained this meant a cow that tried to hurt a human. I had always thought of cows as docile, but apparently the men who handled them had to be alert for aggressive animals to avoid being injured.

We drove back home and found Charlene cooking dinner, after which the whole family assembled for a portrait. As we were sitting around talking, I noticed a car's headlights coming up the driveway. A large, heavy Cheyenne woman and her daughter came in and went into the kitchen with Charlene. Shortly afterwards, Charlene showed me some crude Indian beadwork the two women had brought—and strongly implied that I had to buy it. I forked over fifteen dollars for a poorly worked bracelet, and the woman and her daughter left. Charlene explained that this was a common practice on the reservation—poor women trying to pick up a few dollars by coming around to people's houses peddling trinkets. People bought as an act of charity.

The next morning we were up at six for the cattle drive. We ate a cowboy breakfast at Earl's ranch, prepared by Earl's wife, Maria, and then headed out. Earl saddled his horse, loaded it into a trailer, and drove up a deeply rutted dirt road to the hills of the backcountry where the corrals were. The corrals were primitive enclosures formed by a rickety collection of branches, sticks, and boards loosely wired together. Joe and Earl unloaded their horses and rode off into the hills, leaving me alone—but only for about thirty minutes, when two more Cheyenne horsemen arrived and followed them. The goal of the drive was to bring a herd of some ninety head of cattle down from the high country and to separate out the calves, which would be loaded into trailers and driven to a pen near the highway. The unfortunate calves would be trucked to Belle Fourche, South Dakota, to be sold to a feed lot. I waited for the cowboys to return with the herd, planning to photograph quickly and capture the action.

Finally, the first cattle moved down a steep trail toward the corrals, flanked by the cowboys on their horses, yelling and whistling to keep the cattle moving. The men shooed the animals into the corral, where they milled around, lowing and mooing. There followed a scene of organized chaos as the cowboys set about separating the calves and driving their mothers out of the corral, where they cried piteously for their calves. The calves were then driven into the chute to be loaded on the truck trailer. I watched in fascination until the operation was over. I had never seen a cattle ranch operation or cowboys working cattle. It suddenly occurred to me that all but one of the cowboys were Indians. So much for cowboys versus Indians. Joe told me that the largest Indian rancher on the reservation ran eight hundred head of cattle, a business calling for management skills and mastery of the arts of ranching. I began to understand more fully what many Northern Cheyennes did on the reservation and one reason why the tribe had so firmly rejected strip-mining their lands.

When we returned to the Alden home that afternoon, Joe and I sat around and talked. In the months when snow is on the ground, Joe has a lot of time on his hands, doing some cowboy work, but mostly waiting for the construction season to start. Joe talked about his boyhood, recalling fondly how he milked the cows and then took the cans of cream to the railroad depot to be shipped on the passenger train to Sheridan, Wyoming. He drifted from that topic to the superiority of garden-grown vegetables and then to the fiascos of tribally owned businesses, like the mini-mart and the casino. After several hours of rambling conversation, we both wearied of it.

A call from Charlene put an end to Joe's hopes that she would be home to make dinner. I was headed to Donna Dahle's house for dinner, and Joe looked at me wistfully as I prepared to leave. Then Crystal called from Billings—she would bring Kentucky Fried Chicken home, from a hundred miles away. She was in Billings to get bodywork done on her car. Someone had "keyed" it, run a deep scratch down its side. It seems this was not uncommon on the reservation. The Dahle family home is in Busby, a thirty-minute drive from the Aldens'. Their house was very familiar to me. I had established a close friendship with the Dahles over the years of the coal-mining case, and I had stayed with them many times. Ed Dahle had been the tribe's point man in that fight and was later elected tribal president. Tragically, he died unexpectedly of an aneurism, leaving Donna to run their ranch with the help of their sons.

Donna met me with her usual warmth and cheer, and we hugged in greeting. One of her sons, Zack, was living at home and he shook my hand with a bone-crushing grip. Zack was enormous—six foot two and I'd guess more than 250 pounds. He had been a wrestler and body builder and had a massive torso and a tree-trunk neck, but his size apparently didn't intimidate some Cheyenne kids. He had been a substitute teacher at the school in Lame Deer, where he tried without success to get four students who were being disciplined to do an assignment. His efforts provoked defiance, insults, and profanity. Zack was uninterested in a teaching career after that.

Donna was a fine cook. She served a delicious beef stew that had been simmering all day, mashed potatoes, vegetables, milk, bread and butter, and finally an apple crisp for dessert. The meal was huge, but was a typical Montana offering, with some form of beef as the centerpiece. Before I left, Donna invited me to come stay with them. I had been feeling uneasy about spending the my entire two weeks with the Aldens, even though they assured me they were happy to have me there. Still, I knew that my presence, though occasionally diverting for them, was a disruption. I accepted Donna's offer and said I'd call to work out the details.

The following morning, I was back with Joe at Francis Harris's ranch, where this time Joe was helping to round up some horses so they could be broken in to wear bridles. The roundup began at eleven and the action was fast and furious. Five riders drove a herd of unbroken horses down from the hills into strongly fenced corrals. Groups of five or six horses at a time were separated out and moved into one of the corrals where the cowboys, using whips, got them running along the railing. The horses ran together, wheeling in unison when they reversed direction. The cowboys seemed to know exactly what they were doing as they separated out a single horse and ran it into a different corral. Joe was in his element; he rode his horse easily, and when he dismounted he worked alongside his companions moving confidently in the center of a whirling mass of running horses. It was a fascinating scene for an urban ex-lawyer and a rich opportunity for a photographer.

Photographing a community calls for an inquiring spirit and patience. Driving around Lame Deer later that day, I used my photographer's eye to scan for people or objects that were beautiful or interesting or meaningful, telling something about the life of that community. Along one of the back streets, I saw several derelict cars that intrigued me. I got out of my car and walked closer to them, but before I could raise my camera I was accosted by a belligerent young man, emerging from a dilapidated trailer house and walking toward me aggressively.

"Hey you!" he yelled, "What are you taking pictures for?" He was in his twenties, tall and very thin, wearing a beaten and torn straw cowboy hat and displaying badly broken front teeth. I had encountered similar reactions before when I was taking pictures, so I took the initiative. I called him over, saying, "C'mere." When he came up to me I said, "Hi. My name's Al Ziontz. I'm not here as a tourist. I'm a photographer and I want to try to show life here on the reservation in a realistic way..."

I got no further. My antagonist interrupted: "Hey, you people have raped the Indians and stolen our land and now you want to make pictures of us. No way!"

"Look," I said, "I've spent forty years working as a tribal attorney and I know something about the way the Indians have been exploited. Our law firm stopped the strip-mining on your reservation."

That didn't mollify him. Instead he got nastier: "Oh, so you work for that fucking tribal council and you're with Chestnut, that lawyer who got rich off the tribe."

He was filled with inarticulate wrath over the injustices suffered by Indian people, the perfidy of the tribal council, and hatred of white tribal lawyers. Every word he said reflected his hatred. Trying to be rational, I asked, "What do you think should be done?"

"The United States should make all the Cheyennes rich and the tribal government should be disbanded," he said. He claimed to be a Sun Dance priest and spoke vaguely of the nobility of the Cheyenne Way—a free society, without government, without laws, and living with wealth transferred to it by America in payment for the crimes it had committed against the Indian people.

When I tried to respond, I was met with more anger; rational discourse was impossible. He refused even to tell me his name. Finally, I broke off the encounter. It was going nowhere and he had no interest in anything I might say. I later learned from Steve Chestnut that he was the husband of a woman named Maria Sanchez, leader of a faction on the reservation—the disaffected, angry, radical militants. Such groups are found on many reservations. Scapegoating is common among them. Sadly, the creation of such bitterness is a by-product of the long history of injustice suffered by the Indian people. The encounter nevertheless left me with a bad taste in my mouth. But it was the only extreme hostility I met with in all the time I was on the reservation.

In sharp contrast to that unpleasant confrontation was a charming exchange I had with a little Cheyenne boy. I had gone to the mini-mart and as I stood near the counter, a four-year-old Cheyenne tyke looked up at me and said soberly, "Hi, Grampa." I smiled down at him and said, "Hi." The store was decorated for Halloween, including ubiquitous artificial spider webbing. I was standing in front of some of this webbing when my little friend spoke to me again: "Grampa, watch out for the spider," he warned. I assured him I would be careful not to get bit, and his mother moved off with him.

The next morning, Joe and I drove over to the college cafeteria where we met Charlene for breakfast. I noticed a young man with a distinctive European appearance working in the kitchen. When he spoke, I heard his unmistakable French accent. What was a young Frenchman doing here, working in a restaurant on the Northern Cheyenne reservation in Montana?

"His name is François," Charlene told me, confirming he was French. He was fascinated by Indians and had come to the reservation to see the tribe that had fought General Custer at Little Big Horn. Then he met a forty-year-old Cheyenne woman and, though he was in his early twenties, he fell in love. He may or may not have known that she had been married three times—he simply fell in love with her. He returned to France, where he spent a year making her a beaded buckskin dress, following the traditional Cheyenne style. When his father died and left him a fair amount of money, he returned to Lame Deer and married his Cheyenne love. According to Charlene, it took her a year to go through his inheritance, and then she left him. Broken and dispirited, François decided to stay on in Lame Deer, taking a job as a counterman in the college cafeteria. The Cheyennes felt sorry for him. But after a year, he met another Cheyenne woman, and he and his new girlfriend seemed happy. François was perpetually caught up in romance with the Cheyennes.

When I awoke at six thirty Saturday morning, the power was out. The hillsides were a winter wonderland, snow blanketing everything and the trees bent over. It was only the end of October, but Joe said it would be like this the rest of the winter. Car travel was impossible without chains; only trucks and four-wheel-drive vehicles were moving. I was scheduled to photograph Charlene's mom and dad, and I was worried about getting there. Joe sat at the dining room table working on leather saddle straps, as he did most days. He assured me there would be no problem—he would drive me in his big truck.

When we arrived at the home of Phillip and Florence White Man, Phillip was sitting in his big armchair near the living room window. He wore a western shirt, cowboy boots, and a cowboy hat, just as he did when I first came to their house for Thelma's birthday party. His face was craggy and he wore a thin mustache. The cuffs of his shirt were rolled up and there were two large rings on his left hand. He and Florence knew I was coming over to take their pictures and they knew who I was. They were courteous and understood their own importance and my reason for being there.

Without any questions from me, Phillip launched into the history of the family name, White Man. The name began, he said, in the time when the Cheyennes were driven out of Montana and put in a stockade in Oklahoma. Then they were marched to Fort Keough, which is now Miles City, Montana. There his grandmother worked as a maid, cleaning the quarters of the white officers. This led to physical intimacy, whether consensual or forced was not mentioned, and she became pregnant. After the birth of a little boy, the Cheyennes called him Little White Man. So now his descendants carry the White Man family name.

Then, again without my urging, Phillip told me the story of the Cheyenne family name, Limpy. The Cheyennes had been in a fight, and one of their warriors was badly wounded in his hip. It was torn so badly that people expected him to die. But a medicine man treated him and the women nursed him, changing his dressings frequently. He recovered, but afterward always had a severe limp. The people began to call him by the Cheyenne word for "limpy." And that became the family name of many Cheyennes.

Phillip told me these stories while chewing on his gums and smoking a cigarette. Partly because of his toothlessness and partly because of his Cheyenne clipped style of speech, he was difficult to understand. He was a proud man and clearly the Cheyenne history of war and struggle was a part of him. He obviously thought it was important for this white man who had been the tribe's attorney to learn something about the Cheyennes.

Florence, meanwhile, had been in her room, but now she came out. She had lung cancer and sometimes used a portable oxygen tank. But when she joined us in the living room, she wanted no impediments and so didn't have it with her. Florence taught the Cheyenne language at Dull Knife College, and she brought out a large box of drawings and photographs illustrating Cheyenne words that were also phonetically spelled out. She told me about how she had initiated the program and how proud she was to help perpetuate the language of the Cheyennes. This work gave her deep satisfaction.

Finally, I decided it was time to make some portraits. I took several shots of Phillip and Florence in their living room, looking serene and distinguished. Afterward, it was Florence's turn to tell me some Cheyenne lore. She proceeded to tell me the story of a Cheyenne battle against the Utes in which a Cheyenne warrior rode into the Ute camp, seized a small Ute boy, and made off with him. The warrior was severely upbraided by the Cheyenne chiefs when he returned to the war party. But the warrior was stubborn; he insisted on bringing the boy back to the main Cheyenne camp. A long debate ensued, which resulted in a decision: the boy would be raised as a Cheyenne and would never be told of his Ute origins. Everyone kept the secret, and he grew into a fine young man and a great warrior. He died in a Cheyenne battle with American soldiers. I was somewhat surprised that this elderly, dignified woman should proudly tell such a tale. But it clearly reflected her Cheyenne pride in the tribe's warrior history. I think it also reflected pride in tribal culture: they took an alien child, and the Cheyenne culture turned him into an outstanding Cheyenne.

On another afternoon, I visited the home of Florene and James Walks Along, Charlene's sister and brother-in-law. James was born in Lame Deer, but moved with his family to South Dakota when he was eight. His father was a Mennonite minister and James attended a Mennonite community college. After living in Sioux Falls and Yankton, he returned to Lame Deer and the Cheyenne reservation, where he met and married Florene. James was devoted to his family and stayed home with the children when Florene worked. He was also deeply committed to the tribe and its culture. He was chairman of the school board and belonged to the Kit Fox Society, a traditional Cheyenne warrior society.

I was curious about James's work background, and what he told me revealed something not only about himself, but also about the kind of work a Cheyenne man has to do to support a family. James had acquired many job skills. He was a qualified oil-field roustabout, a coal-drying plant operator, a thermoelectric plant operator, a timber thinner, a cowboy, a farmhand, a ranch hand, and a feed lot manager. He had also run asphalt paving crews and, until the previous year, had operated a pilot plant that processed coal to remove impurities. This last job, he told me, made him sick. He thinks the chemicals gave him high blood pressure and this, combined with having to be away from home and family, had finally induced him to quit.

Florene and James spoke with me at length about their decision to reject material values in favor of a simple, family-oriented life. Then their eleven-year-old son Wesley came in and sat down, staring at me with hostility. Florene told me that in his early childhood he had problems; he had nightmares of soldiers killing everybody and he stuttered. But, she said, they had taken Wesley to the Sun Dance, where he fasted and danced, the youngest Sun Dancer in sixty years. The Sun Dance experience cured him, she said, and he no longer stuttered. James said his son showed great athletic ability and was a good student. Wesley finally spoke up, and asked me in an openly aggressive manner what I was doing photographing people. I explained my purpose to him, seriously and candidly, and he seemed to relax. He became almost friendly. That afternoon with the Walks Along family gave me a rare opportunity to know something of the lives of two people—Cheyennes who embraced traditional life and managed to maintain a deep serenity while coping with the daily challenges of family and work on the Northern Cheyenne reservation.

After ten days with the Aldens, I went to stay in the Dahle home. With the help of Donna Dahle, who was the director of the reservation's

Head Start Program, I obtained permission to photograph Cheyenne children in the program. Permission slips were signed by the parents, and I spent an entire day photographing these delightful kids in their classes and at play. The Head Start teachers, all Cheyenne women, were skilled at holding the children's attention, teaching them and stimulating their imaginations. I saw great love radiating from these teachers, a part of Cheyenne life that was a delight to see.

Then I moved from the very young to the very old: I went to the senior center, actually called the Wendell Turkey Shoulderblades Senior Center. The center was in a modern complex, with housing units consisting of apartments for each resident grouped around a central courtyard. These clusters were connected to a main building containing administrative offices, a kitchen, a large dining room, and a day room with comfortable chairs and couches and, of course, a large TV set. I met first with the administrator, a young Cheyenne woman named Michelle Three Fingers. She gave me permission to set up in the facility and announced to the residents that I would be available to take pictures of anyone who wished to be photographed. At first there were few takers, but gradually, the senior Cheyennes approached me and I had the privilege of photographing them.

Halloween on the Northern Cheyenne reservation is not just a children's holiday. The grown-ups also love putting on garish costumes and parading around the community. The parade ended in the high-school gym where a dance was in progress. I photographed young Cheyenne men and women wearing outlandish masks and costumes dancing with each other on the gym floor.

As my two weeks on the reservation drew to a close, I reflected on what I had seen. There was a powerful sense of tribal identity there. Cheyenne history, culture, and tradition were a part of the lives of young and old alike. Family life was probably similar to what would be found anywhere in rural America, but with some profound differences. Almost every Indian home had some Indian art or artifact on display. Many of the members of the tribe were interrelated—sisters, brothers, uncles, aunts, cousins, nephews, nieces, stepchildren. Beneath the surface of normality lay evidence of tragedies caused by alcoholism, family violence, and bad health. There was also simmering anger, which occasionally erupted in violence. At the same time there was a great deal of striving: young and old attending colleges, universities, and training institutions in an effort to improve their lives. Overall there was a sense of being at home—home on the historic land of the Cheyenne people. Perhaps this, more than anything else, explains why they passed up the wealth that coal mining offered, opting instead for poverty but also the wealth of their land.

TWENTY-EIGHT

The Makah Whale Hunt

ONE EVENING IN THE SPRING OF 1997, I RECEIVED A PHONE CALL at home from Ben Johnson Jr., chairman of the Makah Tribe. It was very unusual to get a call at home from the chairman, especially because it had been three years since I had retired. The tribe wanted me to help them in connection with the whaling controversy that had erupted. I was puzzled. John Arum, one of my former partners at the firm, was dealing with the legal aspects as far as I knew, and I told Ben that.

"No," he said, "we want you to handle public relations." This was even more puzzling. I asked Ben to be more specific.

"Well, you know there's a lot of people writing articles and attacking us because we plan to go whaling, and we feel our side of the story needs to be told."

"But Ben," I replied, "you need a public relations firm. I'm not a public relations expert, I'm a lawyer. I can get you the names of some very good PR firms if you'd like me to."

"No, we don't want no PR firm," Ben said. "Our whaling commission and the council decided that you're the best person to explain our history and our rights. We've been getting a lot of calls from the media, wanting to come out here and interview us, and we've turned them all down because we don't trust them. We would like you to handle the media."

I reflected on Ben's request. After I retired, I hadn't looked back. My contacts with the people in the firm were infrequent and, after moving into photography, I had distanced myself psychologically from my identity as a lawyer. I certainly didn't want to go back to the active practice of law. Besides, I had made a rule for myself: I won't do anything that I don't *want* to do. Surprisingly, when I applied this rule to what Ben was asking, I found it made the answer simple. I *wanted* to help the Makahs. So I said yes.

What were the Makahs proposing to do and why? They wanted to conduct a hunt for a gray whale. Doing this was extraordinarily complicated, though the Makahs' reasons were not. The Makahs had been the premier whalers of the Pacific Northwest coast for centuries. The artifacts that had been excavated at the Ozette dig clearly showed that. The historical record was also unequivocal. In the nineteenth century, before the discovery of petroleum, whale oil was in great demand as a lubricant. The Makahs were in the happy circumstance of being able to supply a commodity that had a ready market. To sell whale oil meant cutting the blubber and boiling it in large kettles, or "trying it," and then pouring the resulting oil into barrels, which the Makahs transported by oceangoing canoes to the Hudson's Bay Company post on Vancouver Island. In one year, the Makahs reportedly sold twenty thousand gallons of whale oil. All of this was well known to the federal government.[1]

In the 1850s, commercial whaling was a thriving industry on the East Coast. To encourage settlement of the West, the government printed flyers touting the abundance of whales in the waters of the Pacific, in hopes of enticing some of the New Bedford fleet to the Northwest. That did not happen, leaving the Makahs with a near monopoly of the whale-oil trade, at least until commercial whaling interests were attracted to the area much later.

When Territorial Governor Isaac Stevens was given his instructions on making a treaty with the Makah, protection of their lucrative whale-oil commerce was specifically provided for. The treaty contained a clause explicitly guaranteeing the continued right to take whales, as well as fish.[2] It was the only treaty he negotiated with the Northwest tribes containing such language; indeed it was the only treaty ever negotiated by the United States that contained such a promise. Not only did Stevens assure the Makahs that the United States had no intention of interfering with their whaling, he went further. He promised them that the federal government would supply them with equipment to help them with their whale-oil industry.[3]

This happy picture was marred when whaling fleets expanded into the Pacific starting in the 1860s. The Makahs found themselves unable to compete, and the whale populations declined. The United States never kept its promise to help the Makah whale-oil industry, and they were displaced. That did not mean that the tribe stopped whaling. They continued to hunt for their own consumption. Whale meat had always been an important part of their diet and that continued. By 1925, commercial whaling had so decimated the herds of gray whales that it was no longer feasible for the Makahs to conduct a hunt, and their whaling came to an end.

Commercial whaling continued in the North Pacific and around the world, but the decline in whales of all species became a matter of international concern.[4] In 1946, the United States signed the International Convention for the Regulation of Whaling.[5] As its name implies, the convention's purpose was not to eliminate whaling, but to regulate it. But forty years of regulation proved ineffectual, and in 1986 the convention banned commercial whaling altogether. Meanwhile, by 1969, the population of gray whales had dropped from its historic high of thirty thousand to two thousand, and the U.S. government placed it on the endangered species list.

As the regulatory body under the whaling convention, the International Whaling Commission met regularly to review biological data on the health of world whale stocks and to allow limited whaling. Subsistence whaling by aboriginal people, such as the Inupiat of Alaska, was permitted, as was whaling by the Chukchi peoples of eastern Siberia. Some nations, such as Norway, refused to accept the total ban and continued commercial whaling. Meanwhile, animal lovers and others came to view all whale hunting as barbarous and insisted on banning all hunting regardless of how numerous the whale population became.

As for the gray whale, thirty-five years of protection allowed the species to rebound, and by 1993 its numbers had reached almost 26,000, close to their historic high. The Makahs had never forgotten their whaling heritage and had watched the data on the gray whale closely. When the animal's numbers demonstrated a healthy population, the Northwest Indian Fisheries Commission petitioned the government to remove the gray whale from the endangered species list. The whale was removed from the list and the Makahs notified the government that they intended to resume whaling.[6]

This news was not greeted with joy by the affected federal agencies. The United States had been a world leader in advocating a total end to all commercial whaling and now they were in the awkward position of having to approve a domestic whale hunt. But the United States had defended the hunting of the bowhead whale by Inupiats, and the Makahs were also an indigenous people, seeking only a subsistence hunt. What was more, the Makahs had a treaty right to hunt whales. Denying the Makahs their treaty right would rouse the ire of many American Indian tribes. So the National Marine Fisheries Service decided to support the Makahs, but only subject to several conditions.

First and foremost, the United States would have to obtain the approval of the International Whaling Commission, or IWC, a tricky political undertaking. Then the Makahs themselves would have to reg-ulate the whale hunt. The hunt would have to comply with conditions set by the IWC. Finally, the Makahs had to agree that there would be no commercial use of the whale meat, that it would be locally consumed and not sold.

When the issue of Makah whaling reached the IWC at its 1996 meet-ing in Aberdeen, Scotland, there was a storm of opposition. France, the Netherlands, Australia, China, and other countries spoke against the Makahs. The stated reason was that since the tribe had not hunted whale for seventy years, whale meat could not be claimed as a staple of the Makah diet, and thus there was no subsistence justification. The real reasons were more complex. Among them was concern that opening up whaling to a new participant on cultural grounds would provide Japan the opening it sought. Japan had long argued that its culture included whale meat as a staple of its diet, and the Japanese had continued to hunt whale on the pretext that it was conducting scientific research.

The opposition to the U.S. proposal for Makah whaling did not make the United States back down. Instead, U.S. negotiators entered into discussions with the Russians. The Russians had a gray whale quota of 165 for the Chukchi people, and it was known that these indigenous people were not using the entire quota. The United States proposed joint quotas: twenty bowhead whales could be taken by the Chukchi from the existing Alaskan Inupiat bowhead five-year quota, and twenty gray whales could be taken by the Makahs over a five-year period from the existing Chukchi gray whale quota. This kind of agreement was entirely within the legal framework of the IWC. The IWC set quotas by species, not by nations, and if two nations wanted to allocate the species quota between them, the commission could not object.[7]

The joint quotas were approved at the IWC's 1997 meeting, and the Makahs were overjoyed. The consequences were immediate: the Makahs began serious preparations for a hunt, and the animal-rights community prepared to do battle. For the Makahs, preparations meant arduous training for the crew that would man the whaling canoe. The Makahs had no intention of using the standard industrial weapon, a ship-mounted cannon that fired a projectile into a whale and killed the animal. Instead, the tribe wanted to reenact their ancestral hunting method: pursuing the whale in a dugout canoe manned by seven men, and then hurling a harpoon into the whale. The only concession to modernity was the use of a high-powered rifle to bring instant death. This was done to comply with the regulations of the IWC that the animal be killed in the most humane manner possible.

But the prospect of the Makahs killing a whale inflamed the animal-rights community. Over 250 organizations, with hundreds of thousands of members, vowed to fight the tribe. The leading opponent was the Sea Shepherd Conservation Society, with 35,000 members and an annual budget of over one million dollars. Their leader was a colorful and charismatic figure who designated himself "Captain" Paul Watson. Watson operated with a converted U.S. Navy minesweeper that he had used in guerilla warfare against Norwegian whaling ships, reportedly scuttling one of these vessels. He also had another oceangoing vessel.[8] Now Watson was heading for Neah Bay to fight the Makahs.

The Makahs faced a serious public relations problem. Articles by naturalists and animal-rights activists attacked the Makahs, appearing not only in Seattle newspapers, but also in national publications. From the Makah side there had been no rebuttal, and the tribe was losing in the court of public opinion. This is when Ben Johnson called on me to help.

I had read some of these articles with growing frustration, and when I accepted the challenge to get into the fight I had some specific ideas. Knowing the Makahs as I did, and knowing the history and treaty background, convinced me that the tribe had a persuasive and appealing story to tell. How to tell it was the challenge. I went out to Neah Bay and met with the tribal whaling commission. Many of its members were old friends, and I soon got to know the younger members as well. I made a little speech: "Look, you guys, nobody is hearing your side of the story. It's like a football game with one team running up and down the field scoring touchdowns, while the other team sits in the locker room. You've got to get out there and tell the press what this is all about. I am completely confident you can do it and do it well."

They asked me exactly what I had in mind. I asked whether they had ever met with the press. They had not. There had been many calls seeking interviews, and they had turned them all down. "Why?" I asked. The answers varied only in their wording. The substance was that they didn't trust the press and didn't want to risk getting bad publicity. I assured them they could present their case in such a way that they would get favorable publicity. So the planning began for a press conference at the reservation.

The Makah Whaling Commission wanted me to handle all communications with the press. I knew the news media was slavering for a chance to get a story. There had been many articles already. I also understood the attractiveness of the Makah side: a Native people preparing to conduct a whale hunt, something none of them had ever done, using traditional methods and sending young men out to sea in a canoe to harpoon a forty-ton animal, which could be highly dangerous when attacked. When I began phoning the newspapers and radio and TV stations, announcing the time and place of the press conference, there was an eager response—they would all be there.

The Makahs have a natural sense of drama, and they had planned well for the press conference. It was held in the Makah Cultural and Research Center, the museum where whaling artifacts were prominently displayed. As the reporters and TV camera and sound technicians filled the room, the tribal whaling commission took their seats at a table facing their audience. I opened the conference and introduced George Bowechop, a Makah elder. If the press thought this was going to be another formulaic press conference, they were in for a surprise. George announced that, to begin, some Makah singers and drummers would sing welcoming songs. I could see the TV cameramen licking their chops at the prospect of this colorful footage, but George dashed their hopes by announcing that the songs were family property and the Makahs did not want them filmed. The cameras would have to be put down. The gaggle of media people were beginning to get the idea that this was an Indian reservation and the tribe had its own rhythm.

A group of seven or eight Makahs wearing traditional headdress filed into the room, carrying drums. They began their chants and accompanied themselves with drumming. The atmosphere was transformed. This was not Seattle, nor was this your standard political or corporate press conference. The press was impatient; they wanted to get their story and leave, but had no alternative but to sit and listen respectfully. When the drumming and chanting ended, George Bowechop then told his visitors that in accordance with Makah custom the Makahs would feed them with a lunch that had been prepared. Once again the non-Indian "all business" attitude was confronted by the Indian way. Chairs were pushed back, tables were brought in, and servers carried in trays of broiled salmon, dishes of vegetables, and bread and butter. Pitchers of fruit drink were set out, and a large coffee urn was placed on the buffet table. Soon some fifteen or twenty reporters and technicians were holding plates on their laps while they ate a generous Makah lunch.

Finally, at about two in the afternoon, the press conference began. As planned, three Makah speakers rose and explained in a clear and strong message the meaning of whaling to the tribe and the tribe's determination to exercise the right their forefathers had secured for them. One of the speakers was a crewmember who described the rigorous training they had undergone to prepare for the hunt, paddling twenty miles out to sea and back in all kinds of weather. He held up the harpoon, an eight-foot-long wooden shaft holding a metal spear that detached when the whale was struck. The harpoon head would carry a line tied to floats. One of the crewmen would dive overboard into the frigid waters of the Pacific and sew the whale's gigantic jaws shut so it would not fill with water and sink. The canoe, they explained, would be accompanied by a chase boat on which a Makah would be carrying a .50 caliber rifle to accomplish a quick, humane kill.

The Makahs had engaged Allen Ingling, a retired professor of veterinary medicine at the University of Maryland. His specialty was the humane killing of animals, and he was also a weapons expert. He had been the one who advised the Makahs to use this rifle. He had come to Neah Bay for the press conference and explained that it was far more humane to fire a shot or two into the base of the whale's skull than to use the traditional method of repeatedly spearing the whale until it died of blood loss. He opened a carrying case and removed the rifle, which he held up as the TV cameras filmed and the still cameras clicked.

When the presentations ended, the questions began. Any trepidation I may have had about the Makahs' ability to field hard questions vanished. They were confident and spoke easily and with mastery. I could sense that the edginess and confrontational style of the press had largely disappeared. Perhaps this resulted from the Makahs' obvious sincerity, perhaps from the ceremony and meal, but for whatever reason, I felt the Makahs had won for themselves, if not a sympathetic, at least an understanding press.

But the public relations war was just beginning to heat up. Sea Shepherd, the Progressive Animal Welfare Society, the Humane Society, and other activist organizations were pouring out reams of material attacking the Makah whale hunt. As one might expect, truth was often sacrificed in the passion of a cause, which to these groups seemed almost holy. The Makahs were accused of a secret pact to sell whale meat to the Japanese, their cultural explanations were denigrated, and the whale was portrayed as having near-human intelligence. The language of these attacks was always inflammatory and filled with hyperbole. The internet was humming with blogs, and the newspapers regularly carried passionate letters to the editor.

Even the federal government tried to dissuade the Makahs. A ranking official of the National Oceanic and Atmospheric Administration, the federal agency representing the government, came to Neah Bay for high-level talks with the tribe. At a joint meeting of the tribal council and the whaling commission, he presented a proposal. If the Makahs would drop their whale hunt, the government would support a major funding effort to construct a tourist center at Neah Bay, with whale watching as its main attraction. The council and the commission members listened respectfully and then, without hesitation or debate, informed him that the tribe was not interested in becoming a tourist attraction; that the whale hunt did not equate with material benefits and that the tribe's decision to go forward with the hunt was irrevocable. A similar proposition was received from Craig McCaw, the billionaire cell phone magnate, and his offer met with the same response.

As the summer of 1998 arrived, the Makahs were gearing up for a fall hunt, practicing almost daily and planning for the momentous event. I was busy too. Feeling the need for a clear and cogent explanation, I wrote a fact sheet for publication that tried to answer all the questions that had been raised. The fact sheet received wide distribution and helped inform the general public about what the Makahs planned to do and why they wanted to do it.

By that summer, the Makah whale hunt was a matter of worldwide interest. Since the tribe had designated me as the contact person, I was inundated with calls from local, national, even international television networks and from reporters who saw the hunt as rich material. The drama was obvious to all. I tried to be helpful to all the callers, giving them the names and phone numbers of contacts at Neah Bay, providing general information, and answering questions.

The antiwhaling forces brought demonstrators to tiny Neah Bay, and the local police braced for violence. Many of the demonstrators had shown themselves willing to use force in their cause. The Clallam County Sheriff organized a task force, which included representatives from the Washington State Patrol, the Coast Guard, the National Marine Fisheries Service, the National Guard, and the Bureau of Indian Affairs Law Enforcement Division. The highway leading into Neah Bay was patrolled and any group that appeared to contain large numbers of protesters was observed.

How did the Makah people react to all this notoriety? Most were distressed. They had never seen their tribe vilified in this way, and they reacted with anger, fear, and anxiety. But ultimately, they rallied to the cause, which to them was as sacred as any their opponents invoked— their treaty rights. If anything, the attacks increased feelings of tribal cohesiveness and unity. They were also encouraged by the growing support from other Indian tribes throughout the state and, indeed, the nation. Indians everywhere saw the Makahs as heroes for reclaiming their historic tradition. Indians have never been sentimentalists about the hunting and killing of animals for food. But they have felt a spiritual connection with the natural world and its animal inhabitants. The Makah whaling crew prayed, sang, and purified themselves in preparation for the hunt—a renewal of ancient spiritual connection.

The whale hunt threw me back into the fray for Indian rights. I was writing articles and public relations pieces and I was also speaking out publicly. I appeared on television talk shows, on radio, and in talks and debates at universities and colleges. In my public appearances I was confident. I debated Captain Paul Watson before a large audience of students at Western Washington University, a campus that was strongly pro-environment. But I was able to refute the conservation argument with well-established scientific data that showed the gray whale stock at an all-time high, able to handle a hunt of five whales a year from its population of thirty thousand. My task was to communicate the deep cultural meaning this hunt had for the Makahs. Here I had the advantage over Watson. He found himself in the uncomfortable position of trying to disparage Indian culture. The audience was won over to the Makah side, and their applause showed it.

On another occasion I spoke to an audience of students and faculty at the University of Washington School of Fisheries. When I began, I sensed they were inclined to oppose the Makah hunt. I turned to the blackboard behind me and wrote one word on it: *ethnocentrism*. Then I asked members of the audience what it meant. As they gave its meaning—the view that one's own culture is superior to others, viewing the practices of another culture through the lens of one's own culture—they began to see the issue more clearly. I was able to isolate the issue to one of ethical beliefs: they had to confront the question of imposing their ethical belief that it was morally wrong to kill this mammal on a Native culture that had killed and eaten that mammal for thousands of years. I pointed to the incongruity of opposing the killing and eating of a whale with the fact that they likely ate beef with no qualms and wore shoes of cowhide with no thought of morality. When my talk was finished, the questions and comments showed I had at least made the audience understand the cultural dimensions of the conflict.

In the public arena, I felt deeply gratified that the fight was no longer one-sided. The tenor of newspaper articles was informed and respectful—all I could hope for. On the water, though, things were tense. The Makahs had barred Sea Shepherd from tying up its two vessels at the tribal dock, so the group had anchored at the mouth of Neah Bay and regularly blasted messages to the Makahs over their loudspeakers. Public expectation was mounting too. In anticipation of the hunt, a small army of reporters encamped at Neah Bay. But as day after day passed without a hunt, most left. The whalers did not find the hunting conditions right throughout that fall. The first successful hunt didn't take place until the following spring.

On May 17, 1999, a whaling canoe manned by eight men successfully harpooned the first whale that had been taken by the Makahs in seventy-five years.[9] There was wild jubilation throughout the village as hundreds trooped down to the beach to see the object of so many hopes and efforts. To many Makahs it was like a dream, their ancestral past brought to life.

To celebrate the historic occasion, the Makahs invited hundreds of friends and well wishers to a festive meal in the high-school gymnasium the following Saturday. Chairman Ben Johnson called to invite me personally. Lennie and I arrived at the gym to find the parking lot crammed with cars and a long line waiting to enter the building. We were ushered to a table at the front of the hall, and the festivities began in the traditional way—with a meal. The hall was filled with Indian people from all over the state, some of whom I knew. After lunch, there was a prayer followed by ceremonial dances. I was somewhat pressed for time because we had an engagement in Seattle that evening and had to leave by three o'clock. As my deadline neared, I quietly made my way to the speaker's platform to make my farewells. When I spoke to Ben Johnson, the chairman asked me not to leave yet, but to come up to the stage where the tribal officials and the whaling commission members were seated.

On the stage I was uncertain why they had invited me up there, until Ben called on me to speak. I was stunned when he introduced me as "the man who made all this possible." When I stepped forward to speak, I was not prepared for what happened. The audience rose to its feet cheering and applauding. I had expected some polite applause, but they wouldn't stop—they went on and on as they stood giving me a standing ovation. I suddenly realized the place I held in the emotions of the Makah people, and as I stood there, I knew it was a defining moment in my life.

After an eternity of applause, I finally had to ask them to stop. When the tumult died down, I began:

You Makah people have a right to be proud today. Once again you have won back your sacred rights. Many of you remember the fight to save Ozette from those who wanted to sweep it into the Olympic National Park. You won that fight and Ozette is Makah today, along with everything that came out of the ground there and now sits in the Makah museum. You won back Tatoosh and Waadah, your ancient lands, which the federal government tried to take from you. You won the right to fish in the Hoko, and with the Boldt decision you have won the right to use your treaty rights in all Makah usual and accustomed places, on the rivers and on the ocean. And now today, you celebrate the treaty right your ancestors preserved for you—the right to hunt the whale. You faced powerful enemies in this, and the fight may not be over, but I know that in the end the Makahs will win. It is a happy day for me and I'm happy to be here with you for this celebration.

As I turned to leave the podium, the audience rose to their feet again and continued their applause until I had descended from the stage and made my way out of the gym. The next day, I wrote in my biographical log: "Saturday, May 22, 1999. The most wonderful day of my life."

Whaling remains unfinished business for the Makahs. Their success in the hunt resulted in protracted litigation. Animal-rights groups challenged the government's action in approving the hunt. The case went to the Ninth Circuit Court of Appeals and ended with a decision requiring the Makahs to go through a lengthy process to receive a permit under the Marine Mammal Protection Act. At this writing, they are deeply engaged in the permit process and there is every likelihood that if the permit is issued, more litigation will follow. But the Makahs have demonstrated their determination to restore their whaling tradition. They are law abiding and patient. They have waited eighty years and they will wait as long as they have to. But they will not give up.

TWENTY-NINE

A Life in Being

I AM OLD NOW, EIGHTY AT MY LAST BIRTHDAY. OFTEN I REFLECT on my improbable career. As a shy, only child of middle-class Jewish parents, ambiguous about my Jewishness, certain only of my idealism, I seemed to drift into the profession of law. Starting at the lowest rung, I struggled to teach myself the skills of a lawyer. Often I was fearful and uncertain. I paid a high emotional price during those early years of lonely apprenticeship. The badge of inferiority that was implanted by my law school experience never left me, no matter the many triumphs I had. But I was driven to achieve—by my sense of responsibility to my client and, in my Indian work, by my deep sense of the righteousness of what I was doing. The moral vacuum that the University of Chicago Law School left was filled by my work representing Indian tribes.

Looking back, it is clear that being a tribal attorney was the most important and most fulfilling part of my adult life. It meant more than being a specialist in an arcane branch of the law. For me, and for my partners, it meant being a part of a movement for the reconstruction of Indian life in America. It was a political movement, and I shared the Indians' feeling of being beleaguered by the forces of the dominant society. I could not avoid feeling that our opponents were the "bad guys"— that they represented the forces that wanted to see Indians disappear, even though many of them were principled people representing the interests of their own communities and their own clients. This is one of the hazards facing the tribal attorney: adopting a Manichaean view in which the Indians symbolize the good and their opponents evil. Over the years, that simplistic view was clouded by conflicts between tribes and by a more nuanced awareness of the real problems of an ethnic government asserting authority over outsiders.

While the work of a tribal attorney is the work of a lawyer, not a polemicist, still our firm's political philosophy regarding the American Indian, his history and his victimization, shaped our legal thinking and our language. So we argued passionately for the recognition of tribal sovereignty, for the territorial integrity of Indian land, for the preservation of tribal resources—air quality, water quality, healthy fish stocks, and an unpolluted environment. Again and again we found ourselves pitted against state governments trying to impose their authority over tribes.

But not all the work of a tribal attorney is concerned with external forces. Tribal governments are now emerging from their infancy and they must be able to provide a just society for their own members and for nonmembers who come under their authority. We were often called on to draft tribal laws and constitutions and to conduct training for tribal judges with an eye toward due process and fairness.

Joblessness and poverty are big problems on most reservations, so tribes often turn to their attorneys to help them find solutions. I spent innumerable hours in negotiation with mining companies, manufacturing companies, timber companies, and fish-processing companies to develop businesses on the reservation. One business we did not deal with was Indian gaming. With the exception of the Mille Lacs Band, none of the tribes we represented operated casinos. While the Mille Lacs do operate big casinos, they rely on the law firm retained by their contractor, a specialist in this area of law.

Frequently my work for tribal clients took me to the nation's capital to meet with senators and congressmen and to testify before congressional committees. I tried to explain the tribe's views to federal agencies and to persuade them to help the tribe. I took pride in saying, "I represent the such and such tribe." It always commanded respect. An Indian tribe is like no corporate client; it has a historic identity, and the nation's history of victimizing Indians is well known.

I believe that being a tribal attorney is a calling. It demands that the attorney place himself unequivocally on the side of the Indian people, not just for one case, but for his life's work. I like to think that a model for tribal attorneys is William Wirt, the lawyer who represented the Cherokees in their epic legal struggle to preserve their tribal existence. William Wirt (1772–1834) was retained by the Cherokee Tribe in their desperate effort to avoid expulsion by the state of Georgia. He was one of the most distinguished lawyers in America. He had served as attorney general of the United States for twelve years and had argued more than 150 cases in the U.S. Supreme Court. Taking the case of the Cherokees pitted him not only against Georgia, but against the president, Andrew Jackson.

In the landmark case of *Worcester v. Georgia*, he was victorious. The Supreme Court ruled that the state of Georgia had no authority over the Cherokees on their lands. But *Worcester v. Georgia* turned out to be a Pyrrhic victory. The state ignored the decision, in fact, didn't even appear in court to contest the case. Andrew Jackson, who was infuriated by Wirt's temerity in opposing Indian removal, had no intention of enforcing the court's decision, giving rise to the apocryphal, "John Marshall has made his decision, now let him enforce it." The Cherokees won the court battle, but they lost the fight against expulsion. Shortly after, they were driven out of Georgia and sent packing on the Trail of Tears.[1]

It would be scant comfort to William Wirt or the Cherokees that 150 years later, the rule of *Worcester v. Georgia* has become a bedrock principle of Indian law, protecting Indian tribes against the incursions of state authority. But I think Wirt and the Cherokees would be pleased to see that, despite the disappearance of many tribes, the Indian nation in America has survived and now comprises more than four hundred tribes and bands with over two million members. The Cherokees, I think, would take particular satisfaction in seeing many tribes functioning as full-blown governments, just as they did before being crushed by state power.

When I began my work for the Makah Tribe in 1964, Indian law was such a little-known branch of American law that few American lawyers had heard of it. Today it is an established field, a subject taught in many law schools in America, with a body of literature that includes two casebooks for law students, several treatises, and innumerable publications and articles dealing with every facet of Indian activity. Not only has the field grown, but so have the number of Indian lawyers. There are over two thousand Indians practicing law and many others with law degrees.[2] Indian law is a specialty practiced by attorneys in some of America's largest law firms. Wirt and the Cherokees would be amazed.

I am optimistic about the future of American Indian tribes. They have grown into functioning governments and Indian tribes have become embedded in the laws of the nation as governmental service providers. In the index to the United States Code, there are more than five thousand entries under "Indian Tribes and Tribal Governments." Even state governments recognize the important role that tribal government plays in public affairs, from fish and wildlife management to environmental protection. Tribes are becoming steadily more accepted as members of the American family of governments.

Tribes long ago realized that their lives, even their very existence, depends on decisions taken in the nation's capital. So they have learned how to make their voices heard there. Today they have strong representation in Washington, D.C. The National Congress of American Indians is a recognized voice of the Indian people and actively lobbies Congress. Many tribes have hired their own lobbyists. Indian gaming has provided some tribes with money far beyond the wildest dreams of even a few years ago. This has attracted some unscrupulous exploiters. But tribes are using their wealth to play the great American political game of helping your friends and defeating your enemies. When Senator Slade Gorton of Washington—the dedicated opponent of Indian rights whose views were not changed even by Supreme Court defeats—ran for reelection in 1996, the tribes of the state threw their financial support behind his Democratic opponent, Maria Cantwell. And Gorton was defeated.

For Indian tribes to survive in the American environment, they have to find support from all three branches of government. Because their very existence is dependent on legal principles, they must have very good tribal attorneys. But, as we have seen in the Cherokee case, politics trumps law. Widely held beliefs that are hostile to tribes will find their way into court rulings on Indian cases, as I think happened in *Oliphant v. Suquamish Tribe*. So tribes must rely on the sympathetic ear of Congress. Perhaps their best asset is the support and good will of the majority of the American people.

Indians enjoy a positive image in contemporary America. There is widespread appreciation of the injustices they have suffered. There is also widespread awareness of their military service in the armed forces. But perhaps most important is the place they occupy in the American narrative. Indian tribes are an integral part of the history of the nation and the nation's romance with that history. Most Americans respect that Indians are America's indigenous people and enjoy the spectacle of Indians celebrating their heritage in traditional regalia. Indians are American icons. If you destroy a cultural icon, you destroy part of your *own* heritage.

So now I come to the end of my story. I look back on the twists and turns of fortune that led to my career as a lawyer for Indian tribes. There was serendipity in the youthful wanderlust that brought me to Seattle in the summer of 1950; there was serendipity even in being drafted into the army, because it led me to begin my career in Seattle instead of Chicago. Practicing in Chicago would never have led me to Indian law, and who knows what mundane, tedious legal backwater I would have ended up in. Even working for a manic-depressive lawyer was serendipitous; I grew swiftly from a young law clerk into a confident attorney with the ability to conduct important cases concerning almost any legal problem. And of course, that West Seattle law office led to meeting the Wilkie family, which put me on the road to Neah Bay.

Even my background as a Jew has been important. For many years I regarded my Jewish identity as peripheral, but over time I came to appreciate that it lent special meaning to my work with Indians. We Jews are also a tribe. Though we don't have any membership rolls, we too have a common history of oppression and discrimination. We too have our customs and rituals. And we too feel the strain of ethnic survival in the American "melting pot." So for me, tribal sovereignty is a shield against oppression and at the same time a force for ethnic survival.

There is a phrase used in the common law of estates to measure the term of a life: "a life in being." Literally, it means the duration of one person's life. I have not come to the end of mine, but I can take its measure. It has been a life defined by making an important contribution to the Indian people in ways both direct and indirect. I feel that my father and mother would have been proud. I didn't seek out the circumstances that led me to the Indian people and I had little control over the direction of my career. In the end I am unable to answer the question of whether I was just a swimmer swept along by the currents of chance, or whether I was the author of my own fate. Perhaps the question no longer has any importance, because that was my history and this is my story.

Notes

CHAPTER FOUR

1 Executive Order no. 6260, August 28, 1933; *Trading with the Enemy Act*, 12 U.S.C. sec. 95a (1917); *Gold Reserve Act of 1934*, 38 Stat. 337 (1934).
2 *Bauer v. U.S.*, 244 F.2d 794 (9th Circuit, 1957).

CHAPTER FIVE

1 *General Allotment Act of 1887 (Dawes Act)*, 24 Stat. 388 (1887).

CHAPTER SIX

1 For press reports of the police misconduct hearing, see *Seattle Post-Intelligencer*, January 23, 1965, and *New York Times Magazine*, December 5, 1965, p. 61.

CHAPTER SEVEN

1 For a full description of the role that Billy Frank played in Indian resistance to Washington State's violation of treaty rights, see Charles Wilkinson, *Messages from Frank's Landing* (Seattle: University of Washington Press, 2000), 34–38.

2 This incident is described by Marlon Brando in his autobiography, *Songs My Mother Taught Me* (New York: Random House, 1994), 375–78.

CHAPTER EIGHT

1 Dennis L. Noble, "Native Americans in the U.S. Coast Guard," U.S. Coast Guard web site, www.uscg.mil/history/NativeAmericans.asp; Sharon E. Wilkerson, "Station Neah Bay Breaks Ethnic Barriers at the Turn of the Century," *Commandant's Bulletin* (U.S. Coast Guard) (November 1995): 27.

2 For a description of the Makah people and their culture, see Ann M. Renker and Erna Gunther, "Makah," in *Handbook of North American Indians*, vol. 7, ed. William Sturtevant (Washington, D.C.: Smithsonian, 1990), 422–30. See also Elizabeth Colson, *The Makah Indians: A Study of an Indian Tribe in Modern American Society* (Minneapolis: University of Minnesota Press, 1953).

3 For a description of the effects of the War on Poverty on tribal governments, see Charles F. Wilkinson, *Blood Struggle* (New York: W. W. Norton, 2005).

CHAPTER NINE

1 See "Status of the Ozette Indian Reservation, Washington," in *Opinions of the Solicitor of the Department of the Interior Relating to Indian Affairs*, 76 I.D. 14, M-36456 (Supp.), February 18, 1969, p. 1989, describing the decline in population at Ozette.

2 Referenced in *Opinions of the Solicitor of the Department of the Interior Relating to Indian Affairs*, 64 I.D. 435, M-36456, November 21, 1957, p. 1805.

3 See *Opinions of the Solicitor*, supra note 1, pp. 188–93.

4 See Patricia Ward Henderson with Helma Ward and Kirk Wachendorf, *Voices of a Thousand People: The Makah Cultural and Research Center* (Lincoln: University of Nebraska Press, 2002). Visitor data provided to the author by Janine Bowechop, executive director, Makah Cultural and Research Center.

5 M. T. Stevens, *Report of the Commissioner of Indian Affairs*

(Washington, D.C., 1858), 232.

6 *Makah Indian Tribe v. U.S.*, Docket No. 60-A, 7 Indian Claims Commission 477, Final Order (April 15, 1959).

7 *Makah Indian Tribe v. U.S.*, Docket No. 60-A, 39 Indian Claims Commission 97 (October 15, 1976); *Makah Indian Tribe v. U.S.*, Docket No. 60-A, 40 Indian Claims Commission 131, 134 (May 4, 1977).

CHAPTER TEN

1 Reef-net fishing is described in *U.S. v. Washington*, 384 F. Supp. 312, 360 (Western District of Washington, 1974).

CHAPTER ELEVEN

1 *Kennedy v. Becker*, 241 U.S. 556 (1916).

2 For the history of the Pacific salmon industry, see Fay G. Cohen, *Treaties on Trial: The Continuing Controversy over Northwest Indian Fishing Rights* (Seattle: University of Washington Press, 1986), 40–45; Patrick O'Bannon, "Technological Change in the Pacific Coast Canned Salmon Industry." (PhD diss., University of California, San Diego, 1983); August C. Radke, *Pacific American Fisheries, Inc.: History of a Washington State Packing Company*, ed. Barbara S. Radke (Jefferson, NC: McFarland, 2002); Kit Oldham, "The First Salmon Cannery on the Columbia River Opens at Eagle Cliff, Wahkiakum County, in 1866," HistoryLink.org (accessed July 17, 2008).

3 *Tulee v. Washington*, 315 U.S. 681 (1942).

4 For a history of the Northwest Indian fishing rights conflict, see American Friends Service Committee, *Uncommon Controversy: Fishing Rights of the Muckleshoot, Puyallup and Nisqually Indians* (Seattle: University of Washington Press, 1970), and Cohen, *Treaties on Trial*.

5 *Department of Game v. Puyallup Tribe*, 70 Wash. 2d 262 (1979).

6 Undated, privately distributed newsletter received in 1970 (copy in author's possession).

7 "Indians Found Innocent of Fish-In Incident," *Seattle Times*, January 17, 1969.

8   *The Renegade*, June 1971 (publication of the Survival of American Indians Association, copy in author's possession).
9   *U.S. v. Oregon* and *Sohappy v. Smith*, 302 F. Supp. 899 (D. Oreg. 1969).

CHAPTER TWELVE

1   Puyallup I is *Puyallup Tribe of Indians v. Department of Game*, 391 U.S. 392 (1968), and Puyallup II is *Department of Game v. Puyallup Tribe, Inc.*, 414 U.S. 44 (1973).
2   George Dysart, conversation with the author, 1971.
3   Stuart Pierson, conversation with the author, 2007.
4   *The Renegade*, June 1971, 8 (copy in author's possession).
5   Barbara Lane, conversation with the author, 2005.

CHAPTER THIRTEEN

1   The attorney statements and those of Judge Boldt, as well as quoted witness testimony, are all from Transcript of Proceedings, *U.S. v. Washington*, 384 F. Supp. 312 (Western District of Washington, 1974), Civ. No. 9213 (hereafter, Transcript). The record of the testimony and remarks of each individual named begins at the first page and ends at the last page referenced.
2   *U.S. v. Winans*, 198 U.S. 371 (1905).
3   Transcript, 4–18.
4   Transcript, 18–30.
5   Transcript, 32–42.
6   Transcript, 60–73.
7   Transcript, 73–87.
8   Transcript, 99.
9   *U.S. v. Washington*, Civ. No. 9213, Exhibit Nos. USA 20–30 and 53.
10 Opinion in *U.S. v. Washington*, 384 F. Supp. 312, 350 (Western District of Washington, 1974).
11 Transcript, 2519–81.
12 Transcript, 2582–89.
13 Transcript, 2621–94.
14 Transcript, 2896–2912.

15 Transcript, 3004–16.
16 Transcript, 3146–81.
17 Transcript, 3182–90.
18 Transcript, 3190–3226.
19 Transcript, 3474–3521.

CHAPTER FOURTEEN

1 Transcript, 4252–83, 4534–53.
2 Transcript, 4283–4329.
3 *State v. Towessnute*, 89 Wash. 478 (1916).
4 Transcript, 4332–68, 4497–4512.
5 Transcript, 4374–4450.
6 Transcript, 4450–75.
7 Transcript, 4598.
8 *U.S. v. Washington*, 384 F. Supp. 312 (Western District of Washington, 1974).
9 Ibid., 389.
10 Northwest Indian Fisheries Commission, *Annual Report* (1982), 32.
11 *U.S. v. Washington*, 520 F.2d 676 (9th Circuit, 1975).

CHAPTER FIFTEEN

1 *State of Washington v. Washington State Commercial Passenger Fishing Vessel Association*, 443 U.S. 658 (1979).
2 See Jovana Brown, "Treaty Rights: Twenty Years after the Boldt Decision," *Wicazo Sa Review* 10, no. 2 (Fall 1994).
3 Ibid.
4 Northwest Indian Fisheries Commission, *Annual Report* (1987), 14.
5 L. McConnell, *Economic Contributions Made by Indian Tribes to Washington State* (Washington, D.C.: Bureau of Indian Affairs, Branch of Fisheries, March 13, 1987), from table in appendix.

CHAPTER SIXTEEN

1 Alvin M. Josephy and Jeremy Five Crows, *Nez Perce Country* (Lincoln: University of Nebraska Press, 2007), 139.

2   Quoted in Mark H. Brown, *The Flight of the Nez Perce* (Lincoln: University of Nebraska Press, 1967), 407.

3   For a history of the termination policy, see Donald L. Fixico, *Termination and Relocation: Federal Indian Policy 1945–1960* (Albuquerque: University of New Mexico Press, 1986), and Kenneth R. Philp, *Termination Revisited: American Indians on the Trail to Self-Determination, 1933–1953* (Lincoln: University of Nebraska Press, 1999).

4   *Tonasket v. Washington*, 411 U.S. 451 (1973).

5   *Colville v. Washington*, 447 U.S. 134 (1980).

6   *Antoine v. Washington*, 420 U.S. 194 (1975).

7   Act of June 29, 1940, 54 Stat. 703 (1940). For the impact of the Grand Coulee Dam on the Colville Tribe, see Paul C. Pitzer, *Grand Coulee: Harnessing a Dream* (Pullman: Washington State University Press, 1994), 215–30, and Kevin Wehr, *America's Fight over Water* (New York: Routledge, 2004), 135–85.

8   *U.S. v. Winters*, 207 U.S. 564 (1908).

9   The initial U.S. District Court decision in *Colville Confederated Tribes v. Boyd Walton Jr. et al.* is found in 420 F. Supp. 1320 (Eastern District of Washington, 1978). Subsequent appeals and proceedings are reported in 647 F.2d 42 (9th Circuit, 1981), 752 F.2d 397 (9th Circuit, 1985), and 883 F.2d 1023 (9th Circuit, 1989).

CHAPTER EIGHTEEN

1   *Hollowbreast v. Northern Cheyenne Tribe*, 505 F.2d 268 (9th Circuit, 1974).

2   *Hollowbreast v. Northern Cheyenne Tribe*, 425 U.S. 649 (1976).

3   *Northern Cheyenne Lease Cancellation Act*, Public Law 96–401 (October 8, 1980).

4   *New York Times*, January 1, 2006.

CHAPTER NINETEEN

1   *Indian Civil Rights Act*, 25 U.S.C. sec. 1301 et seq. (1968).

2   *Mark David Oliphant v. Suquamish Tribe*, 435 U.S. 191 (1978).

3   *Cherokee v. Georgia*, 30 U.S. 1 (1831); *Worcester v. Georgia*, 31 U.S. 6 (1832).

CHAPTER TWENTY

1 *Indian Civil Rights Act*, 25 U.S.C. sec. 1301 et seq. (1968).
2 *Dodge v. Nakai*, 298 F. Supp. 17 (District Court, Ariz., 1968).
3 Alvin J. Ziontz, "In Defense of Tribal Sovereignty: An Analysis of Judicial Error in Construction of the Indian Civil Rights Act," *South Dakota Law Review* 20, no. 1 (Winter 1975).
4 *Martinez v. Santa Clara Pueblo*, 436 U.S. 49 (1978).
5 Alvin J. Ziontz, "After *Martinez*: Indian Civil Rights under Tribal Government," *UC Davis Law Review* 12, no. 1 (March 1979).

CHAPTER TWENTY-ONE

1 The United Kingdom adopted a Human Rights Act in 1998, incorporating parts of the European Convention on Human Rights. However, it differs significantly from the U.S. Bill of Rights in a number of important respects: it contains no prohibition against self-incrimination, nor any requirement of a warrant for searches and seizures.

CHAPTER TWENTY-FOUR

1 See Veronica E. Velarde Tiller, ed. and comp., *Tiller's Guide to Indian Country* (Albuquerque, NM: BowArrow Publishing Co., 1996), 385–87, and Mille Lacs Band of Ojibwe, *Mille Lacs Band of Ojibwe Fact Book* (St. Paul, MN: Mille Lacs Band of Ojibwe, 2007).
2 *Lac Courte Oreilles Band of Chippewas v. Voigt*, 700 F.2d 341 (7th Circuit, 1983).
3 *Mille Lacs v. Minnesota*, 124 F.3d 904 (8th Circuit, 1997).
4 For a comprehensive description of the events leading up to and including the Supreme Court hearing, see Charles Otto Rasmussen, *Ojibwe Journeys* (Odanah, WI: Great Lakes Fish and Wildlife Press, 2003).
5 *Mille Lacs v. Minnesota*, 526 U.S. 172 (1999).
6 Mille Lacs Band of Ojibwe, "Grand Casino Mille Lacs," www.grand casinomn.com/Hotels/Hotels.aspx (accessed September 24, 2007); Mille Lacs Band of Ojibwe, "Economic Impact of the Mille Lacs

Band, Grand Casino Mille Lacs, and Grand Casino Hinckley as of March 2008," www.millelacsojibwe.org (accessed March 2008).

CHAPTER TWENTY-FIVE

1 *Boswell v. Sherburne County*, 849 F.2d 1117 (8th Circuit, 1988).

CHAPTER TWENTY-SIX

1 See *Shoshone Tribe of Indians of the Wind River Reservation v. U.S.*, 85 U.S. Court of Claims 331 (June 1, 1937) (No. H 219), awarding damages to the Shoshone Tribe for the land occupied by the Arapahos. The Arapahos were granted legal authority to settle on the Wind River reservation with the Shoshone by the 1896 Big Horn Hot Springs Land Cession Agreement with the Shoshone and Arapaho Tribes of Indians in Wyoming. For a general history of the Arapahos, see Loretta Fowler, "Arapaho," in *Handbook of North American Indians*, vol. 12, ed. William Sturtevant (Washington, D.C.: Smithsonian, 1998), 840–43, Jeffrey D. Anderson, *The Four Hills of Life: Northern Arapaho Knowledge and Life Movement* (Lincoln: University of Nebraska Press, 2001), 9–13, and Hank Stamm, "Land Cession of 1896," Chief Washakie Foundation Web site, www.windriverhistory.org/archives/treaty_docs/cession1896com. html.

CHAPTER TWENTY-EIGHT

1 See Dr. Barbara Lane's report on the Makahs, *U.S. v. Washington*, supra, Exhibit No. U.S. 20; and the *Columbian* (newspaper published in Olympia, Oregon Territory), September 11, 1852, pp. 2–3, archived in Journal III, Records Group E-198, U.S. National Archives, Washington, D.C.
2 See "Treaty with the Makah, 1855," in Charles J. Kappler, ed. and comp., *Indian Affairs: Laws and Treaties*, vol. 2, *Treaties* (Washington, D.C.: GPO, 1904), 682.
3 Transcript of Journal of Proceedings, Treaty of Neah Bay, Treaty File, Letters Received 1855, Washington W537 (enclosure), p. 5,

Records of Bureau of Indian Affairs, Washington, D.C.

4 See John R. Twiss Jr. and Randall R. Reeves, eds., *Conservation and Management of Marine Mammals* (Washington, D.C.: Smithsonian, 1999), 181.

5 International Convention for the Regulation of Whaling, December 2, 1946, in Phillipe Sands and Paolo Galizzi, *Documents in International Environmental Law* (Cambridge: Cambridge University Press, 2004).

6 *New York Times*, November 19, 1991, p. 2; *Seattle Post-Intelligencer*, January 1, 1993, p. D2.

7 John Arum, attorney for the Makahs who participated in the International Whaling Commission proceedings, conversation with the author, 2008.

8 For stories about Paul Watson and the Sea Shepherd Conservation Society, see the *Guardian* (London), June 3, 2002, p. 13, *Sydney Morning Herald* (Australia), September 7, 1996, p. 37, and Raffi Khatchadourian, "Neptune's Navy," the *New Yorker*, November 5, 2007, p. 59.

9 For a description of the Makah whale hunt and its background, see Robert Sullivan, *A Whale Hunt* (New York: Scribner, 2000).

CHAPTER TWENTY-NINE

1 See Jill Norgren, *The Cherokee Cases* (Norman: University of Oklahoma Press, 2004), Robert V. Remini, *Andrew Jackson and His Indian Wars* (New York: Penguin Books, 2001), and Gregory K. Glassner, *Adopted Son: The Life, Wit and Wisdom of William Wirt, 1772–1834* (Madison County, VA: Kurt Ketner Publishing Co., 1997).

2 *The Lawyer Statistical Report* (American Bar Foundation, 1985, 1994, 2004).

Selected Bibliography

American Friends Service Committee. *Uncommon Controversy: Fishing Rights of the Muckleshoot, Puyallup and Nisqually Indians.* Seattle: University of Washington Press, 1970.

Anderson, Jeffrey D. *The Four Hills of Life: Northern Arapaho Knowledge and Life Movement.* Lincoln: University of Nebraska Press, 2001.

Bordewich, Fergus M. *Killing the White Man's Indian.* New York: Doubleday, 1996.

Brando, Marlon. *Songs My Mother Taught Me.* New York: Random House, 1994.

Brown, Dee. *Bury My Heart at Wounded Knee.* New York: Bantam, 1972.

Brown, Jovana. "Treaty Rights: Twenty Years after the Boldt Decision," *Wicazo Sa Review* 10, no. 2 (Fall 1994): 1–16.

Cadwallader, Sandra, and Vine Deloria Jr., eds. *The Aggressions of Civilization.* Philadelphia: Temple University Press, 1984.

Cohen, Fay G. *Treaties on Trial: The Continuing Controversy over Northwest Indian Fishing Rights.* Seattle: University of Washington Press, 1986.

Colson, Elizabeth. *The Makah Indians: A Study of an Indian Tribe in Modern American Society.* Minneapolis: University of Minnesota Press, 1953.

Deloria, Vine, Jr. *Custer Died for Your Sins.* New York: Macmillan, 1969.

Fixico, Donald L. *Termination and Relocation: Federal Indian Policy 1945–1960.* Albuquerque: University of New Mexico Press, 1986.

Fowler, Loretta. "Arapaho." In *Handbook of North American Indians*, vol. 12, ed. William Sturtevant, 840–43 (Washington, D.C.: Smithsonian, 1998).

Frazier, Ian. *On the Rez*. New York: Farrar, Strauss, Giroux, 2000.

Gibson, Arrell Morgan. *The American Indian: Prehistory to the Present*. Lexington, MA: D. C. Heath and Co., 1980.

Glassner, Gregory K. *Adopted Son: The Life, Wit and Wisdom of William Wirt, 1772–1834*. Madison County, VA: Kurt-Ketner Publishing Co., 1997.

Grinnell, George Bird. *The Fighting Cheyennes*. Norman: University of Oklahoma Press, 1956.

Henderson, Patricia Ward, with Helma Ward and Kirk Wachendorf. *Voices of a Thousand People: The Makah Cultural and Research Center*. Lincoln: University of Nebraska Press, 2002.

Josephy, Alvin M., and Jeremy Five Crows. *Nez Perce Country*. Lincoln: University of Nebraska Press, 2007.

Kroeber, Alfred L. *The Arapaho*. Lincoln: University of Nebraska Press, 1983.

Llewellyn, Karl N., and Adamson Hoebel. *The Cheyenne Way*. Norman: University of Oklahoma Press, 1973.

Mille Lacs Band of Ojibwe. *Mille Lacs Band of Ojibwe Fact Book*. St. Paul, MN: Mille Lacs Band of Ojibwe, 2007.

Noble, Dennis L. "The Makah Influence: Native Americans in the Early Coast Guard." *Commandant's Bulletin* (U.S. Coast Guard) (November 1996): 18–19.

Norgren, Jill. *The Cherokee Cases*. Norman: University of Oklahoma Press, 2004.

Pevar, Stephen L. *The Rights of Indians and Tribes: The Authoritative ACLU Guide to Indian and Tribal Rights*. 3rd ed. New York: New York University Press, 2004.

Philp, Kenneth R. *Termination Revisited: American Indians on the Trail to Self-Determination, 1933–1953*. University of Nebraska Press, 1999.

Pitzer, Paul C. *Grand Coulee: Harnessing a Dream*. Pullman: Washington State University Press, 1994.

Rasmussen, Charlie Otto. *Ojibwe Journeys*. Odanah, WI: Great Lakes Fish and Wildlife Commission, 2003.

Remini, Robert V. *Andrew Jackson and His Indian Wars*. New York: Penguin, 2001.

Renker, Ann M., and Erna Gunther. "Makah." In *Handbook of North American Indians*, vol. 7, ed. William Sturtevant, 422–30 (Washington, DC: Smithsonian, 1990).

Spicer, Edward H. *A Short History of the Indians of the United States*. New York: D. Van Nostrand Co., 1969.

Sullivan, Robert. *A Whale Hunt*. New York: Scribner, 2000.

Tiller, Veronica Velarde, ed. and comp. *Tiller's Guide to Indian Country*. Albuquerque, NM: BowArrow Publishing Co., 1996.

Wehr, Kevin. *America's Fight over Water*. New York: Routledge, 2004.

Wilkerson, Sharon E. "Station Neah Bay Breaks Ethnic Barriers at the Turn of the Century." *Commandant's Bulletin* (U.S. Coast Guard) (November 1995): 27.

Wilkinson, Charles F. *Blood Struggle*. New York: W. W. Norton, 2005.

———. *Messages from Frank's Landing: A Story of Salmon, Treaties and the Indian Way*. Seattle: University of Washington Press, 2000.

Index

aboriginal title, establishing, 70, 75

ACLU. *See* American Civil Liberties Union (ACLU)

Adams, Hank, 49–50, 52, 95

Adler, Stella, 55

"After *Martinez*" (Ziontz), 179

Air Force base, 63

Alaska fishermen, 198–202

alcoholism, 60

Alden, Charlene (born White Man), 238–39, 240, 242, 243

Alden, Crystal, 238, 242

Alden, Joe, 238–39, 242–43

Alden, JP, 238

Alden, Leslie, 238

Alden, Shannon (later Wilson), 238, 239

Aleut Native Corporation, 199

Allotment Act, 42, 159, 161

American Civil Liberties Union (ACLU): board member service, 46; election as affiliate president, 46; fishing rights support, 86–87; Indian rights work, 172–74, 177–78; joining of, 38–39; police department case, 46–48

"American Indian Separatism" (Ziontz), 87

American Legion, 63

Anderson, Margie, 209

Anderson, Steve, 139

animal rights community, Makah whale hunt, 257, 260, 262–63

anti-Semitism, 9. *See also* bigotry/racial prejudice

Antoine family, hunting rights case, 139–40

aquaculture project, Lummi tribe, 80–81

Arapaho Tribes, 277n1 (ch 26). *See also* Northern Arapaho Tribe

archeological site, Ozette, 72

Arkansas, District Court opinion,

170
Army Corps of Engineers, 81, 135, 140–42
Army years, 21–23, 269
artwork, 154, 195–96, 201
Arum, John, 210, 212
Attorney General's Office, Washington: Boldt decision response, 124–25, 127, 128; cigarette taxes, 139; criminal jurisdiction case, 168, 169; hunting rights case, 140
automobile taxes, 139

Baldus, David, 182
bar exams, 21, 25, 26
barristers, England, 187, 189–90
Baskin, Leonard, 195–96
Bauer, Harold, 31–32, 33–34
Beartusk, Kenneth, 148, 156–57
Becker County, Boswell case, 220
Belgarde, Daniel, 168
Belli, Melvin, 30
Berley, Rich, 227, 229, 230, 232–33
BIA. See Bureau of Indian Affairs (BIA)
Biggs, John, 53
bigotry/racial prejudice: childhood experiences, 9, 10–11; against Indians generally, 64–65; Lummi testimony, 81; Makah testimony, 109; against Mille Lacs people, 207–8, 212–14; Seattle police department, 46–48; in Suquamish case, 166–71. See also Northern

Cheyenne Indian Tribe, coal lease case
Birge, Peter, 162
birthday celebration, White Man household, 238–39
The Birth of a Whale (painting), 196
Blackmun, Justice, 127–28
Black Wolf, James, 240–41
Block, Rose (born Bolasny, later Ziontz), 8–9, 44
boat buy-back program, 131–32
Bolasny, Rose (later Block, then Ziontz), 8–9, 44
Boldt, George H.: closing remarks, 122; decision, xii, 123–24; enforcement of decision, 125–26; during Indian testimony, 108–9, 113; integrity of, 132–33; opening statement, 105; pretrial stage, 95–96, 99
Boswell, Wanda, 216–25
Bowechop, George, 258–59
Boyd, Billy Joe, 216, 217, 218, 219, 220–21
Boyd, Joseph, 219
Boyd, Shirley, 218, 219
Brando, Marlon, 50, 51, 52, 53–57, 86
Brennan, Justice, 127–28
Bridges, Alvin, 88
Bridges, Theresa, 88
Bureau of Indian Affairs (BIA): coal leases, 147–48, 152–53; as Indian government, 65, 179; Ozette Reservation, 68–70, 72;

perceptions of, 4; respect for Ziontz law firm, 192; termination program, 135–36; timber management, 42–43, 62

Bureau of Reclamation, 140–41

Burger, Justice, 127–28

Cagey, Sam, 79

canneries, commercial, 84, 119

Cantwell, Maria, 268

casinos, 92, 210, 213, 240, 266, 268

cattle drive, Northern Cheyenne Reservation, 242–44

Cedar River, 14, 114

ceremonies, 61–62, 111, 205, 211

Chambers, Reid, 150–51, 153–54

Chelan Tribe, 134

Cherokee Indian Tribe, x, 267

Cherokee Nation v. Georgia, x

Chestnut, Steve: coal permit work, 149–50, 154, 163, 164; meeting with Northern Cheyenne Tribe, 148, 149; Northern Arapaho Tribe, 226, 227, 229; subsurface mineral rights litigation, 161–63

Cheyennes. *See* Northern Cheyenne Indian Tribe

Chicago: childhood, 8–12; college years, 12–13; law school years, 14–21

Chief Joseph Dam, 135, 140–41

Chief Seattle Days, 167

childhood, 8–12

Chinook jargon, 74, 83–84, 106

Chippewas. *See* Mille Lacs Band, Chippewas

Chukchi, whaling, 255, 256–57

cigarettes, 92, 137–39

City Council, Seattle, 47–48

civil liberties, England, 189

civil rights movement, 93

Claiborne, Louis, 127

claims case, Makah, 75–76

Claplanhoo, Art, 65, 66

Claplanhoo, Ed, 59

Claplanhoo, Thelma, 59

Clinton, Bob, 181, 182

closing arguments, *U.S. v. Washington*, 116–22

coal leases. *See* Northern Cheyenne Indian Tribe

Coast Guard, U.S., 63, 77, 126

Cohen, Felix S., xi

Cold Bay, Alaska, 198

college years, 12–13

Columbia River fishery, 90–91, 94

Colville, Andrew, 134

Colville Business Council, 136–37, 144

Colville Indian Tribe: overview, 134–35; dam conflicts, 135, 140–42; hunting rights case, 139–40; tax cases, 137–39; termination program, 135–37; water rights, 142–44

commercial fishing, pre-treaty, 98, 107, 118

Community Action Program, 66

Confederated Tribes of the Colville Reservation. *See* Colville Indian Tribe

confiscation policy, fishing gear:

Minnesota, 208; Washington state, 51, 89, 108, 110–11

Congress, U.S.: Claims Commission creation, 75; coal lease legislation, 163–64; Indian civil rights, 172–73, 175; island return legislation, 77; mineral rights amendment, 159–60; Ozette case, 70–71; termination program, 135–36

Coniff, Larry, 97, 104–5

conservation, fish: Boldt decision, 123; *Oregon* case, 97; Pullayup cases, 92–93, 101–2, 120; Satiacum case, 50; Seneca Indian case, 85; as state regulation premise, 85–86, 90, 98, 117; tribal management, 130–31; *U.S. v. Washington* testimony, 110

Consolidation Coal Company, 164

constitutional law, teaching period, 181–83

Court of Claims, U.S., 75

Covington, Lucy, 136–37, 144–45

criminal jurisdiction, Suquamish case, 166–71

Crossland, George, 146, 149

Crow Wing County Jail, Boswell case, 220

culverts, fish habitat, 99

Dahle, Donna, 149, 244–45, 250–51

Dahle, Ed, 148, 156–57, 163, 244–45

Dahle, Zack, 245

dams, Columbia River, 135, 140–42

dancing, 61–62, 204–5

Daugherty, Richard, 72

debtor's hearing, with Hile's firm, 26–30

default order, Hile's conflict, 36–38

de la Cruz, Joe, 114

Department of Natural Resources, Minnesota, 208–10

De Raismes, Joseph, 173–74

District Courts: Boswell case, 219–24; Columbia River fishery, 94; Frank's Landing demonstration, 87–89; gold bullion case, 32–33; habitat protection, 99; Mille Lacs Band case, 210–11; mineral rights, 160; Navaho civil rights case, 175, 176; Suquamish case, 168, 170. *See also U.S. v. Washington*

Dodge v. Nakai, 174–75

Dulles, John Foster, 33

Dull Knife College, 240, 249

Durham University, 185–90

Dysart, George, 93–94, 96, 98, 116–17

Earl, from Northern Cheyenne reservation, 243

Eastern Shoshone Tribe, 226–27

Economic Opportunity Act, 65

education: college years, 12–13; graduate school, 21; law school, 14–21

Ehrlichman, John, 57–58
Eighth Circuit Court of Appeals, 211, 221, 229
Eisenhower administration, termination program, 135–36
Elk River jail, Boswell case, 216–24
Elwha River, 107
England, teaching period, 185–88
Ennis, Bruce, 157–58
Entiat Tribe, 134
environmental claim, *U.S. v. Washington*, 98–99
Ernstoff, Barry: Colvilles' meeting, 137; *Oliphant* case, 166–71; retirement ode, 236; subsurface mineral rights research, 151, 161
Ervin, Sam, 175
ethnohistory, in *U.S. v. Washington*, 97, 98, 106–7
European Court of Human Rights, 186
Evans, Dan, 94

Fallon Shoshone-Paiutes, 229
fee policy, Ziontz law firm, 191, 192, 193, 209
Fisher, Llevando "Cowboy," 239
fishing: ACLU's support role, 86–87; Alaska fishermen representation, 198–202; aquaculture project, 80–81; claims case, 76–77; Colville case, 140; dam impacts, 140–41; federal role, 54–55, 85, 93–94; fish-ins/court cases, 50–52,

53–54, 86, 87–90; Indian traditions, 82–83, 106–7, 108; Mille Lacs Band, 203, 207–10; treaty rights, 51, 83–84; Washington state restrictions, 6, 52–53, 84–86, 90–91. *See also U.S. v. Washington*
Fonda, Jane, 58
Fonda, Peter, 58
Fort Gordon, Georgia, 21–22
Fort Monmouth, Georgia, 22
François, from Northern Cheyenne reservation, 247–48
Frank, Billy, Jr., 51–52, 110
Frank's Landing, 52, 87, 88
Friedlander, George, 137
Friedman, Lawrence, 18
Frizzell, Kent, 150, 154, 155, 162
Fulle, Floyd "Frost," 45, 46. *See also* Ziontz, Alvin J., law firm

Gahbow, Art, 204
Game Department. *See* fishing; *U.S. v. Washington* case
gas/oil issues, Northern Arapaho, 227, 229–30
George, Don, Jr., 88
Georgia, Cherokee Nation v., x
Georgia, Worcester v., x, 267
Getches, David, 96–97, 100, 103, 117
Gibbs, George, 83
gift ceremonies, 61–62, 205
Ginsberg, Ruth Bader, 177–78
gold bullion case, 31–34
Gold Reserve Act, 32
Gordon, Jack, 41

Gorton, Slade, 124–25, 128, 139, 168, 169, 268
graduate school, 21
Grand Coulee Dam, 135, 140–42
gray whale. *See* Makah Tribe, whale hunt
Green River, 92, 114
Gregory, Dick, 58
Gronholt, Paul, 199–201

habeas corpus, Indian Civil Rights Act, 173, 175
Halloween, Northern Cheyenne, 247, 251
Hanson, Bill, 86–87
Harris, Dave, 27
Harris, Francis, 242, 245–46
Head Start Program, 251
Heath, Wallace, 80–81
Henry (black man), 10–11
high school, 11–12
Hile, Jerry: absence from practice, 26–28, 30, 34, 38, 39; clerk position, 24–26; gold bullion case, 32; manic periods, 35–38, 39–41; partnership offer, 43
Hinckley, Minnesota, 213
Hines, Bill, 182, 185
historical evidence, *U.S. v. Washington*, 106–7
Hoko River, 49, 86, 107, 109, 110
Hollowbreast v. Northern Cheyenne Tribe, 159–63, 228–29
Hopi Indian Tribe, 164–65
horse roundup, Northern Cheyenne Reservation, 245–46
housing, Makah, 62, 67

Human Rights Act, 276n1 (ch 21)
human rights courses, teaching, 185–88
hunting rights, 139–40, 208, 210–11, 229

Ides, John, 110
income-sharing approach, Ziontz law firm, 46, 191, 194–95, 197
"in common" phrase: Stevens treaties, 84, 85; *U.S. v. Washington* case, 85, 106, 117; Washington court rulings, 85
"In Defense of Tribal Sovereignty" (Ziontz), 176, 178
Indian Civil Rights Act, 167, 168, 172–79
"The Indian Civil Rights Act and ..." (De Raismes), 176
Indian Claims Commission, 75–78
Indian law: claims cases, 75–76; establishment of, 267–68; logging case, 42–43; neglect of, ix–xi; reflections on personal involvement, 265–67; teaching period, 180–81, 183. *See also* tribal sovereignty
Indian Rights Committee, ACLU, 172
Ingling, Allen, 259–60
Interior Department, U.S.: fishing rights role, 93–94; mineral rights case, 159–60, 162; Navaho civil rights case, 175; Northern Cheyenne coal leases, 150–51, 153–56; Ozette

Reservation, 70. *See also*
Bureau of Indian Affairs (BIA)
International Convention for the
Regulation of Whaling, 255
International Whaling Commis-
sion (IWC), 255, 256, 257
Inupiats, 192, 255, 256–57
Iowa City, teaching period,
182–85
Irgun, 55
Irving, Hillary "Zab," 5, 107–10
IWC (International Whaling
Commission), 255, 256, 257

Jackson, Andrew, 267
Jackson, Henry M. "Scoop,"
70–71, 72
Japan, whaling, 256
Jewishness, 8–9, 269
jobs, before law profession, 11–12,
16, 17–20
Johnson, Ben, 253–54, 263
Johnson, Jim, 125, 210, 211
Johnson, Lyndon B. (and admin-
istration), xi, 65–66
Joseph, Chief, 135
Justice Department, U.S., 94–95.
See also U.S. v. Washington

Kanassetega, Jay, 205–7, 216
Karth, Dr., 40–41
Kautz, Nugent, 88
King, Rudolph, 240, 241
King County Law Library, 25
King Cove, Alaska, 198, 199–201
Kinley, Forrest, 112–13
Kit Fox Society, 250

Kitsap County, criminal jurisdiction case, 166–71
Korean War, 19, 21–23
Kosieradzki, Mark, 220, 222,
223–24

*Lac Courte Oreilles Band of Chip-
pewas v. Voigt*, 208
Lacovara, Phillip, 127
Lakes Tribe, 134
Lane, Barbara, 97, 98, 106
Lane, Vernon, 80–81
law practice, with Hile's firm:
clerk position, 24–26; debtor
hearing case, 26–30; default
hearing, 36–38; gold bullion
case, 31–34; during Hile's
manic periods, 35–38, 39–41;
management of, 34–35, 39;
partnership proposal, 43; psychiatric hearing case, 39–41;
Seattle move decision, 23–24;
whiplash case, 30–31; Wilkie
family representations, 4,
41–43. *See also* Ziontz, Alvin
J., law firm
Lawrence, Joe, Jr. "Bobe," 5
law school: classes, 14–15, 18,
20–21; England's approach,
187, 188–89; father's pressures,
13–14; jobs during, 17–20;
social life, 16–17, 19
Legal Services program, 174–75,
193–94
Levi, Edward, 15
lighthouse, Tatoosh Island, 74, 77
Limberhand, Dennis, 148, 156–57

Limpy family name, history, 248–49. *See also* White Man entries

linguistic evidence, *U.S. v. Washington*, 106–7

Littlewolf, Doris, 240

logging case, Bureau of Indian Affairs, 42–43

Long Branch, New Jersey, 22

Lower Brule Sioux Tribe, 229

loyalty policy, Ziontz law firm, 79, 149, 192, 228

Lummi Indian Tribe: aquaculture project, 80–81; attorney selection, 79–80; *Towessnute* case, 119–20; in *U.S. v. Washington*, 95, 98, 112–13, 115, 123–24

Lyre River, 107, 108

Madison, *Marbury v.*, 183

Makah Cultural and Research Center, 72–73

Makah Tribal Council (decisions/meetings): attorney selection, 5–6; claims case, 76, 77; Lummi tribe representation, 79; Ozette case, 68, 70–73; structure of, 66–67; Washington, D.C. conference, 65–66

Makah Tribe: attorney selection processes, 3–7, 49, 196–97; claims case, 75–77; fishing activity, 49–50, 129–31; lifestyle, 59–65, 66–67; on-site attorney, 192, 194; Ozette Reservation, 68–73; Tatoosh Island, 73–75, 77–78; in

U.S. v. Washington, 95, 100, 107–10; Waadah Island, 73, 74–75, 77–78

Makah Tribe, whale hunt: assistance request, 253–54; celebration of, 263–64; historical background, 254–56; opposition to, 257, 260–61, 262–63; preparations for, 257, 261–62; press conference, 257–60; proposal for, 256–57

Manichaean views, Indian clients, 265–66

Marbury v. Madison, 183

Mark David Oliphant v. Suquamish Tribe, 166–71

Markishtum, Quentin "Squint," 5, 49, 60–61

marriage, 21

Marshall, John, x, 183, 267

Marshall, Thurgood, 127–28, 170, 171

Martinez v. Santa Clara Pueblo, 176–77

McCaw, Craig, 261

McCloud, Don, 88

McCloud, Janet, 87–88, 89

McGimpsey, Earl, 97, 105, 121–22

Medicine Bull, Burt, 148

membership rolls: Boldt decision impact, 131; Northern Arapaho proposal, 233–35; Santa Clara Pueblo case, 176–77

Methow Tribe, 134

Michigan. *See* Mille Lacs Band, Chippewas

military bases, 63

military service, 21–23, 63, 269
Mille Lacs Band, Chippewas:
    Boswell case, 216–25; casino
    operations, 210, 213, 266;
    dance experience, 204–5;
    fishing/hunting rights con-
    flicts, 177, 207–13; government
    structure, 205–6; reservation
    challenges, 213–15; reservation
    description, 203–4
Mille Lacs v. Minnesota, 209
mineral rights, legislation,
    159–60. *See also* Northern
    Cheyenne *entries*
mining leases. *See* Northern
    Cheyenne Indian Tribe
Minnesota, 208. *See also* Mille
    Lacs Band, Chippewas
Mitchell, John, 132
Mitchell, Mr., 174–75, 176
Modern Trials (Belli), 30
Montana, coal tax, 150. *See also*
    Northern Cheyenne *entries*
Morisset, Mason, 127, 140, 151
Morton, Roger, 154–56
Moses, Chief, 136
Moses Tribe, 134
Muckleshoot Indian Tribe, 92, 97,
    100, 113–14
Murphy, Diana, 210–11
museum, Makah, 72–73

Nakai, Dodge v., 174–75
National Congress of American
    Indians, 144, 169, 268
National Marine Fisheries Ser-
    vice, 126

National Oceanic and Atmo-
    spheric Administration, 260
National Park Service, 70–71, 72
Navaho Indian Tribe, 164–65,
    174, 176
Neah Bay, descriptions, 3–4, 5.
    See also Makah *entries*
Nelson Lagoon, Alaska, 198,
    201–2
Nespelem Tribe, 134
New Jersey, Army training, 22
New York, Seneca Indian case, 85
Nez Perce Indians, 134, 135
Niemi, Preston, 36–38
Ninth Circuit Court of Appeals:
    criminal jurisdiction, 168–69,
    170; fishing rights, 99, 125,
    128; gold bullion case, 32;
    mineral rights, 159, 160, 161–
    62; water rights, 143; whaling
    activity, 264
Nisqually River, 88–89, 92
Nisqually Tribe, 51–52, 100,
    110–11
Nixon administration, 132,
    154–56
Nooksack River, 80, 98
Nootka language, 64
Norsworthy and Reger, 164
Northern Arapaho Tribe: attor-
    ney selection process, 226–29;
    enrollment change proposal,
    233–35; general member-
    ship meetings, 232–34; and
    Shoshone tribal government,
    226–27, 277n1 (ch 26); sweat
    lodge experience, 230–32

Northern Cheyenne Indian Tribe: casino operations, 240; history, 147; mineral rights conflict, 159–63; in Northern Arapaho presentation, 228–29; reservation description, 146–47. *See also* photography, Northern Cheyenne reservation

Northern Cheyenne Indian Tribe, coal lease case: attorney selection, 146, 149; cancellation legislation, 163–64; industry negotiation efforts, 156–58, 164; permit transactions, 146, 147–50, 151–53; petition for voiding permits, 150–51, 153–56

Northern Cheyenne Lease Cancellation Act, 163–64

Northern Cheyenne Tribal Council, 147–49, 239–40

Northern Cheyenne Tribe, Hollowbreast v., 159–63, 228–29

Northern States Power Company, 157–58, 164

Northwest Indian Fisheries Commission, 255–56

Northwest Indians fishing rights conflicts. *See* fishing; *U.S. v. Washington*

Norway, 255, 257

O'Connor, Sandra Day, 212

oil/gas issues, Northern Arapaho, 227, 229–30

Ojibwe. *See* Mille Lacs Band, Chippewas

Okanogan Tribe, 134

Oliphant v. Suquamish Tribe, 166–71

Olympic National Park, 68, 70–73

Onamia, Minnesota, 213

Oregon, U.S. v., 94, 97

Ozette Reservation and village, 68–73

Palouse Tribe, 134

Parker, David "Ty," 5

partnership formation, Ziontz law firm, 44–46

Peabody Coal Company, 148–49, 150, 156–57, 164–65

Peninsula Marketing Association (PMA), 198–202

Penn, Chris, 114

Perkins, Coie law firm, 45

personal reflections, 265–70

Peterson, Charlie, 5, 60, 64

Pevar, Steven, 178

Phase Two, *U.S. v. Washington,* 99

Phelps, Ed, 156–57, 158

photography, early interests, 236–38

photography, Northern Cheyenne reservation: birthday celebration, 239; cattle drive, 242–44; council meeting, 239–40; horse roundup, 245–46; host family time, 238–39, 242, 243, 244–45, 247–48; hostile confrontation, 246–47; individuals, 240–41, 248–50;

lodge poles, 240; reflections on, 251–52; school-related activities, 241–42, 251; tribal court, 241

Pierson, Stuart, 95–96, 100–103

Pirtle, Robert, 45–46, 138–39. *See also* Ziontz, Alvin J., law firm

Pitkin, Stanley, 95

PMA (Peninsula Marketing Association), 198–202

Police Department, Seattle, 46–48

potlatches, 61–62

poverty problem: Boldt decision impact, 131; Chicago ghetto, 17–18; Johnson administration approach, xi, 65–66; Lummi reservation, 80; Mille Lacs Band reservation, 213; Muckleshoot reservation, 113–14

Powell, Justice, 128

pow-wow, Colville Reservation, 137

pretrial stage, *U.S. v. Washington*, 95–100, 107

The Problem of Indian Fishing (film), 53

publications, Ziontz's, 87, 174, 176–77, 178–79

Public Law 91-489, 71

Public Law 98-282, 77

Puyallup Tribe: fish camp raid case, 89–90; Frank's Landing fish-in, 87–89; Satiacum fish-in, 50–51, 86; state regulation cases, 92–93, 101–2, 120; in *U.S. v. Washington*, 100, 111–12

Pysht River, 107

Quileute Indian Tribe, 42, 53–54, 95, 100, 114

Quileute River, 53–54

racial prejudice. *See* bigotry/racial prejudice

reef-net fishing, 80, 98, 115, 123–24

Rehnquist, William, 128, 132, 169, 170, 212

retirement decision, 236

rice gathering, Mille Lacs Band, 203, 209–10

Riley, Carrol, 107

Rising Sun, Ted, 148

robbery, 20

Roosevelt, Franklin D., 8, 31

Rosebud Society, 160, 163

Rosenbaum, James, 214, 221, 223, 224

Rowland, Allan, 146, 148, 156–57

Russia, 8, 255, 256–57

Sacramento, California, 22–23

salmon, Indian traditions, 82–83. *See also* fishing; *U.S. v. Washington*

Sanchez, Maria, 247

Sand Point, Alaska, 198, 199

San Poil Tribe, 134

Santa Clara Pueblo, Martinez v., 176–77

Satiacum, Bob, 50–51, 86

Satiacum, Suzanne, 88

Sauk-Suiattle Indian Tribe, 97
schools, Indian, 61, 69, 241–42, 251
sealing, 76, 108. *See also* whaling
Sea Shepherd Conservation Society, 257, 260, 262–63
Seattle: move to, 23–24; police department case, 46–48; summer work, 18–20. *See also* law practice, with Hile's firm
Seattle, Chief, 166
Seattle Argus, 87
Seattle Seven, 95
Sekiu River, 110
self-confidence: childhood, 9; with Hile's law practice, 26–27, 34; law school, 15–16, 20; masters program, 21; reflections on, 265
Seneca Indians, 85
Senior Center, Northern Cheyenne, 251
Sennhauser, John, 96–97, 100
"Separatism Should be Accepted as Future Way of Life" (Ziontz), 87
Seventh Circuit Court of Appeals, 208
Sherburne County, Boswell case, 216–24
Shoshone tribes, 226–27, 229, 230, 277n1 (ch 26)
Shoulderblades, Turkey, 148
Signal Corps, 21–22
Sioux tribes, 229
Skokomish Indian Tribe, 97
Slonim, Marc: Alaska fishermen case, 199, 202; Boldt portrait, 133; Boswell case, 221, 223–24; Mille Lacs Band representation, 209, 210–12, 214
smoke shops, 92, 137–39
solicitors, England, 187, 190
South Dakota Law Review, 174, 176, 178
sovereignty principle, masters thesis, 21. *See also* tribal sovereignty
Spang, Alonzo, 153, 240
Spang, Ray, 157, 158
spinal stenosis, 186
Spokane flight, 144–45
sportfishermen: Mille Lacs Band conflicts, 203, 207–10; steelhead interest, 52–53; in *U.S. v. Washington*, 109, 124, 127–28
Squaxin Island Tribe, 97
Standing Rock Sioux Tribe, 229
Starr, Louis, 114
State of Washington v. Washington State Commercial Passenger Fishing Vessel Association, 127–28
State v. Towessnute, 119
steelhead: regulatory approach, 52–53, 99; in *U.S. v. Washington* case, 104–5, 109, 110, 122
Stevens, Isaac, 73, 83–84, 94, 254–55
Stevens, Justice, 127–28
Stewart, Justice, 128
Stillaguamish Indian Tribe, 97
Streetcar Named Desire (movie), 56

strip mining. *See* Northern Cheyenne Indian Tribe, coal lease case

subsistence premise, in *U.S. v. Washington*, 97–98, 102–3, 105

Sun Dance, 250

Supremacy Clause, U.S. Constitution, 104, 117, 122, 193

Supreme Court, U.S.: in claims process, 76; criminal jurisdiction, 169, 170–71; hunting rights, 140, 211–12; mineral rights, 162–63; smoke shops, 138–39; tribal membership, 176–78; water rights, 142

Supreme Court, U.S., fishing rights: Boldt decision, 125, 127–28; Mille Lacs band, 211–12; Puyallup cases, 92–93, 116–17, 120; Seneca Indians, 85

Supreme Court, Washington: Boldt decision, 127; hunting rights, 140; Johnson election, 125; Lummi Indian case, 119–20; Puyallup cases, 50–51, 87; smoke shop case, 138

Suquamish Indian Tribe, 166–71

sweat lodge experience, 230–32

Tallbull, Patsy, 240

Tatoosh Island, 73–75, 77–78

tavern, during childhood, 8, 9–11

taxes, Colville Indian Reservation, 137–39

Taylor, Zachary, 208, 210, 212

teaching period, university courses, 180–90

termination policy, x, 135–36

Three Fingers, Michelle, 251

Title 25, United States Code, 42

Tobin, Tom, 214

Tonasket, Jerri, 138

Tonasket, Leonard, 138

Tonasket, Mel, 144

torts classes, 14–15, 188–89

Towessnute, State v., 119

Trading with the Enemy Act, 31–32

trailer taxes, 139

Treaty of Neah Bay (1855), 73–74. *See also* fishing; Makah, whale hunt; Stevens, Isaac; *U.S. v. Washington*

tribal attorney, as a calling, xv, 265–70. *See also* Ziontz, Alvin J., law firm

tribal court hearing, Northern Cheyenne reservation, 241

tribal government, growth of. *See* Indian law; tribal sovereignty; *specific Indian tribes, e.g.,* Makah *entries;* Northern Cheyenne *entries*

tribal sovereignty: criminal jurisdiction case, 168–70; disregard for, x–xi; and Indian Civil Rights Act, 175–76, 178; logging case research, 42; in presentation to Makah Tribal Council, 5–6; smoke shop case, 138–39; in United States Code, 42; in *Worcester v. Georgia*, x, 267; as Ziontz law

firm foundation, 193, 228, 269.
See also U.S. v. Washington
Troop Information and Education, Army years, 22
Tse Kow Wootl, 68
Tulee, Sampson, 85
Turtle Mountain Band, Chippewas, 43
Twin River, 107

UC Davis Law Review, 178–79
Ukpeagvik Inupiat Corporation, 192
United Kingdom, Human Rights Act, 276n1 (ch 21). See also England, teaching period
University of Chicago Law School, 14–21
University of Iowa Law School, 181–85
University of Washington, 72–73, 180–81, 207, 262
U.S. v. Oregon, 94, 97
U.S. v. Washington: overview, xii–xiii; appeals of, 124–25, 127–28; Boldt's decision, 123–24, 125–26; closing arguments, 116–22; historical evidence, 106–7; impact on tribes, 128–32; Indian testimony, 107–15; joint biological statement, 105–6; linguistic evidence, 106–7; opening statements, 101–5; pretrial stage, 95–101, 107
U.S. v. Winans, 101
U.S. v. Winters, 101–2, 142–43

Vance, Mr., 27–30
Vance, Mrs., 26–30
Veeder, Bill, 142, 143
Vestal, Allen, 182
Vineland, Minnesota, 213
Voigt, Lac Courte Oreilles Band of Chippewas v., 208

Waadah Island, 73, 74–75, 77–78
Walks Along, Florene, 238–39, 241
Walks Along, Jaidell, 239
Walks Along, James, 238–39, 241, 249–50
Walks Along, Wesley, 250
Walks Last, James, 238–39
Walks Last, Johnathan, 238–39
Walks Last, Jolene, 238–39
Walks Last, Luanna, 238–39
Walsh, Thomas, 161
Walton, Boyd, 142, 143–44
Walton rights, 144, 227, 229, 230
Warbrick, Colin, 188
War on Poverty conference, 65–66
Washington, D. C. conference, 65–66
Washington state. See fishing; Makah entries; U.S. v. Washington
Washington State Commercial Passenger Fishing Vessel Association, State of Washington v., 127–28
Washington University, 185
water quality claim, U.S. v. Washington, 98–99

water rights, 142–44, 227, 229, 230–35
Watson, Paul, 257, 262
Wauneka, Annie, 175, 176
Wedll, Don, 208–9
Wenatchee Tribe, 134
Wendell Turkey Shoulderblades Senior Center, 251
Western Washington University, 262
Weston, Burns, 182–83
West Seattle, characterized, 24–25
West Seattle Democratic Club, 38
whaling, 64, 76–77, 78, 108, 254–56. *See also* Makah Tribe, whale hunt
whiplash case, 30–31
White, Bernice, 113–14
White, Justice, 127–28
White Man, Charlene (later Alden), 238–39, 240, 242, 243
White Man, Florene, 238–39, 248–49
White Man, Phillip, 238–39, 242, 248–49
White Man, Phillip, Jr., 239
White Man, Thelma, 238–39
White River, 14, 114
Wilkie, Bruce, 3, 4–5, 60
Wilkie, Nell, 43
Wilkie, Pat, 41–43, 60
Wilkie, Pat, Jr. "Shine," 41–43, 60
Williams, Mr., 29
Wilson, Henry, 239
Wilson, Shannon (born Alden), 238, 239

Winans, U.S. v., 101
Wind River Reservation, 226–27, 277n1 (ch 26). *See also* Northern Arapaho Tribe
Winters, U.S. v., 101–2, 142–43
Wirt, William, 267
Wisconsin. *See* Mille Lacs Band, Chippewas
Woodenlegs, John, 148
Worcester v. Georgia, x, 267
Wright, Benjamin, 111–12
Wright, Judge, 40
Wright Junior College, 12

Yakima Tribe, 100
Yancey, Jimmy, 17
Yellow Magpie, Arapaho (Baskin), 195–96
Yiddish, 8–9, 55

Ziontz, Alvin J.: childhood/youth, 8–12; college years, 12–13; law clerk years, 24–26; law school years, 14–21; marriage, 21; military service, 21–23; personal reflections, 265–70; publications, 87, 174, 176–77, 178–79; retirement decision, 236; solo practice, 44; teaching period, 180–90; Wilkinson on, ix–xiv. *See also* photography, Northern Cheyenne reservation
Ziontz, Alvin J., law firm: Alaska fishermen representation, 198–202; breakup and reformation, 194–97; growth of, 191–92; partnership

beginnings, 44–46; personal reflections, 265–70; practice policies, 191–94, 228; sabbatical proposal, 181; Seattle police case, 46–48; Suquamish representation, 166–71. *See also U.S. v. Washington; specific Indian tribes, e.g.,* Makah *entries;* Northern Cheyenne *entries*

Ziontz, Harry (father of AJZ), 8–11, 12–13, 26, 44

Ziontz, Jeff (son of AJZ), 22, 56

Ziontz, Lenore "Lennie" (wife of AJZ): during Army years, 22; Boswell case, 224; England period, 185; Iowa City period, 181, 182, 183–84; law school years, 20; marriage, 21; Seattle household, 23, 34

Ziontz, Martin (son of AJZ), 22, 195

Ziontz, Ron (son of AJZ), 182, 184, 185, 186–87

Ziontz, Rose (born Bolasny, Block) (mother of AJZ), 8–9, 44